RADICAL

CHRISTIANITY

RADICAL CHRISTIANITY

THE NEW THEOLOGIES IN PERSPECTIVE

With Readings From The Radicals

By

Lonnie D. Kliever

and

John H. Hayes

ACKNOWLEDGMENTS

Grateful acknowledgment is extended to the following authors and publishers for permission to quote from copyrighted material:

MIRCEA ELIADE AND THE DIALECTIC OF THE SACRED by Thomas J. J. Altizer, copyright 1963 by W. L. Jenkins, used by permission of the publisher, The Westminster Press.

"Creative Negation in Theology" by Thomas J. J. Altizer, copyright 1965 by The Christian Century Foundation, reprinted in FRONTLINE THEOLOGY ed. by Dean Peerman, copyright 1967 by M. E. Bratcher, used by permission of the publishers, THE CHRISTIAN CENTURY and John Knox Press.

RADICAL THEOLOGY AND THE DEATH OF GOD by Thomas J. J. Altizer and William Hamilton, copyright 1966 by Thomas J. J. Altizer and William Hamilton, used by permission of the publisher, The Bobbs-Merrill Company, Inc.

THE GOSPEL OF CHRISTIAN ATHEISM by Thomas J. J. Altizer, copyright 1966 by W. L. Jenkins, used by permission of the publisher, The Westminster Press.

TOWARD A NEW CHRISTIANITY ed. by Thomas J. J. Altizer, copyright 1967 by Harcourt, Brace & World, Inc., used by permission of the publisher.

"Can We Manage Without God?" by Kenneth L. Wilson, copyright 1967 by THE CHRISTIAN HERALD, used by permission of the publisher.

"Catholic Philosophy and the Death of God" by Thomas J. J. Altizer, copyright 1967 by Cross Currents Corporation, used by permission of the publisher, CROSS CURRENTS.

THE ALTIZER-MONTGOMERY DIALOGUE, copyright 1967 by Inter-Varsity Christian Fellowship, used by permission of the publisher, Inter-Varsity Press.

THE SECULAR MEANING OF THE GOSPEL by Paul M. van Buren, copyright 1963 by Paul M. van Buren, used by permission of the publisher, The Macmillan Company.

"Christian Education POST MORTEM DEI" and "Straw Men and the Monistic Hangover" by Paul M. van Buren, copyright 1965 by The Religious Education Association, used by permission of the publisher, RELIGIOUS EDUCATION.

"Theology in the Context of Culture" by Paul M. van Buren, copyright 1965 by The Christian Century Foundation, reprinted in FRONTLINE THEOLOGY ed. by Dean Peerman, copyright 1967 by M. E. Bratcher, used by permission of the publishers, THE CHRISTIAN CENTURY and John Knox Press.

"The Dissolution of the Absolute" by Paul M. van Buren, copyright 1965 by Abingdon Press, used by permission of the publisher, RELIGION IN LIFE.

GOD'S REVOLUTION AND MAN'S RESPONSIBILITY by Harvey Cox, copyright 1965 by The Judson Press, used by permission of the publisher.

THE SECULAR CITY by Harvey Cox, copyright 1965, 1966 by Harvey Cox, used by permission of the publisher, The Macmillan Company.

"The Place and Purpose of Theology" by Harvey Cox, copyright 1966 by The Christian Century Foundation, reprinted in FRONTLINE THEOLOGY ed. by Dean Peerman, copyright 1967 by M. E. Bratcher, used by permission of the publishers, THE CHRISTIAN CENTURY and John Knox Press.

"Secularization and the Secular Mentality: A New Challenge to Christian Education" and "Response to Critics" by Harvey Cox, copyright 1966 by The Religious Education Association, used by permission of the publisher, RELIGIOUS EDUCATION.

"An Exchange of Views," "Afterword" and "Beyond Bonhoeffer? The Future of Religionless Christianity" by Harvey Cox in THE SECULAR CITY DEBATE ed. by Daniel Callahan, copyright 1966 by The Macmillan Company, used by permission of the publisher.

"The Death of God and the Future of Theology" by Harvey Cox in THE NEW CHRISTIANITY ed. by William Robert Miller, copyright 1967 by William Robert Miller, used by permission of the publisher, Delacorte Press.

"Why Christianity Must be Secularized" by Harvey Cox in THE GREAT IDEAS TODAY 1967 ed. by Otto Bird, copyright 1967 by Encyclopaedia Britannica, Inc., used by permission of the publisher.

ON NOT LEAVING IT TO THE SNAKE by Harvey Cox, copyright 1967 by Harvey Cox, used by permission of the publisher, The Macmillan Company.

"The Shape of a Radical Theology" by William Hamilton, copyright 1967 by The

TO ARTHISS AND SARAH

TABLE OF CONTENTS

PREFACE

This book presents an historical, comparative and critical study of the six leading proponents of *radical Christianity*--Paul M. van Buren, William Hamilton, Gabriel Vahanian, Harvey Cox, Thomas J. J. Altizer and John A. T. Robinson. The book falls into three divisions. Part One traces the rise of radical Christianity out of a collision between the basic assumptions of traditional Christianity and the modern world's relativism and secularism. Part Two explores the meaning of radical Christianity at the points of faith, revelation, truth, God, man, Christ, church and discipleship. Brief selections from all of the writings of each of the radicals are arranged around these eight themes and prefaced by summary descriptions of the alternative approaches in Orthodoxy, Liberalism and Neo-orthodoxy. Part Three assesses the significance of radical Christianity by summarizing the key insights and contributions of each of the radicals to the contemporary theological revolution. Although this three-fold division reflects a logical progression of thought, some persons may prefer to read Parts One and Three before reading the more difficult material in Part Two since Part Three contains summary statements on each of the radicals. In studying Part Two, some readers may choose to follow the reading selections of a given radical theologian straight through the eight issues discussed. Such rearrangements will do no violence to the substance of the book since each part is relatively independent of the other parts.

This book is designed for the interested reader who lacks an adequate historical and theological orientation for understanding the technical literature and the crucial issues in the radical debate. Thus, the historical discussion in Part One makes as few references as possible to specific theological writings and subtle theological distinctions. The commentary and readings in Part Two are written and arranged to facilitate comparison of the radicals to one another as well as to the theological alternatives in Orthodoxy, Liberalism and Neo-orthodoxy on specific matters of Christian thought and life. The critical evaluation in Part Three highlights only the more crucial issues and alternatives in the radical debate. But, throughout the book, the attempt has been made to strike the delicate balance of presenting alternatives fairly while taking sides personally, and of exploring issues technically while simplifying them appreciably. Whether these goals have been achieved must be left to the judgment of specialist and nonspecialist readers. Because such judgments are called for in a work of this kind, the division of labor on the book should be made clear. Professor Kliever and Professor Hayes collaborated on the over-all plan of the book and on the selection and editing of the readings in Part Two. Professor Kliever wrote the historical, theological and critical commentary throughout the book and is solely responsible for the theological judgments expressed and any errors committed.

Finally, behind every book are a great number of people who deserve far more credit than mere mention in a preface, but naming some of them here is a small way of expressing recognition and appreciation. Mr. Wilton Hall, Jr. of Droke House Publishers must be credited with the idea and invitation to prepare a book which places reading selections from the radicals in the context of alternative theological traditions. Professor Kliever's wife, Arthiss Marie, read the entire manuscript with a keen eye for unnecessary theological and grammatical obscurities. Four Trinity University student assistants, Elizabeth Gonzalez, Toni Griffin, Cathy Rice and especially Karen Keilers, deserve particular thanks for working through very strange ideas and rough drafts in typing and proofreading the final manuscript. Trinity University graciously furnished summer time and library resources for the preparation of this volume. Colleagues, friends and students too numerous to name have shared in these explorations by lending their attention and criticism. Finally, and foremost, gratitude is extended to the men presented in this volume for permitting this use of their writings. Full bibliographical references to the writings quoted in Part Two are included in the Selected Bibliography at the end of this book.

Lonnie D. Kliever

John H. Hayes

PART ONE

THE RISE

OF

RADICAL CHRISTIANITY

Radical questions are disturbing the Church these days. Have most Christian beliefs become unbelievable? Has God's relation to the world changed in our time? Should Christians forget about other-worlds and after-lifes? Can Christianity survive in a post-Christian era? Should the modern Christian admit that God is dead? Was God ever more than a personification of human ideals?

These questions are upsetting not so much because of *what* they ask but because of *who* asks them and *how* they are answered. Similar rhetorical questions have often been put to the Church by her cultured despisers and implacable foes. But today these very questions are being raised within the Church and, in varying ways, answered affirmatively! These questions come from such Christian thinkers as Bishop John A. T. Robinson, Thomas J. J. Altizer, Harvey Cox, Gabriel Vahanian, William Hamilton and Paul M. van Buren rather than as barbs from omnipresent village atheists or materialistic philosophers. Furthermore, these questions are not treated as doubts to be dispelled or as demons to be exorcized. Rather, they are viewed as the only guides and conditions for a Christianity that can survive in the modern world.

These radical proposals have burst like bombshells inside and outside the Church. Not since the "Fundamentalism-Modernism" controversy half a century ago has theological unrest so completely pervaded Christian consciousness and public interest. The battles are being fought in seminary and college classrooms, from church and political pulpits, in sacred and secular publications, in public gatherings and private meditation. Unlike centuries of previous doctrinal controversy, this warfare is no longer waged exclusively by mercenaries or professionals. No longer are theological quarrels "hired out" to philosophers who can battle over faith's quandries without disrupting the Church's citizenry. No longer are doctrinal disputes settled by theologians within the isolated warzones of seminary classrooms and technical publications. The battles of belief are being fought, quite literally, in the streets.

In previous generations, theological debate seldom received such widespread attention. By the time doctrinal changes reached the church pew and the market place, the issues had been thoroughly discussed and the alternatives clearly formulated. These options were, in turn, translated by teachers and ministers into concepts and programs intelligible to laymen. But the modern revolution in communications has changed all of this. Now theological upheaval reaches the general public as quickly as theologians publish or even speak. The paperback explosion and the electronic age have forever ended pastoral protectiveness and radically altered theological style. Consequently, theological debate now confronts clergymen and laymen, engages believer and nonbeliever alike. For good or for ill, the Church can no longer settle her family quarrels out of earshot of her children or her neighbors.

Yet very few people are really comprehending what the radical theologians are saying. Theological interest and study among laymen abounds. But the general public in or out of the Church simply cannot understand, much less join, this new debate until the issues and alternatives are clarified for them. And, although the radicals have been given an astonishing play in the popular as well as the religious press, such clarification seldom has been given. The popular press tends to celebrate while the religious press tends to castigate the radicals on the basis of selected inflammatory quotes and controversial proposals. But neither treatment throws much light on why such radical proposals are being advocated. Consequently, the general public remains largely in the dark about the meaning and significance of this budding theological revolution.

Unfortunately, some churchmen are happy to leave laymen in the dark. The Church's place in the world seems more secure when the general public is insulated against the shocks of such high-voltage theological debate. But pastoral protectiveness belongs to an earlier era of religious authoritarianism and theological professionalism. No longer can the general public sleep securely through theological revolutions. Laymen must be equipped for theological understanding since they can no longer be insulated against theological debate. Furthermore, such equipping can be as beneficial as it is necessary. Properly channeled through laymen, even high-voltage theological debate can bring light into a darkened world and a sluggish Church.

But where and how should this equipping begin? Should laymen immediately tackle the major statements of the radical theologians themselves? Should they first read some scholarly criticisms of radical thought? Neither of these alternatives is the best place for laymen to begin, although such writings are certainly not off limits or entirely beyond comprehension for laymen. The proposals of the radicals and the countertheses of their critics can be appraised best in light of a clash between the traditional faith of the Church and the revolutionary changes of

18

modern life. Radical Christianity purports to detect and overcome infirmities growing out of this clash which threaten to destroy Christianity as a viable faith and power in the modern world. Therefore, laymen should begin their study of radical Christianity by discovering whether traditional Christianity has been undermined by the modern world and how traditional Christianity has been reinterpreted by the radical theologians. Only then will laymen be equipped to follow the continuing debate over radical theology.

But is this ideal beginning beyond reach for all but the few? How can most laymen comprehend the highly complex and variegated movements of life and thought represented by the terms "traditional Christianity," "modern world" and "radical Christianity"? Are ambitious reading programs covering all the mainline interpretations of Christian faith through the centuries and all the far-reaching revolutions in human life during the past two centuries the only way to understand the conflicts that have arisen for modern Christians? Are detailed studies comparing all the varied formulations of Christian doctrines to the proposed reconstructions of radical theology the only way to understand the options that are available to modern Christians? While the problems represented by these questions are real, they are less formidable than they first appear. Laymen can readily grasp the clash between traditional Christianity and the modern world if these are reduced to their basic underlying assumptions. Furthermore, laymen can grasp the basic differences between radical interpretations of Christianity and other theological approaches if these are compared succinctly at particular doctrinal points. Finally, laymen can provisionally assess the implications of radical Christianity for personal faith if these are suggestively outlined for them.

This book hopefully will provide these perspectives on radical Christianity. These requirements for an adequate understanding of the new theologies conveniently divide the material of this book into three parts. Part One will trace the rise of radical Christianity by analyzing the clash between traditional Christianity and contemporary culture. Part Two will survey the meaning of radical Christianity by comparing radical thought to the theological approaches of Orthodoxy, Liberalism and Neo-orthodoxy on specific Christian doctrines. Finally, Part Three will explore the significance of radical Christianity by relating its major concerns to the life and thought of contemporary Christians. This rough map of radical Christianity's relationship to the modern world and to earlier interpretations of Christian faith should equip the venturing layman for further reading, intelligent discussion and personal evaluation of the new theologies.

Of course, even detailed and accurate maps have their limitations. Every map is an abstraction since depth, novelty and complexity are excluded. But the function of any map is to portray in general rather then to picture in detail. Maps are never ends in themselves. They serve as guides for exploring and working through a territory. Thus, mapping the main features of the modern world, traditional Christianity and radical Christianity can never capture their living depth, novelty and complexity. But this limitation is a liability only if we forget the purpose of our map.

One limitation in mapping cultural outlooks and belief systems may prove debilitating. Plotting the relationships between the modern world, traditional Christianity and radical Christianity is like mapping a region in the midst of territorial conflicts or frontier expansion. The modern world, traditional Christianity and radical Christianity all represent shifting boundaries and changing territories. Mapping their relationships must, therefore, be somewhat tentative and provisional. But, if we are to make some sense *today* out of the collision of these three world views, we must run this risk of map-making.

Acknowledging these limitations and weaknesses of encompassing surveys, we must first trace out the rise of radical Christianity. Here we are not interested in detailing the appearance and remarkable development of radical Christianity in the last five years. This story is full of human interest with its charismatic figures, unlikely coincidences, ideological conflicts and astounding impact. But, for our purposes, we need only discover how the conflict between the underlying assumptions of traditional Christianity and of modern life set the stage for radical Christianity's advent.

I. THE CONTEXT OF RADICAL CHRISTIANITY

No movement in history or thought arises out of nothing. The radicals themselves are the first to admit that they are not saying something entirely new. They all find forerunners in the past century and a half and, curious as it might sound, they all trace the roots of radical Christianity to the Bible itself. In addition, they all recognize that radical Christianity has emerged out of the encounter between tradional Christianity and the modern world.

This unlikely parentage justifies calling radical Christianity a *new Christianity*. Even the most extreme expressions of radical thought claim kinship with traditional Christianity. But radical Christianity as a whole breaks with decisive beliefs and experiences of the Christian past because of a revolution in human life and thought during the last one hundred and fifty years. Whether radical Christianity is genuinely "Christian" or really "new" remains to be seen. Here we are interested only in finding out why some theologians are calling for a new Christianity.

The call for a new Christianity issues out of a confluence and collision of fideism and exclusivism with relativism and secularism. These abstract terms are often used to describe systematic statements of belief or consciously held ideologies. But here they stand for styles of life and thought. They denote the underlying though seldom noticed assumptions of human behavior. In short, these four terms are descriptive of the way certain people think and act today, whether they are aware of it or not.

Herein arises the need for a new Christianity according to the radicals. Fideism and exclusivism are characteristic of life in the Church while relativism and secularism are characteristic of life in the world. But, as we shall see presently, these two sets of basic assumptions simply do not fit together. Since these assumptions are at odds with one another, persons who are adherents of traditional Christianity and citizens of the modern world face a dilemma. The modern Christian must choose between or compartmentalize Church and world. But neither option is viable because men cannot escape the modern world and should not live divided lives. For this reason, the radicals have undertaken the task of rethinking the basic assumptions underlying both Christian faith and modern life in hopes of bringing them together.

Indeed, the nature of this undertaking is the reason for calling them *radical* theologians. In this context, "radical" does not mean irresponsible, unstable, flamboyant, immoral, reductionistic or materialistic although these epithets and worse have been hurled at the radicals. "Radical" designates neither emotional states, political leanings nor philosophical commitments. Rather, "radical" denotes both a special kind of problem and a special method of problem-solving. A *radical problem* strikes to the very roots of our being, calls into question the very essence of human life. Hence, *radical problem-solving* must resolve those impasses in our belief systems which have become obstacles to productive life and thought or to authentic faith and belief.

21

According to the radical theologians, changes in human life and thought in the last one hundred and fifty years have raised *radical problems* for Christian believers. These problems go to the very roots of how one can be both human and Christian. The Church has certainly been aware of these problems. This awareness is evident in the continuing succession of reformations and reformulations within the recent past—the rise of Protestant Liberalism, the struggles between science and religion, the historical-critical treatment of the Bible, the aborted experiments in Catholic Modernism, the influence of the Social Gospel, the impact of Neo-orthodoxy, the growth of the ecumenical movement and the innovations of Vatican II. But, according to the radicals, none of these attempts to solve the problems for faith raised by the modern world has been *radical*. None of them has gone to the roots of the problems—to the conflicting basic assumptions of traditional Christianity and the modern world! Laudable as these continuing attempts to relate faith and life have been, they have all been useless patches on worn-out garments. Nothing less than *radical* adjustments can remove the *radical* obstacles to being a Christian in the modern world.

But why have these theologians detected radical problems and prescribed radical solutions for contemporary Christians? Are the assumptions underlying life in the modern world really inescapable? If not, why are the adjustments to the modern world already represented in Protestant Liberalism and Neo-orthodoxy and presently being explored in Roman Catholicism inadequate? An answer to these questions requires explicit attention to what is meant by fideism, exclusivism, relativism and secularism.

1. Fideism

Traditional Christianity in its many forms has usually been committed to fideism. This term comes from the Latin word *fides* which means faith. But more is meant by fideism than the claim that man is related to God through faith rather than through his senses or intellect. While agreeing that man is related to God through faith, fideism further holds that faith is based upon a totally supernatural, infallible and unquestionable revelation.

Certain varieties of traditional Christianity have argued for an additional source of human knowledge of God. Roman Catholicism and most Protestant theologies prior to 1800 claim that natural evidence and even rational proof of God's reality can be found in the existence, design and purposiveness of the natural world. But these demonstrations do not furnish complete and saving knowledge. As the Westminster Confession representatively puts it: "Although the light of nature and the works of creation and providence do so far manifest the goodness, wisdom and power of God as to leave men inexcusable, yet they are not sufficient to give that knowledge of God and of his will which is necessary to salvation." Thus, even for those who claim that some knowledge of God is available to all men everywhere, this natural understanding is insufficient and condemning apart from supernatural revelation and redemption.

Furthermore, most Protestant theologians since the early nineteenth century have rejected the idea of natural evidence or rational proof for the existence of God. This rejection rests on philosophical and religious grounds. Philosophically, these theologians have accepted the critique and rejection of natural theology set forth in the writings of David Hume and Immanuel Kant. These eighteenth century philosophers argued that all human efforts to discover and prove God are doomed because of the inherent limitations of all human reasoning. Natural or rational knowledge of God is also rejected on religious grounds. All human reasoning is limited and distorted by sin. But surrendering a belief in man's natural or rational capacities to know God has not disrupted Protestantism's claim to know God. Rather, man's knowledge of God rests wholly on God's revelation to man. God can be known only when, where and how he makes himself known. And for traditional Christianity God has revealed himself to faith–supernaturally, infallibly and indubitably.

The source of this divinely given and guaranteed revelation for traditional Christianity as a whole is the Bible. The Bible furnishes man saving knowledge of God's superrational nature, of Christ's supernatural accomplishments, and of history's supertemporal consummation. In addition, Roman Catholics recognize church tradition as a source of revelation. For them, "tradition" denotes a body of truths revealed to the disciples of Jesus, some after the resurrection, which were not written down. These traditions were handed down orally by the successors of the Apostles until a later time in the Church's history when they were recorded. But Roman Catholic theologians insist that tradition contains nothing necessary for salvation in addition or contradiction to the Bible.

Formally, Protestants and Catholics agree that the whole counsel of God concerning his own glory and man's salvation is expressly set down or may be deduced from Scripture. Furthermore, the Bible's unique authority rests on none other than God himself. The Bible is authoritative because it is the Word of God authored by God. Faith has *no* basis and needs *no* assurance other than Scripture.

Certainly this position recognizes the need to interpret and appropriate the Scriptures. All things in the Bible are not equally clear in themselves or to everyone. But the interpretation and appropriation of the Scripture is always under the guidance of God's Spirit speaking through Scripture. Once again, the Westminster Confession speaks representatively: "The infallible rule of interpretation of Scripture is the Scripture itself, and therefore, when there is a question about the true and full sense of any Scripture (which is not manifold, but one), it may be searched and known by other places that speak more clearly. The Supreme Judge, by whom all controversies of religion are to be determined, all decrees and councils, opinions of ancient writers, doctrines of men, and private spirits, are to be examined, and in whose sentence we are to rest, can be none other but the Holy Spirit speaking in the Scripture." Hence, even at points of disagreement and difficulty, there is no appeal beyond the Scriptures.

Finally this position does offer a kind of proof for itself. Biblicists defend the supernatural character of the Bible by appealing to the distinctiveness of Israel, the fulfillment of prophecy, the evidence of miracles, the ministry of Jesus, the resurrection of Christ, the growth of the Church, the witness of the apostles and even the claims of the Bible for itself. But these "proofs" are all circular. The proofs for the authority of the Bible are derived from the Bible itself. Once again, faith has no appeal beyond Scripture for the Bible is self-grounding.

As we shall see later in the discussion of secularism and relativism, numerous difficulties have arisen for this uncompromising biblicism in the last one hundred and fifty years. Doubtlessly, the majority of laymen in the Church are oblivious to these difficulties. But all Protestant theologians today save the most hidebound fundamentalists have modified their view of revelation to take account of the scientific error, historical inaccuracy, theological diversity, moral unevenness and confessional character which becomes apparent in a historical-critical study of the Bible.

The usual approach has been to make a distinction between the *words* of the Bible and the *Word* of God. The Bible is composed of the words of ordinary men and thus manifests the idiosyncrasies, limitations and foibles of all things human. But through these frail words the very Word of God is spoken and may be heard. Revelation means encountering God through the Bible rather than finding information about God in the Bible.

But this contemporary adjustment, so typical of Protestant Neo-orthodoxy, is often simply fideism in another garb. Now instead of basing faith on a supernatural, infallible and indubitable book, faith is based on a supernatural, infallible and indubitable revelation mediated through a fully human, fallible and questionable book. The Christian can know that he has received such a revelation only when he has indeed received it. In other words, a self-grounding experience has become the ground of faith. Similar to earlier appeals to experience in Mysticism, Pietism and Revivalism, a self-convincing and self-authenticating experience becomes the only and final court of appeal.

Perhaps we can already see traditional Christianity riding a collision course with the modern world. Faith based on a self-grounding revelation, whether written or encountered, is only as secure as the alleged revelation. If insoluable problems are posed or convincing counter explanations are offered for these revelations, Christians are left with only two options. They must either dogmatically reaffirm or skeptically reject the reality of their revelation.

But fideism is not the only basic assumption of traditional Christianity which runs counter to the basic assumptions of life in the modern world. Not only does the Church traditionally claim to have a supernatural, infallible and indubitable ground for faith; it also regularly claims that this ground *alone* offers the true knowledge and saving power of God.

2. Exclusivism

Traditional Christianity is an exclusive though militant religious faith. Salvation for men is available only through Jesus Christ. Other religious ways and systems offer at best preparatory faith and truncated truth. More typically, they are condemned as idolatrous and truthless. But the salvation given by Jesus Christ potentially includes the whole human family. Therefore, the Church has always recognized a missionary mandate to take her exclusive Gospel to the ends of the earth. In fact, these two impulses are usually thought to entail one another. The Church's mission to the world is goundless unless Christianity is the only true faith and since Christianity is the only true faith it must share its good news with the world.

Some rather stern and unsavory consequences follow from traditional Christianity's exclusive and militant character. God's redemptive purposes and benefits are denied to all except those who share in the salvation history of the Old and New Israels. The whole history of mankind is a story of idolatry and condemnation except for a single strand of people who have received true understanding and eternal salvation. The many are doomed to find no purpose in this life and eternal punishment in the life to come. Only the few chosen and redeemed find eternal life here and hereafter. In addition to these admitted features of traditional Christianity, less acknowledged consequences of exclusivism have often followed. Exclusive claims to God's truth and grace have repeatedly invited and sanctioned religious intolerance, racial prejudice, economic exploitation and political colonialism.

In various ways, traditional Christianity has tried to soften these harsh features. The exploitive tendencies of exclusivism are condemned as aberrations when they are recognized and acknowledged. In addition, limited exceptions to a wholesale condemnation of non-Christians are provided in appeals to an age of accountability, invincible ignorance and the baptism of desire. Protestants remove some of the sting of exclusivism by teaching that children are not condemned in God's sight until they can distinguish between right and wrong. Catholics go further by excepting morally upright ancients and pagans who remain ignorant of God's full revelation in Christ or who are deprived of God's saving grace in the sacraments. Of course, a doctrine of universalism retains exclusivism while avoiding its usual inequities. But traditional Christianity has resolutely rejected the belief that all men will eventually be saved through Christ because this universalism would deny the reality of free will, the purposiveness of history and the seriousness of sin. Therefore, while disclaiming the unsavory aspects and softening the sternness of exclusivism, traditional Christianity remains committed to the claim that Christians are the sole recipients of God's saving truth and grace.

But why is the Church committed to this "scandal" of particularity? Traditional Christianity enjoys the glory and suffers the stigma of this scandal partly because of its historical character.

26

Fideism's claim to a supernatural, infallible and indubitable revelation of God need not be wedded to exclusivism if this revelation were available to all men everywhere and everytime. But traditional Christianity is not a religion of ideas universally discoverable by men. It is a religion of events uniquely wrought by God. The only saving truth and grace of God were given originally in the concrete events of Israel and Christ and are mediated to the present through the concrete witness of the Church. The particularity of revelatory events and witnessing communities seems to require that absolute claims be exclusive as well.

But even a revelation which is both historical and fideistic need not be exclusivistic. One could believe, for example, that God reveals himself through history differently in ways appropriate to diverse cultures. Actually, traditional Christianity's exclusivism may depend as much on logical and psychological considerations as on biblical and theological assumptions. Logically, the claim that Christianity is the only true religion rests on an absolute divison of beliefs into separate categories of truth and error. The very concept of degrees or approximations of truth is rejected since every belief about anything is supposed either true or false. In addition to this mathematical ideal of truth, exclusive claims for Christianity find support in the psychological need to belong to an intimate community of persons. This need is most often met by the creation of in-groups. But there can be no in-groups apart from out-groups. Exclusive groups must exclude to retain their distinctiveness. In short, the Church's claim to have the only true religion may be as much a reflection of the way people customarily think and live as an intrinsic demand of Christian faith itself.

Once again, we can anticipate traditional Christianity's collision with the modern world. Can a historical yet exclusive faith be intellectually or morally defended in the face of history's variety and vastness? Does viewing the whole sweep of history in the light of one event make any sense? More important, can God's truth and grace be restricted to Christian history without rendering God morally unthinkable? These questions strike at the very foundations of Christian exclusivism and hence cannot be ignored.

Merely spelling out what fideism and exclusivism mean has already exposed traditional Christianity's vulnerability to the modern world. We need no conscious understanding of the basic assumptions underlying modern life and thought to sense the gulf between Church and world. And, if we find ourselves uncomfortable and perhaps impatient with the Church's claim to an infallible and privileged access to God, we betray our own citizenship in the modern world. In either case, we must pursue further why traditional Christianity and the modern world have reached an impasse. We must see precisely why relativism and secularism have raised radical problems for an exclusivistic and fideistic Christianity. Only then will we be in a position to understand why and how the radical theologians are calling for a new Christianity.

3. Relativism

The discovery of spatial and temporal relativity has made a profound impact on modern life and thought. For centuries, men have believed in universal truths, values and institutions. Differences between cultures and changes within cultures were scarcely noticed because of their geographical isolation and gradual amelioration. But the development of modern means of travel, communication and education brought such parochialism to an end. Men have become aware of the diversity and the changes in human life through the past two centuries of historical research, comparative study and philosophical criticism of human life in all of its expressions. Such intellectual activity laid bare the diversity of social institutions, life styles and belief systems found in different times and places. More recently, men have realized not only that politics, ethics and religion are relative but scientific propositions, logical rules and perhaps sensory perceptions as well. Both the social and natural sciences have acknowledged that scientific laws are not absolute. Philosophy has shown that we think and even perceive with conditioned categories. In short, a sobering realization that there are no universal institutions, values, beliefs, truths or experiences has dawned in the twentieth century.

Although the full meaning and consequences are far from clear, great strides in understanding and accommodating relativism have been made. The bases and manifestations of relativism are being explored in such intellectual disciplines as physics, psychology, sociology, history, rhetoric, ethics and theology. Numerous theories have been formulated which explain why men not only *do* but *must* differ in their views of things and ways of life. While each theory has its own distinctive features, they all share one common denominator. All theories of relativism center in the claim that men are limited *to* and *by* their own viewpoints. Every viewpoint is marked by distinctive spatiotemporal, physiopsychic and sociohistorical features. These distinctive features are, in turn, reflected in all truth claims, faith affirmations, value judgments and social institutions growing out of that point of view. Therefore, absolute accuracy, exact agreement and universal applicability are impossible because no two perspectives are identical.

Accommodating relativism is proving more difficult than explaining it. The question of what relativism implies for our usual claims about Truth, Goodness and Beauty is still being debated. Three lines of philosophical argument are discernable in this clash of opinion. *Subjective* relativism denies all objectivity to judgments of fact and value. Every human claim is hopelessly subjective because of the limitations and isolation of individual viewpoints. *Contextual* relativism avoids such skepticism and nihilism by recognizing that people who share the same broad intellectual and cultural standpoints can make truth claims and value judgments. But these claims and judgments are objective only within their given frame of reference since there are no universal frameworks. Finally, *objective* relativism goes further still by anchoring claims of fact and value in the real world. Admittedly these claims are always imperfect and incomplete because of their perspectival character. But they are significant of and related to objective reality. These three alternatives, however, are not mutually exclusive nor always consistently adopted. Relativism with respect to knowledge is often treated separately from the relativity of value judgments. Thus, for example, the knowledge claims of science may be judged *objectively* relative while the value judgments of ethics may be portrayed as *contextually* or even *subjectively* relative. In short, the question of how relative claims relate to objective reality has not been conclusively resolved.

Although the debate will continue for some time, a significant corner seems to have been turned in the last decade or two. Relativism has been freed from the onus of skepticism and nihilism. Both contextual and objective theories of relativism have shown how man's quest for what is true, good and beautiful can be fruitful even though relative. In addition, subjective relativism is declining as a serious option, although fresh converts and diehard opponents to relativism seem bent on preserving it. Of course, skepticism or nihilism may serve as useful antedotes to dogmatism and they still occur as intellectual rationalizations for egoism. But consistent skepticism and nihilism are increasingly difficult to defend and impossible to practice, because they are self-contradictory and self-defeating.

Thus, a way has been opened to accept relativism without abandoning life to ignorance and savagery. Relativism disclosed the partial and changing character of all scientific descriptions, moral opinions, religious beliefs, aesthetic canons and social institutions. But relativism also teaches that we can live with approximate descriptions of the world, consensus opinions about morality, shared outlooks in religion, prevailing tastes in art and tentative structures of society. We can function in a relative environment if we demand less than final answers and expect nothing more than pragmatic assurances. We can, because we *have* and *must!*

The full scope and implications of relativism are slowly but surely pervading public consciousness and behavior. Judging from the prevalence of all manner of contemporary absolutisms, relativism has yet to leaven all areas of modern life and thought. But it has penetrated the public domain at two vital points. Both morality and religion have become increasingly relativized in theory and in practice. The erosion of doctrinal distinctives, the disappearance of denominational exclusivism, the crises over moral values, the relaxing of moral rigidity all betray a ferment of relativism. Indeed, the American traditions of moral and religious individualism and political and ecclesiastical pluralism have long expressed and nourished a tacit relativism.

Nor is it accidental and insignificant that relativism has "surfaced" first in morality and religion. Contrary to what some suggest, these areas of thought and life have become relativized because of their omnipresence rather than their absence. Relativism has become apparent in morality and religion precisely because people are involved and concerned with them daily. The vast majority of people have yet to realize the relativity of politics and science because they are not directly involved in these activities. But only time stands in the way of relativism pervading every area of life and thought.

Needless to say, relativism raises radical problems for traditional Christianity. It strikes at the roots of fideistic and exclusivistic claims to God's truth and grace. The idea of timeless truths, unchanging values and permanent institutions appears hollow in a world increasingly committed to relativism. Worse yet, claiming *sole* access to the divine nature, will and favor echoes presumption in a world increasingly comfortable with relativism.

The day of proclaiming any point of view final much less exclusive is rapidly fading away.

The Church certainly has not been oblivious to this challenge to her life and thought. Two significant theological movements have arisen in response to relativism—Liberalism and Neo-orthodoxy. In the nineteenth century, Protestant Liberalism developed a thoroughgoing accomodation to the discovery of historical and social relativism. Liberalism as a whole acknowledged both that Christianity is firmly embedded in history and society and that other religions are authentic purveyors of faith and morality. But two distinct ways of accommodating these concessions emerged within the liberal movement. The majority of Liberalism's adherents conceived of Christianity in terms of "abiding truths in changing categories." The Church does possess eternal verities of faith and morality but these treasures are always contained in earthen vessels. The means for communicating and implementing faith and morality are always culturally conditioned and hence subject to change when intellectual and social conditions change. But these changes are dictated by the strategy of *relevance* rather than governed by the whim of *relativity*. Furthermore, although Christianity has no monopoly on truth, Jesus did disclose the highest understanding of God and his will for men. Therefore, Christianity has priority and responsibility for the spiritual and social concerns of men everywhere. In contrast, a minority voice within the liberal movement viewed Christianity as only one expression of the universal human phenomena of faith and morality. Both religion and ethics grow out of the dynamics of man's rational and social life as ways of understanding and controlling his environment. Since faith and morality, then, are functions of their cultural contexts, religioethical perspectives should never become permanently formulated and can never be comparatively ranked.

Liberalism of one variety or another became the dominant voice in Protestantism by offering a way for the Church to retain much of classical Christianity while accommodating herself to the intellectual and social revolutions reshaping the modern world. But Liberalism's strength proved to be her undoing or at least her temporary eclipse. During the 1920's, a powerful reactionary theological movement appeared in Protestantism. Neo-orthodoxy indicted Liberalism for conceding too much to the modern world in accepting relativism as a working principle for faith and life. Once relativism is accepted, Christianity can only become a reflection and function of culture as, indeed, Liberalism's extremist minority admitted. And, since the Church largely under the tutelage of liberal theology offered little resistance and guidance to a world in turmoil and change, Neo-orthodoxy became a prophetic ferment and finally the prevailing theology in contemporary Protestanism.

Neo-orthodoxy, as the name implies, gained both its prophetic power and pre-eminent status by refurbishing traditional Orthodoxy's fideism and exclusivism. Neo-orthodoxy fully acknowledges the relativism of all human concepts, institutions and relationships. But, unlike Liberalism in any of its varieties, Neo-orthodoxy further claims that faith must rest on absolutes to be saving and healing. Therefore, faith can rest on nothing human. No *humanly* formulated beliefs, established structures or sustained relationships can deliver man from selfishness and separation, despair and death. Only a *divinely* given and guaranteed revelation can bear the weight of man's eternal salvation and reconciliation. Unlike the older Orthodoxy, however, Neo-orthodoxy does not simply equate the Bible or Chruch *as such* with this supernatural revelation. Both the written and the lived witness of the Chruch are human and hence not absolute. But in sovereign power and gracious condescension God offers his love and reveals his will *through* these imperfect channels. The absolute and unchanging Word of God freely and surely speaks through these relative and mutable words of men.

Neo-orthodoxy seems to have won a place for traditional Christianity in the modern world. By clearly distinguishing without separating the divine and the human in history, the contemporary Christian can admit the relativity of all things human and criticize the idolatry of all false absolutes. At the same time, the contemporary Christian can enjoy the presence of the Absolute God and further God's purposes in a relative world. Thus, Neo-orthodoxy claims to have come to terms with relativism by circumventing rather than denying it.

But, despite its compelling power and established place within Protestantism, Neo-orthodoxy remains quite vulnerable to the modern world. Neo-orthodoxy may appear to have taken the measure of relativism but modern secularism raises radical questions for this refurbished traditional Christianity. By striking at the roots of fideism whether old or new, secularism challenges both the place of the Chruch and the reality of God in the modern world.

4. Secularism

Secularism is the most important and comprehensive feature of life and thought in the modern world. This term should not be confused with philosophical or practical materialism, although some secularists happen to be materialists. Secularism neither singles out matter as the only reality nor exalts material possessions as man's highest good. Rather, secularism limits thought and life to this world. This limitation is reflected in the derivation of the term from the Latin *saeculum,* which means "of this age" or "related to this world." Secularism means thinking 'from below' and living 'from below.'

As such, secularism stands in bold contrast to the ways men have understood and conducted themselves for centuries. From primitive times, men have oriented their thinking and managed their affairs 'from above.' They have assumed that the world of time and space is surrounded by an eternal and transcendent world. Life in the time-space world is derived, governed and fulfilled from the eternal-transcendent world. But the connection between these two separate worlds is established and maintained only through special means. *Religious* authorities, institutions and activities link the physical and the spiritual worlds. Consequently, men have depended upon religion to establish truth, define morality and control society in this world while looking to the other world to explain mysteries, correct injustices and fulfill destiny.

Against this enduring outlook, secularism dispenses with religions and other-worlds as sources for understanding and resources for controlling life. This rejection is due more to the irrelevance than to the incredibility of two-world thinking. Men have less and less need for supernatural explanations, ecclesiastical tutelage and religious consolations. Men grow more and more confident in their ability to understand their world, control their environment and solve their problems. While life is still full of residual mystery, challenge and suffering, these are believed manageable without benefit of clergy or deity. Secular man looks no further than his own universe for all the purpose and fulfillment life affords.

Secularism has been making these inroads into social and mental structures for centuries. But this process has dramatically accelerated in our time and the ferment in the minds of the few has finally spread to the masses. The assumptions of secularism are operative even in the life and thought of persons and institutions who officially deny and resist secularism. Thinking and living from above has been gradually but surely squeezed out of the modern world by the rise of science, the achievements of technology and the power of revolution.

Modern science has taught men to explain things from below. Appeals to other-worldly powers, metaphysical postulates, and miraculous interventions have become unnecessary as man has learned to explore and explain nature and life without them. Beginning from experience, proceeding by imagination and ending with application, man has pulled more and more of the real world into an intelligible and functioning explanation of the ways and whys of the universe. First the world around and then the world within have come under patient and painstaking human investigation and human interpretation. In the process, the boundaries "beyond which science cannot go" have continually receded. In the physical world, the conquests have been spectacular— motion, matter, energy and space. In the psychic world, the boundaries of thought, relationship, want and guilt have successively fallen and even the frontiers of life and death are being explored. Man needs no help 'from above' in explaining why things happen.

Modern technology has furnished men the equipment for controlling things from below. Men will always be dependent upon a natural environment. But they are less and less plagued by the limitations, discomforts, fickleness and ravages of their environment. Mechanical technology has transformed life and society by harnessing energy and creating tools almost beyond imagination. Medical technology has made great strides in extending life's enjoyment, productivity and longevity. Environmental technology is making dramatic breakthroughs in multiplying natural resources and regulating natural processes. Of course, technological advances have multiplied the world's risks and problems — accidents, warfare, pollution and overpopulation to name a few. But even the liabilities of technology are believed soluable by technological means. Man needs no help 'from above' in controlling when things happen.

Finally, social revolution has enabled men to change things from below. Men will always be dependent upon a social environment. But no longer do kings rule by divine right or enjoy amnesty from redress. No longer must the oppressed endure injustice as a whim of Fate or a judgment of God. The modern era was ushered in by social revolution as much as by scientific and technological advance. The masses have learned how to be makers rather than victims of history and society. They have learned that organized power exercised in a variety of ways can bring about social, political and economic changes. This lesson has profoundly altered the structures and underpinnings of society. Representative and pluralistic societies attempt to build orderly and perpetual revolution into the fabric of political institutions and cultural purposes. But, regardless of the prevailing social embodiments and philosophies, men no longer wait for other-worldly deliverance or recompense for the indignity, suppression and exploitation they suffer. Man needs no help'from above' in changing how things happen.

For these reasons and in these ways, modern life has dissolved man's primitive dependence upon divine providence and subservience to ecclesiastical authority. Secularism strikes at the roots of the claim and content of fideistic Christianity. The very notion of supernaturally given and guaranteed truth finds no place in a world committed to thinking from below. The day of accepting anything on authoritative testimony without empirical and experiential corroboration soon will or already has passed away. The 'authority crisis' in both Church and world is an irreversible fruit of secularism.

Secularism plays even greater havoc with the content of fideism's claim to supernaturally given and guaranteed revelation. Traditional Christianity belongs to the two-world orientation discussed above. As an other-wordly Being and Power, God works both through and apart from natural process and human agency to achieve his purposes. But the keystone for fideism has always been a belief in God's miraculous intervention or direction in life. For centuries the miraculous element in traditional Christianity was thought of in terms of supernatural interruptions of nature. More recently, this venerable concept has given way to the idea of God "acting in history." But secularism challenges both translations of miracle. Were not miracles in the old sense of supernatural interruptions of nature merely prescientific explanations of strange phenomena or fanciful exaggerations of pious imagination? Are not miracles in the modern sense of God acting in history merely value judgments about meaningful events or verbal doubletalk by compromising theologians? The idea of God as a miraculous problem-solver and need-fulfiller finds no place in a world capable of controlling and changing life from below. The day of waiting for God to show the way, do the work or transmute the failure of making life fully human has begun to pass. Secularism has laid the world at the door of *human* initiative, resourcefulness and responsibility.

Understandably, secularism's corrosive effect on traditional Christianity has been stubbornly ignored or only gradually acknowledged by the Chruch. Two notable efforts were made in the past to come to terms with man's growing capacity to understand, control and change things from below. Eighteenth century Deism and nineteenth century Liberalism both sought to harmonize Christian faith with the new science, technology and politics of their time. While these theological movements differed in many ways, they modified the traditional view of God in much the same way and for much the same reason. Both reinterpret the mode and locus of God's relationship to men. No longer could God be portrayed as solving problems and fulfilling needs by miraculously interrupting or manipulating happenings in the physical world. Science had shown the world too orderly and predictable to permit or expect God to abrogate cause and effect sequences. Thus, biblical and theological claims to such miracles were systematically reinterpreted as prescientific explanations, pious exaggerations or symbolic expressions of faith.

But, while giving up the idea of miracle in *physical* space, both Deism and Liberalism retained a kind of miracle in *psychic* space. Both portrayed God as solving problems and meeting needs by intervening or interacting in man's spiritual life. The "inner" miracles of communion, conscience and conversion were taken as immediate and certain experiences of God. Furthermore, these miracles of the inner life freed men from the terrors of nature and strengthened men for the tasks of life. Thus, religiousness became the bridge between God and man, heaven and earth, spiritual and physical.

Even Neo-orthodoxy, which differs in so many ways from Liberalism, accepts much of this partial accommodation to secularism. New terms have been introduced and fresh emphasis has been placed on God's sovereign and free creation of faith. Thus, for Neo-orthodoxy, God encounters man in history rather than man finding God in inwardness. God addresses man in the crises of life rather than man knowing God through conscience. God liberates man in the moment of decision rather than man receiving salvation at conversion. But Neo-orthodoxy, in material agreement with Liberalism, locates God in human experience rather than natural process. While miracles do not occur in nature, God does act in history. But God's presence and power in history can be apprehended only by faith.

36

It was only a matter of time, however, until man's ability to explain, control and change things from below spilled over into psychic and historical space. Sociology, psychology, literature and philosophy began to explore and explain the depth dimensions of life in terms of causal and natural dynamics. Politics, psychotherapy, education and communications began to shape and redirect psychic energies and historical events through human and natural techniques. Gradually, the distinctively human dimensions of life, which Deism and especially Liberalism and Neo-orthodoxy thought an inviolable sanctuary, began to yield less and less room and need for God.

Secularism continues to narrow the range of natural happenings and human experiences which require God for their occurrence or explanation. Until quite recently, most theologians were unwilling to admit how far this secularizing process could go. In the past fifty years, only a few men like Ernst Troeltsch, Paul Tillich and H. Richard Niebuhr saw and sought to work through the radical implications of secularism for Christian life and thought. But even their reformulations finally rest on mystical validation of religion's special role (Troeltsch), on divine ground for man's ultimate concern (Tillich), or on special revelation within life's religious depths (Niebuhr). Thoroughgoing secularism was held at bay by reserving such special 'unsecular' places for God and faith.

But one theologian prior to the midpoint of the twentieth century did call for an uncompromising acceptance of the secularizing process. Dietrich Bonhoeffer, executed by the Gestapo in 1945 for his role in the German resistance movement, has keynoted our current theological revolution more than any other man. He drew little notice outside his own circle as a young theological professor and author. His impact came after his death and through fragmentary writings–an incomplete book published posthumously as *Ethics* and a few personal letters smuggled out during his imprisonment which were later published by one of his friends under the title *Letters and Papers from Prison.* These fragments, especially the letters, exploded like a delayed time bomb on the theological scene of the mid-fifties. This explosion set off a chain reaction that is still rocking the Church and the world.

In a letter written in the Spring of 1944, Bonhoeffer declared his own intention to face secularism without any kind of pious escapes. Acknowledging the surprising and disturbing character of this turn, he wrote:

We are proceeding toward a time of no religion at all: men as they are now simply cannot be religious anymore. Even those who honestly describe themselves as "religious" do not in the least act up to it, and so when they say "religious" they evidently mean something quite different. Our whole nineteen-hundred-year-old Christian preaching and theology rests upon the "religious premise" of man. What we call Christianity has always been a pattern—perhaps a true pattern—of religion. But if one day it becomes apparent that this *a priori* "premise" simply does not exist, but was an historical and temporary form of human self-expression, i.e., if we reach the stage of being radically without religion—and I think this is more or less the case already...—what does that mean for "Christianity"? *(Letters and Papers From Prison, pp. 162-63).*

At last the question had been asked radically. Can Christianity survive when its linchpin of religiousness is removed by the secularizing process?

Bonhoeffer believed that only a "religionless Christianity" could survive in "a world come of age." The Church simply must accept the fact that God as the solution to those problems which arise when human understanding fails and human resources end has become superfluous. Reserving 'special places' for God like moral consciousness, boundary situations or religious depths are last-ditch efforts to make room for God which are doomed to fail. Claiming special experience of God through God's sovereign and free acts in history is even more vulnerable to the secularizing process. The wave of the future in a world freed from adolescent dependence upon God belongs to a faith freed from the wornout garments of religiousness. Contrary to some interpretations of Bonhoeffer, he meant something far more radical by "religionless" than an end to otherwordly piety, individualism and inwardness. He meant a Christianity freed from the view of God as a *miraculous* problem-solver (whether in physical or psychic space), from the view of Christ as the fulfillment of a *special* depth (whether a moral or religious depth) and from the view of the Church as the custodian of a *saving* power (whether a revelatory or sacramental power).

Bonhoeffer did not live to work out a consistent theology, ecclesiology and liturgy for such a religionless Christianity. His letters are filled with tantalizing suggestions and tentative sketches. But moving through all of them are two different and perhaps contrary assessments of secularism. Sometimes the

38

secularizing process is viewed as God's way of teaching men to live in and for the world without him. More typically, Bonhoeffer sees secularism as God's way of confronting men in *all* of life rather than in some *special* place. In either case, Bonhoeffer welcomed secularism as the will rather than the enemy of God. But different styles of Christian life and thought were certainly implied in his two approaches to secularism.

Precisely because of the fragmentary and ambivalent character of Bonhoeffer's call for a religionless Christianity, he became the harbinger of a theological movement which reflects an even greater diversity. Bonhoeffer marks the beginning of the radical theologies but his influence is preparatory rather than pervasive, catalytic rather than determinative. All the radical theologians begin with a Bonhoefferian acceptance of the world come of age and commitment to a religionless Christianity. But they end up offering a variety of interpretations of Christian faith for the modern world.

II. THE VARIETIES OF RADICAL CHRISTIANITY

Radical theology has emerged out of the collision of traditional Christianity and the modern world. By reducing these complex and variegated movements of life and thought to their underlying assumptions, we have seen how incompatible the Church's fideism and exclusivism are with the world's relativism and secularism. We have also seen how Liberalism and Neo-orthodoxy sought to resolve this impasse by partially accepting and partially circumventing these basic features of modern life. But, following Bonheoffer's inspiration and slogans, a small group of theologians have rejected liberal and neo-orthodox realignments for not going far enough. Both fail to treat the problems raised by the revolutions in modern life and thought *radically*. Liberalism and Neo-orthodoxy alike postpone the total relativizing and secularizing of Christian life and thought by reserving 'special places' for a problem–solving and need-fulfilling God. But these modifications of traditional Orthodoxy did not halt this process. Therefore, the radicals call for the Church to abandon her policy of strategic retreat and reentrenchment. Nothing less than a complete restructuring of faith's foundational beliefs and behavior can revitalize the Church in the modern world. Only a *radical* theology can resolve the *radical* problems disrupting life and thought for men who are both moderns and Christians.

But, as we shall see in the following chapters, radical Christianity is not a monolithic movement. Strikingly different interpretations of the Christian faith are offered by the spearheads of the radical movement. Such dissonant notes as the Church's significance and irrelevance, God's nearness and absence, Christ's divinity and humanity, man's immortality and finitude, and even God's vitality and death can be heard in the cacophony of sounds called radical Christianity. Not only are these polyphonic sounds pointed out by the critics of the radical theologies. The radicals also fully acknowledge and vigorously debate these differences between themselves.

How then can we speak of radical Christianity even in a collective sense? Do the radicals share a core commitment which is the source both of their unity and diversity? These questions can be fully answered only by comparing the actual writings of the radicals at specific points of concern. Such an analysis follows in Part Two of this book. But a preliminary sketch here of the unity and diversity within the radical movement will introduce the format and facilitate the analysis of the following chapters.

The radicals are bound together by their common acceptance of the modern world's relativism and secularism. They all regard religion, in Bonhoeffer's three-fold sense of the term, as unessential and even detrimental to faith. Relativism and secularism have brought an end to believing and behaving as if God miraculously transmutes human lacking, as if Christ uniquely fulfills spiritual depths and as if the Church exclusively mediates saving power. Thus, radical Christianity properly includes all those theologians who relinquish *absolute* standpoints for man and *special* places for God in nature, history or inwardness. Only by virtue of this rejection may radical Chrisitianity be called a unified movement.

Although unified by an uncompromising acceptance of relativism and secularism, the radicals disagree over how these features of modern life and thought came to pass and what they mean for faith. These disagreements are often obscured and easily overlooked because the radicals confront common problems, explore similar themes and sometimes employ identical terminology. But, despite agreements at numerous points, the avant-garde spokesmen for radical Christianity present distinctive and distinguishable responses to the modern world's relativity and secularity.

How then can we characterize the diversity of the radical

movement? Often movements of life and thought may be best described by being circumscribed. Substantive differences and subtle nuances may become visible only at the outer perimeters where the alternatives are clear and definite. Thus, the inner complexity and diversity of the radical movement can be grasped in the light of two apparently opposite ways of handling the loss of absolute standpoints and transcendental experiences.

On the one hand, relativism and secularism can be interpreted *theocentrically*. The modern world can be accepted without losing faith's soul because ultimately God stands at the center of the relativizing and secularizing process. Admittedly, the traditional concepts of God, Christ and Church have been rendered obsolescent by the developments of the last two hundred years. But these traditional concepts were imperfect to begin with and have become increasingly inadequate vehicles for understanding and expressing faith. Thus, relativism and secularism actually clarify and strengthen rather than obscure or destroy the realities of faith. Relativism republishes the biblical view of God's sovereignty and man's limitations. God alone is absolute and no human institution, cause or relationship can claim absoluteness without usurping God's sovereignty. Relativism has once and for all unmasked the pretensions of all egoistic, political and even religious absolutisms. Relativism is the counterpart of all divine injunctions against idolatry. Similarly, secularism reflects the biblical view of God's purposes for human life. God intends nothing less for man than free and responsible life in and for the world. Secularism has forced man to stop restricting faith to special places and to stop stultifying life by inflexible structures. Secularism is the equivalent of God's original command to subdue the earth and have dominion over it. From such a theological vantage point, faith is more vital and God more real in the modern world than ever before.

On the other hand, relativism and secularism may be interpreted *anthropocentrically*. These achievements are the fruits of human curiosity, ingenuity and courage. Through his own efforts, man has eliminated the need and possibility of looking beyond human resources for life's purpose and fulfillment. The universe as a whole and the distinctiveness of human life can no longer be experienced or understood in *any* theocentric way. No room remains for God in the modern world, not even for a God who wills or permits the relativizing and secularizing process. While these momentous consequences may not have been foreseen by any of life's modernizers, relativism and secularism leave men completely alone in the universe. But, despite this loss of God, faith remains vital and necessary for this radical view. Fyodor Dostoevsky, a 19th century forerunner of radical Christianity, explored the theme that "everything is permitted if there is no God" in several novels. Radical Christians who place man at the center of modern life and thought reject this reading of God's disappearance. The 'death' of God means that men have become solely responsible for humanity. Stripped of otherworldly anchorage and orientation, men must establish and nuture human relations in all their emotional intensity, enriching mutuality and sacrificial nobility. Anthropocentric faiths are the life styles men have evolved for making and keeping life fully human. Although many forms of human faith are possible, Christian faith denotes that distinctive way of maintaining human life which was first envisioned and embodied by the man Jesus. Herein lies the claim of this approach to be a *Christian* atheism or a *godless* Christianity.

Radical Christianity then coheres and diverges in response to relativism and secularism. The radicals share in common the disappearance of absolute standpoints and transcendental experiences in human life and history. But their reactions to this shared loss run the gamut from clearly theocentric to strictly anthropocentric reformulations of Christian life and thought. Between these rather clearcut positions, a number of distinguishable alternatives offer creative alliances and tensions between theocentric and anthropocentric motifs. By paying careful attention to how these divergent motifs are defined and deployed, radical Christianity's unity and diversity can be comprehended.

The usefulness and correctness of this characterization will only become apparent in the following chapters when the radicals will be compared with one another and against the views of Orthodoxy, Liberalism and Neo-orthodoxy at specific points of belief.But before this fuller comparison is undertaken, the representative spokesmen for radical Christianity should be introduced.

Keeping in mind the fluidity of meanings and combinations of theocentric and anthropocentric motifs among the radicals, the radical movement is circumscribed by the secure theocentrism of Bishop John A. T. Robinson, and the unabashed anthropocentrism of Paul M. van Buren. Robinson, the most celebrated ecclesiastic among the radicals, sees radical theology as the most recent of an endless succession of remolding the earthen vessels which mediate

God's reality for a time. But the reality safeguarded and enshrined in these outmoded containers remains unquestioned and unchanged. Van Buren, a former Episcopal priest who now teaches religion at Temple University in Philadelphia, differs sharply from Robinson by leveling all religion down to man. The rise of relativism and secularism has merely revealed that even Christian beliefs about God have never been more than vivid parables of human and cultural values.

The remaining spokesmen for radical Christianity represent a variety of creative alliances and tensions between theocentric and anthropocentric concerns. While defining and combining these concerns somewhat differently, their respective positions permit a kind of arrangement between the clearcut positions of Robinson and van Buren. Thomas J. J. Altizer, Episcopalian layman and religion professor at Emory University in Atlanta, attributes the disappearance of divine transcendence and the emergence of human maturity to *God's* will and work. Nevertheless, Christian faith must be radically reconstructed because God has become totally intimate and incarnate throughout human life and thought in the relativizing and secularizing process. Baptist Harvey Cox of Harvard Divinity School calls for a relative and secular theology which can celebrate the modern world and human responsibility as the fruition of biblical man's understanding of God and Christ. But all the major theological categories must be reworked to preserve the freedom and openness of history and life. God can find a place in such theology only by making possible a future for which man alone is responsible. Gabriel Vahanian, a French Calvinist who teaches religion at Syracuse University, also claims that the reality of God can no longer be grasped by modern man through Christian concepts. But theology must grapple with relativism and secularism is such a way that God and man remain sharply distinguished though inseparably related. Otherwise, human life will be engulfed by enslaving ideologies. Finally, William Hamilton, who formerly taught at Colgate-Rochester Divinity School and now teaches at New College in Florida, calls for an end to all reinterpretations of faith in terms of God. Human experiences of meaning and transcendence, which remain as important as they ever were in classical Christianity, must now be understood and fulfilled within human community. Appeals to God are irrelevant or misleading for man's religious needs and concerns.

We can now see why and how radical Christianity has arisen in our time. The radicals believe that traditional views of God, Christ and Church have been thoroughly undermined by modern life and thought. Orthodoxy has chosen to ignore these revolutionary changes in human behavior and understanding while Liberalism and Neo-orthodoxy have only partially accepted and accomodated these features of modern life. But the radicals insist that relativism and secularism can neither be ignored nor circumvented. Indeed, these irrevocable features of modern life and thought can lead to a more mature, responsible and *Christian* faith for our time. Only broad agreements over how Christian faith can and should be reinterpreted for the modern world exist among the radicals. But they speak as one in calling the Church and the Christian to a radical overhauling of faith's basic assumptions, specific beliefs and concrete practices.

PART TWO

THE MEANING

OF

RADICAL CHRISTIANITY

Radical Christianity represents a decisive break with all preceding ways of understanding and implementing Christian faith. This break centers in the conviction that all expressions of traditional Christianity have been rendered inadequate and irrelevant by the modern world. Orthodoxy as a theological option understandably has no place for relativism and secularism since its classical formulations predate the seventeenth century. Orthodoxy came from a time when Christianity's two-world orientation was unchallenged by thinking and living from below. But the perpetuators of Orthodoxy are faulted for their resistance to all alliances with modern life and thought. Liberalism and Neo-orthodoxy, on the other hand, were consciously developed as responses to the challenges of relativism and secularism. Both forged ingenious syntheses of Christian faith and modern life by partially accepting a this-worldly orientation while reserving special places in this world for God. But these privileged sanctuaries have also fallen under the pervasive pressures of modernity. Consequently, the radicals have summoned the Church to rethink faith's foundations as well as restructure faith's expressions. Faith can no longer be based on other-worldly realities or directed toward other-worldly goals. Faith must be gounded and functional in this-worldly experience. Only such *radical* reconstruction can offer an adequate belief system and responsible life style to modern men.

Of course, the radicals are fully aware of the persistence of more traditional ways of interpreting and expressing Christian faith. Orthodoxy, Liberalism and Neo-orthodoxy give little outward indication of losing their followings. Each has countless adherents and staunch defenders. Among church leaders, conservative Protestants and Catholics remain thoroughly committed to Orthodoxy. The major theological voice among ecumenical Protestant and liberal Catholic leaders for the past quarter of a century has been Neo-orthodoxy. Although Liberalism among the clergy suffered an eclipse during the 1940's and 50's because of the criticisms of Neo-orthodoxy, a chastened Liberalism shows signs of a resurgent vitality among some theologians and ministers. By contrast, a somewhat different alignment prevails among laymen in the churches. Orthodoxy and Liberalism predominate while Neo-orthodoxy claims strikingly few. Church members who are still influenced by residual denominationalism generally accept Orthodoxy's biblical literalism and other-worldly piety. Less doctrinally oriented laymen hold to a simplified liberal affirmation of the fatherhood of God and brotherhood of man. Only a comparatively small number of laymen have assimilated the basic commitments of Neo-orthodoxy. Therefore, radical Christianity contends against theological systems and styles which still enjoy the devotion of the vast majority of contemporary Christians.

But, as the discussion in Part One has shown, the radicals claim that most modern believers do not and can not "practice what they preach." Few churchmen would deny the striking disparity between belief and behavior in the contemporary Church. Scores of books and countless sermons during the past decade have catalogued and lamented the simultaneous revival of religion and spread of secularism. Doctrinal distinctives and other-worldly piety have diminished as religious concern and church attendance have increased. This anomaly is usually attributed to theological shallowness and personal hypocrisy among contemporary Christians. But the radicals offer a different diagnosis of this gulf between creed and deed. The erosion of doctrinal distinctives reflects the irrelevance of prevailing belief systems rather than the theological illiteracy of contemporary laymen. The breakdown of other-worldly piety is due more to integrity than to hypocrisy among modern churchmen. The old devotional and moral patterns are being abandoned because they are no longer meaningful. Although confusion and guilt accompany this separation, the distance between official policy and actual practice grows because the Church's prevailing belief systems and life styles no longer illumine and support the week-day lives of their adherents. Therefore, the radicals call for a thoroughgoing reformulation of Christian faith in the interest of faith's vitality and life's wholeness.

But thus far we have only seen why radical Christianity has risen to challenge more familiar patterns of belief and behavior. Little more than a general characterization of the actual substance of this theological ferment has been offered. Nothing has been said about radical Christianity at particular points of belief and behavior. We must now examine the specific proposals for reformulating the Christian faith which are advocated by the radicals.

Our investigation will take the form of an inquiry. A series of questions concerning theology's task, faith's framework and religion's role will be addressed to the radicals. Each question will be prefaced by a brief survey of the thinking of Orthodoxy, Liberalism and Neo-orthodoxy on the issues at stake. Against this background, radical Christianity's new and diverse answers will be presented in the form of brief selections from the writings of the radicals. These excerpts will be collated to form summary statements of the specific beliefs and practices of the six radical theologians introduced in the preceding chapter.

Three important purposes will be served by structuring our inquiry in this way. A prefatory survey of Orthodox, Liberal and Neo-orthodox thinking on major theological issues will illumine the differences between radical Christianity and these more familiar forms of faith. This comparison will offer a sweeping view of the various formulations of the Christian faith current in the Church today. Furthermore, the arrangement of materials from the radicals by authors and themes will reveal the unity and diversity within the radical movement. Their shared diagnoses but differing prescriptions for the ills besetting the Church will be set forth in some detail. Finally, the use of selections from the writings of the radicals will underscore the distinctiveness and tentativeness of their search for a new style and vocabulary of faith for our time. The crucial emphases, unresolved obscurities and important shifts in their thought will be catalogued by letting the radicals speak for themselves.

I. WHAT IS THEOLOGY'S TASK?

The first series of questions that must be put to the radicals concern theology's task. What is the relation of theology to faith? What is the source and substance of theological claims? How are theological statements proved or evaluated? Beginning with such general questions may seem like an unnecessary detour in getting to the particular proposals of the radicals. But an overview of the relation of theology to faith, reality and truth will prove quite helpful in dealing with the specific features of radical thought.

In every theological system, specific doctrines are spelled out in terms of basic principles or guidelines. These general assumptions function like the foundations of a building. A finished building is certainly more than its foundations, but these underpinnings affect and reflect the completed edifice. Since they shape and sustain, foundations are important structural elements in a building even though they are usually later hidden and forgotten. Similarly, every theological system is undergirded by certain foundational principles. All specific beliefs rest on basic decisions about why theological understanding is sought, how it is derived and when it is trustworthy. And, as in material buildings, these undergirding foundations are usually ignored and obscured by all but the architects and builders of belief systems. But they shape and sustain these buildings of the mind nonetheless.

Furthermore, specific differences and conflicts between rival theological systems are largely due to disagreements over foundational principles. Strikingly different foundational concepts of theology's subject matter and method lead to widely different specific beliefs about faith's realities and relationships. Questions of truth and error over specific religious beliefs are largely debates over appropriate foundational principles. The role that basic assumptions play in the knowing process furnishes the major occasion for error in all human understanding. Inappropriate assumptions about how a given subject matter must be approached invariably produce inadequate understanding of that subject matter. Moreover, the occurrence of such distortion often goes unrecognized because most people are simply not aware of their underlying assumptions. Thus, inappropriate foundations can both produce error by distorting understanding and compound error by obscuring detection.

The decisive role that foundational principles play in all religious understanding and controversy dictates our present starting point. Serious clashes of religious opinion finally rest on conflicting presuppositions which shape and sustain these opinions. Therefore, we must begin our analysis of the radical theologians by investigating their basic assumptions about the place, the sources and the criteria of theology. Only by laying bare these foundational principles for radical as well as more familiar modes of Christian thought will we be equipped to compare and understand these diverse theological positions at particular points of belief and behavior.

1. The Place of Theology

Theology furnishes the intellectual rationale for religious

devotion and obedience. The term comes from two Greek words, *theos* which means "deity" and *logos* which means "discourse." But theology has seldom dealt exclusively with the nature and existence of God. The word has taken on a much broader meaning through centuries of Christian usage. Theology embraces the whole range of man's religious concerns. It seeks to make every aspect of the meaning, basis and consequences of religious faith intelligible.

As such, theology and faith are broadly related as theory and practice. Faith is certainly more than intellectual inquiry or understanding. Faith denotes distinctive attitudes, actions and relationships. But putting a living faith into practice is always intimately related to some religious beliefs. Beliefs without practice are dead but practice without beliefs is impossible. Some beliefs are operative in all but the most elemental human feelings, actions and relationships. These beliefs may not always be clearly formulated, cogently supported or consistently followed. But they are conditions and conditioners of all significant human behavior. Theology, then, seeks to present a coherent and convincing account of the beliefs which are invoked or implied in religious behavior.

But disagreements have prevailed throughout church history over precisely *how* theology and faith are related as theory and practice. Faith always involves belief and behavior but different theological traditions stress and relate these components of faith differently. These differences typically fall between two extremes. On the one hand, faith may be understood primarily as the acceptance of a body of beliefs which does result in a changed life. On the other hand, faith may be interpreted as the adoption of a style of life which is illumined by a belief system. Theology obviously has a very different status in these different ways of defining faith. In the former, theology furnishes faith's object while in the latter theology merely clarifies faith's realities. These limiting definitions of faith's relation to theology will become visible in the following comparative analysis.

Orthodoxy looks to theology for the content of faith. Man's relation to God and to his fellow man is based upon knowledge of God's will and work on man's behalf. Such saving knowledge involves more than an intellectual understanding of certain propositions about God, Christ and man. Saving knowledge means accepting personally and living consistently with these beliefs. Since Orthodoxy defines faith as knowledge of saving truths, everything depends upon precise and correct formulations of these truths. The very word "orthodoxy" comes from two Greek words which mean "right belief." Therefore, theology has the important task of defining the beliefs which are absolutely necessary for salvation. This solid core of beliefs does not permit theological diversity and innovation. Differences and shifts of opinion may arise over the implications of faith in concrete social circumstances. But no changes or disagreements are permitted in the saving fundamentals of belief. Theology promulgates and protects the "faith once delivered" through history's changing times and places.

Liberalism reacts to this intellectualism and dogmatism of Orthodoxy. Faith is first and foremost a way of life rather than a body of beliefs. Faith is a living relationship characterized by the reign of God in human hearts and the reality of love among human beings. This intimate relationship to God and man is illumined but not established by religious beliefs. Such beliefs simply help to clarify and communicate the dimensions and duties of faith. Therefore, theology for Liberalism neither reworks a fixed content nor requires a dogmatic certitude as in Orthodoxy. Theology seeks to make faith's living relationship to God and man relevant to all human activity and consistent with all human knowledge. Since faith's relationships are situationally conditioned, theologies must change when faith's circumstances change. And, since faith's realities are personally experienced, theologies can vary without distorting faith's relationships. Theology then has the continuing task of integrating faith with man's total experience.

Neo-orthodoxy offers a more subtle and complex rendering of theology's importance for faith than Orthodoxy or Liberalism. Neo-orthodox theologians consider Orthodoxy's definition of faith as intellectual knowledge and Liberalism's interpretation of faith as personal relationship overly simple concepts of faith. As we have seen, both Orthodoxy and Liberalism find a place for intellectual knowledge and personal relationship in their views of faith. But Neo-orthodoxy insists that these components are not related as cause and effect or as fact and interpretation. Rather, they are distinguishable but inseparable aspects of *personal* knowledge. Knowledge of persons is different from knowledge of things precisely because persons are known only in and through an intimate relation to them. Orthodoxy's analysis of faith models man's relation to God on the analogy of man's knowledge of things with its great stress on faith as intellectual assent. But, while Liberalism rightly protests that faith is a personal relation to God, it fails to appreciate the integral role knowledge *about* persons play in all knowledge *of* persons. Faith is personal knowledge of God, but this intimate relationship is established and sustained through correct knowledge about God's will and work. This proper understanding is given in and through the preaching of Word and Sacraments in the Church. Therefore, theology in the Neo-orthodox scheme has the important responsibility of testing the accuracy of preaching. Theology spells out the content of preaching by explicating the foundations and responsibilities of faith. New forms for communicating may be required from time to time since preaching always occurs in a live context. Theology then has the neverending task of relating an unchanging message to changing situations.

PAUL M. VAN BUREN

It is a common-place to say that most church-goers are either wrong or confused about the nature of faith. Some take faith as assent to a group of peculiar assertions, as did the Red Queen when she said she had mastered the art of believing six impossible things before breakfast. Others take faith to be a sort of inner glow that makes you feel good all over. Since the language of faith, traditionally, is so often associated with things which no man has ever seen, it is not surprising if a somewhat empirical age finds faith to be at best a bit fuzzy. All of this is widely known and often decried. Little seems to be done about it. ("Christian Education *Post Mortem Dei*," p. 8).

[Bonhoeffer's] question still lies before us: How can the Christian who is himself a secular man understand his faith in a secular way? We intend to answer this question with the help of a method far removed from Bonhoeffer's thought. The answer will be reached by analyzing what a man means when he uses the language of faith, when he repeats the earliest Christian confession: "Jesus is Lord."

Our proposal to answer Bonhoeffer's question by analyzing the language of faith has been suggested to us by the work of philosophers, of whom there are now many in the English speaking world, who practice "linguistic analysis." *(The Secular Meaning Of The Gospel, pp. 2-3)*.

The problem of the Gospel in a secular age is a problem of the logic of its apparently meaningless language, and linguistic analysists will give us help in clarifying it. We dare to call *our* problems *the* problem not because we have access to what everyone or anyone else means by "secular age" or "Gospel,"but because we dare to hope that what we have found helpful for our own understanding may prove helpful for others, who may then identify the problem to some extent as we have identified it. *(The Secular Meaning Of The Gospel, pp. 84-5).*

According to linguistic analysts, if we wish to know the meaning of a word or statement, we must look at the way it functions in actual use. The meaning of a word is not some invisible presence behind the word, some "ghost in the machine" (to use Gilbert Ryle's phrase). The meaning of a word is identical with its use. We shall apply this deceptively simple, but (as we shall see) far-reaching, thesis of the linguistic analysts to the problem of a contemporary understanding of the Gospel, and it will clarify and help to dissolve some of the apparently insoluable conflicts which mark the current discussion in theology. *(The Secular Meaning Of The Gospel, p.16).*

A careful, functional analysis of the language of the New Testament, the Fathers, and contemporary believers will reveal the secular meaning of the Gospel. *(The Secular Meaning Of The Gospel, p. 19).*

Linguistic analysis, although it is related historically to the Logical Postivism of the Vienna Circle of the 1920's, should not be confused with the somewhat dogmatic spirit and teachings of that philosophy. Indeed, its deepest roots lie in the tradition of British empiricism. It is more accurate to speak of linguistic analysis as a method than a school or movement of philosophy, for what its practitioners share is only a common interest and a common logical method. Their interest is in the function of language, and their method lies in the logical analysis of how words and statements function, both in normal and in abnormal use. Linguistic analysts are not opposed in principle to the use of religious or theological language, as the logical positivists were. Indeed, some of them have produced interesting studies of religious and theological statements in the last ten years or so. *(The Secular Meaning Of The Gospel, p.14).*

[R. M.] Hare has invented the word blik for a fundamental attitude... The basic presuppositions we have about the world are not verifiable, ... and yet everything we do depends on them..."Bliks" are serious matters for those who hold them, whether we judge any particular "blik" to be right or wrong, and everyone has a "blik."...[Thus, the statements of faith are] expressions of a "blik," an orientation, a commitment to see the world in a certain way, and a way of life following inevitably upon this orientation. What Hare is suggesting is that a man's faith and his theology have a meaning, even though the theistic rug has been pulled out from under him. *(The Secular Meaning Of The Gospel, pp. 85-7)*.

[Ian T. Ramsey] offers support for and further elaboration of Hare's concept of a "blik." He argues that the language of faith combines the language of discernment, of an admittedly special sort, with the language of commitment, of a sort which covers the totality of life and the world. Statements of faith direct our attention to certain kinds of situations: situations of disclosure, when "the light dawns," and the situation becomes alive and new. The emphasis is not only on the disclosure or discernment, but also on the resulting commitment, whereby what we now "see" becomes important and determines our subsequent seeing. *(The Secular Meaning Of The Gospel, p. 87)*.

Ramsey has made in effect a further development of Hare's concept of "blik." A "blik" involves a perspective entailing commitment, and Ramsey has clarified this with his analysis of the language of discernment and commitment. *(The Secular Meaning Of The Gospel, p. 91)*.

One of the most radical contributions to the analysis of the language of faith has been made by R. B. Braithwaite...Religious assertions are in fact *used* as moral assertions. Moral assertions share with religious ones the characteristic of being neither logically necessary nor empirical; yet they have a use: that of guiding conduct. *(The Secular Meaning Of The Gospel, pp. 92-3)*.

But more important, for Braithwaite, is the following distinction: "A religious assertion will...have a propositional element which is lacking in a purely moral assertion, in that it will refer to a story as well as to an intention." Consequently, "to assert the whole set of assertions of the Christian religion is both to tell the Christian doctrinal story and to confess allegiance to the Christian way of life." He notes that what he calls "story" has also been called by other names: parable, fairy tale, allegory, fable, tale and myth. He prefers the word "story" because it is neutral, "implying neither that the story is believed nor that is is disbelieved." The Christian story includes straight history and also material clearly not historical. But Braithwaite insists that belief in the empirical truth of the stories "is not the proper criterion for deciding whether of not an assertion is a Christian one. A man is not, I think, a professing Christian unless he both proposes to live according to Christian moral principles and associates his intention with thinking of Christian stories; but he need not believe that the empirical propositions presented by the stories correspond to empirical fact."   *(The Secular Meaning Of The Gospel, p. 95).*

What is the function of these stories and how are they related to this intention to act? Braithwaite answers that the stories have a psychological and causal relationship to the intention: to say that an action is "doing the will of God" helps us to carry it through, and Braithwaite feels that theologians need to keep in mind the psychological fact that men's behaviour is determined not only by intellectual considerations, but also by phantasies, imaginations, and hopes.   *(The Secular Meaning Of The Gospel, pp. 95-6).*

"Religious belief," he concludes, is not "a species of ordinary belief, of belief in propositions. A moral belief is an intention to behave in a certain way: a religious belief is an intention to behave in a certain way (a moral belief) together with the entertainment of certain stories associated with the intention in the mind of the believer."   *(The Secular Meaning Of The Gospel, p. 96).*

Not all analytic philosophers, of course, have approached the language of faith in the way we have presented. A number of philosophers have argued that faith is a kind of knowledge and that faith-statements are to be understood cognitively...Christianity, they argue, is not essentially a conviction, commitment, or attitude, but entry into and living in a relationship with a transcendent being, and it stands or falls with the meaningfulness of its assertions concerning that transcendent being.   *(The Secular Meaning Of The Gospel, p. 96).*

We judge the cognitive approach to theological language to be inadequate to the character of secular thought and to the heart of the Gospel.

We cannot argue, of course, for some objective, normative definition of verification or of the Gospel. When we call this approach inadequate, we are exposing our own categorical commitments which we see reflected in some modern kerygmatic theology, some modern analytic philosophy, and indicated by the word "secular." We can only acknowledge that our commitments

56

are such as to lead us to reject a search for a religious preserve to be investigated by a special religious way of knowing, and we are commited to a Gospel which begins, not with an argument for undifferentiated theism, but with the impact of whatever it was that happened on Easter in the context of a particular history. With such commitments, we have no choice but to return to the consensus of such analysts as Hare and Braithwaite about the character of the language of faith and to assess its possibilities as a tool for determing what we have called the secular meaning of the Gospel.

The first point of consensus is that "simple literal theism" is wrong and that "qualified literal theism" is meaningless. The second agreement lies in the implicit or explicit conviction that the language of faith does have a meaning, and that this meaning can be explored and clarified by linguistic analysis. The third consensus is a concern to take Christianity seriously as a way of life, even though a straightforward use of the word "God" must be abandoned. *(The Secular Meaning Of The Gospel, pp. 99-100).*

This attempt to define a consensus does justice to no single position of the language analysts, yet our summary indicates the trend of their interpretations of Christianity. It remains to evaluate the method and results of these philosophers for a reconstruction of the kerygma and Christology. *(The Secular Meaning Of The Gospel, p. 101).*

WILLIAM HAMILTON

We have been aware for some time that modern atheism has become a subject of special theological concern to Christians, but only recently has it moved so close to the center of theology and faith itself. The British publication of Bishop Robinson's *Honest to God* partly created and partly released forces that may well be coming together into a new theological movement in that country. And there is an American counterpart to this British movement, though it goes back in time a bit before *Honest to God.* This American movement is the death of God theology. It is a movement, though until quite recently there was no communication between the participants. But they have begun to talk to each other and to discover that there are a handful of people here and there who one day may all contribute to a common theological style. ("The Death of God Theologies Today," pp. 23-4).

57

It is perhaps worth while to distinguish between the theological or "hard" radicals I am talking about and the "soft" radicals. Soft radicals tend to have difficulty not with the message but with the medium through which the message should be passed. They worry about adequate institutional embodiment, the problem of communication, hermeneutics, secularism and modern man. They have the gospel, but they don't like the old words. They have God, but sometimes for strategic reasons they may decide not to talk about him.

The hard radicals are really not interested in problems of communication. It is not that the old forms are outmoded or that modern man must be served but that the message itself is problematic. The hard radicals, however varied may be their language, share first of all a common loss. It is not a loss of the idols, or of the God of theism. It is a real loss of real transcendence. It is a loss of God. ("The Shape of a Radical Theology," p. 1220).

There are two schools of interpretation of Protestant religionlessness. In the moderate, Honest-to-God, ecclesiastical school of interpretation, religion generally means "religious activities" like liturgy, counselling, going to church, saying your prayers. To be religionless in this sense is to affirm that the way we have done these things in the past may not be the only way, or may not be worth doing at all, and that radical experiments ought to be attempted in the forms of the church and ministry. Bishop Robinson's lectures on "The New Reformation" delivered in America in the spring of 1964 are an able presentation of this moderate radicalism. A good deal of the material out of New York, Geneva, and the denominational headquarters on the church and ministry reflects this promising line, and a good many religious sociologists and radical religious leaders on the race issue tend to use Bonhoeffer and religionlessness in this way.

This is an important trend, and we need more and not less experimentation on these matters of the ministry, for we are well into the opening phase of the breakdown of organized religion in American life, well beyond the time when ecumenical dialogues or denominational mergers can be expected to arrest the breakdown.

The religionlessness I wish to defend, however, is not of this practical type. At no point is the later Bonhoeffer of greater importance to the death of God theology than in helping us work out a truly theological understanding of the problem of

58

religionlessness. I take religion to mean not man's arrogant grasping for God (Barth) and not assorted Sabbath activities usually performed by ordained males (the moderate radicals), but any system of thought or action in which God or the gods serve as fulfiller of needs or solver of problems. Thus I assert with Bonhoeffer the breakdown of the religious *a priori* and the coming of age of man. ("The Death of God Theologies Today," pp. 39-40).

The movement toward secularism, autonomy, away from God, is approved not so that secularists will applaud, but for theological reasons: *i.e.,* dependence and need are not proper descriptions of man's relationship to God. Bonhoeffer invites us to accept the world without God as given and unalterable. If there is to be a God for the modern world, he will not be found by renouncing the world that can do without him.

There is also, in Bonhoeffer's vision of the world come of age, a rejection of religion as salvation either by transmitting the individual to some protected religious realm, or even as protection from something that, without religion, a man might fall into, like despair or self-righteousness. Put more clearly, Bonhoeffer states that in the world come of age, we can no longer be religious, if religion is defined as that system that treats God or the gods as need-fulfillers and problem-solvers.

There are thus no places in the self or the world, Protestants who listen to Bonhoeffer go on to say, where problems emerge that only God can solve. There are problems and needs, to be sure, but the world itself is the source of the solutions, not God. God must not be asked to do what the world is fully capable of doing: offer forgiveness, overcome loneliness, provide a way out of despair, break pride, assuage the fear of death. These are worldly problems for those who live in this world, and the world itself can provide the structures to meet them.

Familiar intellectual worlds are being rejected by Bonhoeffer and by those who are using him as their navigation chart today—Protestant theologies of correlation, for example, where worldly forms of art and knowledge are used to illustrate the incompleteness or brokeness of the world without God. It need hardly be added that the vulgar world of the problem-solving preacher, the pro-God subway ad, and the slick, vulgar world of the clever T.V. commercial for God, are being set aside as well.

Technically, what Bonhoeffer is saying is that in the modern world that can do without God, the idea of the innate religiousness of man, the religious *a priori*, must be rejected. ("Dietrich Bonhoeffer," pp. 116-7)

The breakdown of the religious *a priori* means that there is no way, ontological, cultural or psychological, to locate a part of the self or a part of human experience that needs God. There is no God-shaped blank within man. Man's heart may or may not be restless until it rests in God. It is not necessarily so. God is not in the realm of the necessary at all; he is not necessary being, he is not necessary to avoid despair or self-righteousness. He is one of the possibles in a radically pluralistic spiritual and intellectual milieu.

This is just what man's coming of age is taken to mean. It is not true to say, with Luther, *entweder Gott oder Abgott.* It is not true to say, with Ingmar Bergman, "Without God, life is an outrageous terror." It is not true to say that there are certain areas, problems dimensions to life today that can only be faced, solved, illumined, dealt with, by a religious perspective.

Religion is to be defined as the assumption in theology, preaching, apologetics, evangelism, counselling, that man needs God, and that there are certain things that God alone can do for him. I am denying that religion is necessary. ("The Death of God Theologies Today," pp. 39-40)

There are perhaps three possibilities for radical theology and the radical theologians.

1. They could move to the left, the way many of their Christian critics think they will move, to a candid atheism or humanism without any of the Christian claims. Perhaps Marxist, perhaps Freudian, perhaps new left — but Jesus will become as dispensable as God, and the Christian community will not be the one in which they find their comrades.

2. They could move to the right, and the birth or resurrection of God could be experienced. I cannot see how one can rule out this possibility. As far as the present theological situation in Protestantism goes, the radicals are in closest debate and discussion with two other groups, neither of them "death of God" types: with secular theology as done by Harvey Cox, and with Bishop Robinson and his explorations. This is the most exciting theological triangle I know about.

3. They could move to different items on the theological agenda. Right now, the radical theology is still in its polemic, offense-giving, publicity-oriented phase, a phase spearheaded by

the phrase "death of God" and by the radicals' insistence that that is what they mean. I think it quite likely that this emphasis will fade, and that there will be less emphasis on the specific fact of God's disappearance, the mode of it, and the reasons for it, and more emphasis on the positive requirements for living as a Christian without God. Some have gods that need to die; some don't and we must not get fixated on the phrase or the event, however true. Some other items on the agenda that interest me are:

a. Christology, and the possibility of replacing the doctrine of the two natures with a historically understood *imitatio Christi* approach.

b. The doctrine of man; sin, guilt, and optimism in the radical theology.

c. The problem of the institutional embodiment appropriate to the radical theology: church, sacrament, ministry.

d. The dialogue with the Jew, both believing and unbelieving, and the dialogue with Buddhism as another godless religion.

("Questions and Answers on the Radical Theology," pp.238-40)

GABRIEL VAHANIAN

Man is not an atheist, except by contrast with an established theism, whether it be monotheism or polytheism. As Jean Guitton has said, man is essentially an idolater or an "iconoclast," but not an atheist. *(Wait Without Idols, pp. 233-34)*.

The word iconoclasm is used here in what may be considered to be its biblical sense, which greatly differs from its common usage. Basically, the common meaning of iconoclasm refers either to the anti-artistic drive of every kind of religious or ideological puritanism, or to the Promethean or blasphemous revolts against theism, against God as the reality which calls into being the reality of man. *(No Other God, p. 45)*.

Modern iconoclasm is an antidivine manifestation, whereas the biblical form is a deflation of man's natural inclination to deify himself, or his society, or the state or his culture. In this light, any reader of the Bible will discern the relentless exposing of this manifold, constant proclivity to elevate the finite to the level of the infinite, to give to the transitory the status of the permanent, and to attribute to man qualities that will deceive him into denying his finitude. In short, biblical iconoclasm is directed against any latent or overt self-deification and against "ethnolatry" in any one of its forms: racial, national, cultural. Ethnolatry is the reduction of a particular civilization and the religion identifying it to the characteristics of a race and the idolization of its idiosyncrasy. Biblical iconoclasm is directed against man's most subtle and degenerate idol—himself. Whenever this is overlooked, the particularity of biblical thought is by the same token grievously bypassed.

This particularity can, indeed, be seen from the first to the last book of the Bible. The myths of man's creation in the image of God and of the Last Judgment are misunderstood when they are not grasped as implying a conception of man that is the direct antithesis to all sorts of human apotheoses. Unlike common sense, pretension to deity is equally distributed among men. But the biblical position is clear: man is not God and, especially, he may not pull divine rank on his fellowmen. For the same reasons, neither nature nor history, which has a beginning and an end, is endowed with divinity. *(Wait Without Idols, pp. 24-5)*.

Therefore biblical iconoclasm is directed, not against God, but against idolatry in all its forms from superstition to legalism or dogmatism and literalism—against anything that preaches the deification of man, the divinization of culture or history or reason and religion as well as against anything that sacralizes symbolic events or institutions. *(No Other God, p. 46)*.

Iconoclasm is, for all practical purposes, the essential ingredient of monotheism as understood in the biblical tradition. Without this element, faith in God loses its indispensable character, and can result neither in radical commitment to God nor in an equally radical and iconoclastic involvement in the world. *(Wait Without Idols, p. 26)*.

Our present crisis stems from the fact that we have changed the biblical iconoclasm of the Christian tradition into the idolatrous post-Christian religiosity of our cultural institutions, be they social, political, economic, or ecclesiastical. *(Wait Without Idols, p. 234)*.

The "death of God" is the continental divide which separates Christian man from post-Christian man. ("Beyond the Death of God," p. 5).

To say that our age is post-Christian means to acknowledge the emergence of a self-understanding based on such a radically different type of preconception that if it is taken into consideration, as it must be, then one must concede that the preconception on which the Christian world view rests has been neutralized, and is now irretrievable. *(No Other God, pp. 69-70)*.

Governing our worldview and our self-understanding is thus what, by way of contrast, may be called radical immanentism. This kind of immanentism, which has nothing to do with classical metaphysical immanentism, leaves God altogether out of the picture and must be understood in the sense of what is implied, for example, by the notion of immanent justice rather than by any of the various notions of God's immanence. Whether God is or is not, radical immanentism considers him at best irrelevant, and seeks accordingly to define existence and the world without the help of a transcendental reference. *(No Other God, p. 70)*.

The radical immanentism of our cultural religiosity may be only provisional. In the light of Biblical thought, this immanentism can show that God dies as soon as he becomes a cultural accessory or a human ideal; that the finite cannot comprehend the infinite *(finitum non est capax infiniti)*. From this point of view the death of God may be only a cultural phenomenon as though only our religio-cultural notion of God were dead. But this makes even more serious the question whether the transcendental view of man and his culture, as set forth in the Bible, has any chance of surviving the modern presupposition that God is dead. *(The Death Of God, p. 231)*.

It is not surprising therefore that the birth of the post-Christian era coincides with the transfer of the iconoclastic tradition—though perhaps mutilated—from theology to literature, even to Promethean literature. In the wake of this transfer, the traditional conflict between theism and atheism, no longer supported by a transcendentalist framework, has evaporated. The idolatry of religion itself being laid bare, the way is open to the possibility of understanding in a fresh manner the biblical notion that transcendent as God's reality may be, it must be attested in the world and its empirical phenomena through the structures of human existence, of man's works and his word. *(No Other God, p. 47)*.

HARVEY COX

The purpose of theology is to serve the prophetic community. For this reason the place of theology is that jagged edge where the faithful company grapples with the swiftest currents of the age. Any "theology" which occurs somewhere else or for some other reason scarcely deserves the name.

We all sense that there is something wrong in theology. However, contrary to the seminary obituary columns, it is theology, not You Know Who, that is dead. Or if not dead, then very sick. To bring our calling back to health, it is our task as theologians to begin once again to make up our minds at the place of, and for the purpose of, prophecy. This means we must stand between two determinative clusters of events: the demise of religion as an unquestioned cultural ethos and the emergence of revolution as the decisive form of the new world civilization.

The task of prophecy is to illuminate contemporary history, to clarify the crucial options, and to summon man to the responsible stewardship of his world. The task of theology is to guide, criticize, and deepen prophecy. But theology is sick. Its dyspepsia and delirium arise mainly from the fact that theology is still fascinated with religion, either morbidly or stubbornly, and that it still exhibits insufficient interest in discerning the signs of the times—in revolution. Rather than helping the prophets greet a religionless, revolutionary tomorrow, some theologians are more interested in dissecting the cadaver of yesterday's pieties. Instead of scanning the temporal horizon for signs of the new humanity, many of us flee from the bewildering secular matrix where this promised community is taking shape. ("The Place and Purpose of Theology," p. 7)

But what is "Secularization"? The word does have troublesome vagueness. It refers to a wide variety of ideas depending on the context in which it appears. In my own book I have tried to stay close to its etymological source, (i.e."saeculum," "this present world age") and define it as the movement of man's primary interest and attention *from* other worlds beyond or above this one and *to* this world. This includes the loosing of this world from its dependency on mythical, metaphysical or religious dualism of any sort. It means, therefore, taking this earthly realm, with all its health and hope, with all its sickness and sin, in utter seriousness. (" Secularization and the Secular Mentality," p. 83)

When I use the word "secularization," I intend it to mean *both* man's loss of interest in other worlds with a resulting intensification of interest in this one, *and* the newly emergent role of the church as minority and servant rather than as majority and lord. For many people, this movement away from otherworldliness and away from ecclesiastically dominated society is the occasion for hand-wringing and lamentation. I disagree. There can be no question that it poses serious problems for theology, but it also presents unprecedented new opportunities. ("Why Christianity Must Be Secularized," p. 10)

What should theology do in the face of the secularization of our world? Three types of answers have begun to arise to this question in our time. The first group of theologians might be called the pruners. They wish to pare down Christianity to fit within the assumptions of what they take to be the modern scientific world view. Paul van Buren and the so-called death-of-God theologians, Thomas Altizer and William Hamilton, typify this group. ...

At the opposite pole, there are those theologians who feel that Christianity must be retained in its classical philosophical housing whether it be scholastic or idealistic, or some other. They are the preservationists. An excellent and well-argued example of their work can be found in E. L. Mascall's *The Secularization of Christianity*. Oddly, theologians of this type agree with the pruners on what the "essential" components of Christianity are, but unlike the modernists they decide to defend rather than discard. They both agree on what "God" means, but the pruners say he is dead while the preservationists say he "exists." Preserving of course always entails a certain amount of pickling, and pickling prevents further growth. Hence, in order to establish their claim, the preservationists criticize not only the pruners, they also criticize those engaged in the further development of doctrine and its reinterpretation.

The third group of theologians includes all those who see Christianity from a historical or developmental perspective. They deny the idea, held by both pruners and preservers, that there is some timeless and irreducible "essence" to Christianity. They understand it rather as a movement of people, a church moving through history with a memory and a vision, entering into riotously different cultural and social forms along the way. ("Why Christianity Must Be Secularized," pp. 11-2)

I place myself within the third group in the above classification of current theological approaches. I reject as reductionistic any suggestion that we should simply abandon various classical Christian doctrines as archaic residues of the past. But I reject just as vigorously the notion that we should defend them in the form in which we have inherited them. In fact, I would argue that it is the misguided effort to defend Christianity in one or another of its classical forms (and the conservatives hotly differ with each other on which *is* "the" classical form) that unwittingly creates the very atheism it seeks to avoid. Atheism is always the shadow of some form of theism. Most atheists today, including those who still want to be Christians, disbelieve in exactly the same conventional picture of God that orthodox theologians try so vigorously to defend. ("Why Christianity Must Be Secularized," p. 13).

Despite hopes of positivists to find for each word one unequivocal meaning, words are alive. Their meanings are always a product both of their former usage and of their present embodiment. This is even more true of doctrines. The nuances of meaning and language in a living religious community are constantly changing, and theologians must be attentive to these changes. Hence they find themselves not only elucidating doctrines but developing them and giving a purer meaning to the symbols of the community.

How then according to this historical-development view does theology proceed in an age of secularization? *Secularization means that the world of human history now provides the horizon within which man understands his life.* Thus the task of theology is to rethink and develop the doctrines of biblical faith to engage this contemporary sensibility. ("Why Christianity Must Be Secularized," p. 13).

Gibson Winter has described the style of theological thinking we need if we are to take a step forward instead of a step backward. He calls it "theological reflection." It is coming to consciousness about the meaning of contemporary events in the light of history. It is a way of taking responsibility both for the reshaping of the past and the constitution of the future. Reflection is that act by which the church scrutinizes the issues the society confronts in light of those decisive events of the past—Exodus and Easter—in which the intent of God has been apprehended by man in faith. Thus the church looks to the hints God has dropped in the past in order to make out what He is doing today.

But clearly the focal point of such reflection, the issues upon which it must center, are none other than the life-and-death issues of the secular metropolis. It must be reflection on how to come to political terms with the emergent technical reality which engulfs us. These are *political issues,* and the mode of theology which must replace metaphysical theology is the *political* mode. Thus one answer to Bonhoeffer's question is that the way we talk about God in a secular fashion is to talk about him politically.

But are we using the word *politics* too loosely? The word itself, as Paul Lehmann reminds us, was given its classic meaning by Aristotle. For Aristotle, politics was "the science of the polis," the activity which used all the other sciences to secure not only the good for man but the good for the whole city-state, since that is naturally higher than the good of any one man. Lehmann suggests that what God is doing in the world is politics, which means making and keeping life human. Politics also describes man's role in response to God. It is "activity, and reflection on activity, which aims at and analyzes what it takes to make and keep human life human in the world." Theology today must be that reflection - in - action by which the church finds out what this politician-God is up to and moves in to work along with him. In the epoch of the secular city, politics replaces metaphysics as the language of theology. *(The Secular City, pp. 222-3).*

To say that speaking of God must be political means that it must engage people at particular points, not just "in general." It must be a word about their own lives—their children, their job, their hopes or disappointments. It must be a word to the bewildering crises within which our personal troubles arise—a word which builds peace in a nuclear world, which contributes to justice in an age stalked by hunger, which hastens the day of freedom in a society stifled by segregation. If the word is not a word which arises from a concrete involvement of the speaker in these realities, then it is not a Word of God at all but empty twaddle.

We speak of God to secular man by speaking about man, by talking about man as he is seen in the biblical perspective. Secular talk of God occurs only when we are away from the ghetto and out of costume, when we are participants in that political action by which He restores man to each other in mutual concern and responsibility. We speak of God in a secular fashion when we recognize man as His partner, as the one charged with the task of bestowing meaning and order in human history.

Speaking of God in a secular fashion is thus a political issue. It entails our discerning where God is working and then joining His work. Standing in a picket line is a way of speaking. By doing it a Christian speaks of God. He helps alter the word *God* by changing the society in which it has been trivialized, by moving away from the context where "God-talk" usually occurs, and by shedding the stereotyped roles in which God's name is usually intoned. *(The Secular City, pp. 224-5).*

To say that the secular meaning of the Gospel today must be ethical-political does not mean it must be handed down in the form of moral principles. It means, rather, that the church needs to reorder its life so that Christians can come together to consult with each other about what God is doing now in the secular world, so that they may joyfully participate in this secular mission of God. ("Why Christianity Must Be Secularized," p. 18)

THOMAS J. J. ALTIZER

Hopefully a new day has dawned for theology, a revolutionary day in which the gradual but decisive transformation of faith that has occurred in the modern world will be recognized, even though doing so may promise the end of most if not all of the established religious forms of the West. At the moment, and for perhaps well into the future, the most radical theological revolution is promised by the death of God theology, a theology grounded by one means or another in the death of the Christian God. This is not to say that this theology, if such it can be called, is the only new or even revolutionary theology at hand. The majority of Christian theologians, whether Catholic or Protestant, acknowledge the end of Western Christendom as we have known it, and with it the end of those cultural and social forms which once assumed a Christian name. Everywhere today theologians are either struggling for new forms of faith and community or are engaged in a desperate battle to preserve the old forms at whatever cost. Until recently it was possible for many theologians to take a neutral stance in this conflict, but increasingly the crisis at hand is driving both the theologian and the believer to a choice between a strange and largely unknown future and a seemingly archaic and irrelevant past. *(Toward A New Christianity, p. 1).*

Perhaps the most distinctive theological sign of our situation is that theology itself is coming to confess that ours is a time in which God is dead. Thus far the theologian has been unable to speak with clarity of the death of God, but a lack of clarity is an inevitable consequence of the initial expressions of a new and radical theological movement, a movement that must begin by attacking the very possibility of "God language" in our situation. Now that we have learned that we can no longer speak about God we must learn how to speak of the actuality of his death. For to refuse to speak about the death of God is to turn away from the moment before us, to evade the brute reality of our history, and

68

therefore to foreclose the possibility of speaking the Christian Word which is present in our midst. If ours is truly a history in which God is no longer present, then we are called upon not simply to accept the death of God with stoic fortutude but rather to will the death of God with the passion of faith. A faith whose ground lies in the presence of the Word in history has no choice but to open itself to the full reality of history. When we face a moment of history in which God is dead, Christian theology must proclaim the death of God if it is to witness to the Word of faith. No longer may we linger with the dying echoes of God's former presence; we must confess that God has truly and actually died before we can speak the Word which is present to us. ("Creative Negation in Theology," p. 866)

We must not allow an orthodox theology to deny that the proclamation of the death of God can be a Christian confession. The radical theologian will insist that a theology which continues even in our time to proclaim the reality of God is closed to the contemporary reality of the incarnation. A Christian theology of the incarnation cannot view the Word as eternal and unmoving, or inactive or impassive, or unaffected by its own movement and process. The Christian Word moves only by negating its own past expressions. Unlike all forms of non-Christian religion, Christianity celebrates a Word that becomes fully incarnate in a fallen time and space. Furthermore, the Christian Word is a forward-moving process, a Word seeking an eschatological End that transcends a primordial Beginning. But the very fact that the Christian Word is a Word moving forward rather than backward to Eternity means that it is a Word which is perpetually moving beyond its own expressions. ("Creative Negation in Theology," pp. 866-7)

The primary words "God is Dead" are words recording a confession of faith. Let me be clear in emphasizing that as far as our intention is concerned, we intend to be speaking in faith. We do not intend to be speaking as unbelievers, as those who would call the church to abandonment of everything that it once believed, or to an abandonment of its primal faith. But rather we are attempting to speak in the context of the face of a new movement which attempts on the one hand to turn to the primal ground of the Christian faith and on the other hand intends to give expression to that ground in terms of the context of contemporary history and reality.

Now the words "God is dead" or "the death of God" are, of course, of fundamental importance here. I think that, if any attention at all is given to these words, it will be seen that they do not represent ordinary atheism. The ordinary atheist, of course, does not believe in God, does not believe that there is now or ever has been a God. But we are attempting to say that God Himself is God, and yet has died as God in Jesus Christ in order to embody Himself redemptively in the world. In saying that God is dead we are attempting to say that the transcendent Ground, the ultimate, final Ground, of the world, life, and existence has died. He has died in such a way as to embody Himself redemptively in Christ. He has died to make possible final reconciliation of Himself with the world. So the word "death" here is indeed of extreme importance. *(The Altizer-Montgomery Dialogue, pp. 7-8)*

There is solace for us in the fact that Israel once experienced a comparable crisis. Through the catastrophic events of the Exile, Israel lost everything which was the source of order and meaning to an ancient people. Banished from their sacred land and traditions, the exilic Jews were forced to live without their monarchy, their shrines and temple, their cultic priesthood. Today we know that a new form of faith was born out of that crisis. This revolutionary faith may well have had roots in earlier traditions, and was certainly given its initial expression in pre-exilic prophetic circles; but it was only after the Exile that Israel created what we know as the Bible and became a new community of faith existing in opposition to the world about it. Judaism was created out of a faith that dared to negate its original forms and structures. By turning away from a God of worldly strength and power it evolved an interior faith that could withstand the terror of history and affirm the darkness of an alien world as the creation of a Creator whom it now knew as the absolutely sovereign Lord.

Is there any reason to believe that our contemporary Christian crisis is less than that of the ancient Jew in Exile? Just as the Jew was born out of a passage through the death of his own sacred history, may we hope that a new Christian will be born out of the death of Christendom? ("Creative Negation in Theology," pp. 864-65)

There would seem to be little doubt that we are now entering a period in which Christianity must confront the most radical challenge that it has faced since the time of its beginning. Certainly the churches are inadequately equipped to face such a challenge, and if we were forced to rely solely upon ecclesiastical

Christianity to find a way to a new Christian life and witness, then we would very nearly be without hope. But there is no intrinsic reason why Christianity should be identified with its ecclesiastical expressions. Indeed, the identification of Christianity with the Christian Church may well be the major source of the troubles that now beset the Christian faith. This study has chosen to challenge this identification, and to do so with the conviction that there is no other way to a living and contemporary Christian faith. Few Protestants are aware of how much of our inherited Christian faith and witness has its source in an increasingly archaic ecclesiastical tradition, and even fewer theologians are willing to negate all those ecclesiastical norms and traditions which are incompatible with the contemporary life of faith. But there lies no way to a contemporary epiphany of Christ apart from a consistent and thoroughgoing transformation of the language and forms of all ecclesiastical Christianity. *(The Gospel Of Christian Atheism, p. 9).*

JOHN A. T. ROBINSON

The true radical is the man who continually subjects the Church to the judgement of the Kingdom, to the claims of God in the increasingly non-religious world which the Church exists to serve. *(Honest To God, p. 140).*

The revolutionary can be an "outsider" to the structure he would see collapse: indeed, he must set himself outside it. But the radical goes to the roots of his *own* tradition. He must love it: he must weep over Jerusalem, even if he has to pronounce its doom. Any re-formation must start from within, and in the case of the Church must respect the fact that the life it would see renewed is the organic life of a Body deeply rooted in the processes of history. It is not only, I think, because I am an Englishman that I see reformation marked as much by evolution as by revolution. To be realistic we must begin where we are—with the plant, the liturgy, the ministry, the money and the organization we have got. We must be prepared to involve ourselves in the burden and struggle of seeing that it is less irrelevant, less wasteful, less sheerly frustating than it is. Nothing is gained by simply cutting oneself off from the main body and getting out on a limb. Indeed, it is essential to have the humility to see oneself as part of the sin and irrelevance that has to be overcome—from within. *(The New Reformation? p. 79).*

The Christian gospel is in perpetual conflict with the images of

God set up in the minds of men, even of Christian men, as they seek in each generation to encompass his meaning. These images fulfil an essential purpose, to focus the unknowable, to enclose the inexhaustible, so that ordinary men and women can get their minds round God and have something on which to fix their imagination and prayers. But as soon as they become a substitute for God, as soon as they *become* God, *so that what is not embodied in the image is excluded or denied,* then we have a new idolatry and once more the word of judgement has to fall. In the pagan world it was—and still is—a matter in the main of metal images. For us it is a question much more of mental images—as one after another serves its purpose and has to go. *(Honest To God, pp.125-6).*

Without the constant discipline of theological thought, asking what we really mean by the symbols, purging out the dead myths, and being utterly honest before God with ourselves and the world, the Church can quickly become obscurantist and its faith and conduct and worship increasingly formal and hollow. That is why the cast of our theology, the mould of our belief, is in the long run so important. It will condition everything. *(Honest To God, p. 133).*

What looks like being required of us, reluctant as we may be for the effort involved, is a radically new mould, or *meta-morphosis,* of Christian belief and practice. Such a recasting will, I am convinced, leave the fundamental truth of the Gospel unaffected. But it means that we have to be prepared for *everything* to go into the melting—even our most cherished religious categories and moral absolutes. *(Honest To God, p. 124).*

I believe we are being called, over the years ahead, to far more than a restating of traditional orthodoxy in modern terms. Indeed, if our defence of the Faith is limited to this, we shall find in all likelihood that we have lost out to all but a tiny religious remnant. A much more radical recasting, I would judge, is demanded, in the process of which the most fundamental categories of our theology— of God, of the supernatural, and of religion itself—must go into the melting. Indeed, though we shall not of course be able to do it, I can at least understand what those mean who urge that we should do well to give up using the word 'God' for a generation, so impregnated has it become with a way of thinking we may have to discard if the Gospel is to signify anything.

For I am convinced that there is a growing gulf between the traditional orthodox supernaturalism in which our Faith has been framed and the categories which the 'lay' world (for want of a better term) finds meaningful today.   *(Honest To God, pp. 7-8).*

The whole world-view of the Bible, to be sure, is unashamedly supranaturalistic. It thinks in terms of a three-storey universe with God up there, 'above' nature. But even when we have refined away what we sould regard as the crudities and literalism of this construction, we are still left with what is essentially a mythological picture of God and his relation to the world. Behind such phrases as 'God created the heavens and the earth', or 'God came down from heaven', or 'God sent his only-begotten Son', lies a view of the world which portrays God as a person living in heaven, *a* God who is distinguished from the gods of the heathen by the fact that 'there is no god beside me'.   *(Honest To God, p. 32).*

If Christianity is to survive, let alone to recapture 'secular' man, there is no time to lose in detaching it from this scheme of thought, from this particular theology or *logos* about *theos,* and thinking hard about what we should put in its place. We may not have a name yet with which to replace 'theism': indeed, it may not prove necessary or possible to dispense with the term (hence the query in the title of this chapter). But it is urgent that we should work away at framing a conception of God and the Christian Gospel which does not depend upon that projection.   *(Honest To God, p. 43).*

The task of theology may be seen as a form of map making—trying to represent the mystery of *theos* (the incommunicable spiritual reality) by a *logos* or word-picture which can be used for the purposes of communication. It involves a translation or transposition from one dimension to another. And to make a map it is necessary to employ what the geographer calls a "projection." In physical geography the most familiar of these is Mercator's projection, named after the famous sixteenth-century Flemish geographer, which performs the not inconsiderable task of transferring a spherical earth onto the oblong pages of an atlas...Any *logos* about *theos* must also employ some projection to depict or represent the spiritual reality with which it is dealing. Usually we are no more conscious of it than we are when looking at an atlas. Indeed, there is one that has so dominated the tradition in which most of us have grown up that we almost forget that the map is not a direct transcript of reality itself. It has the same effect as the Authorized or King James Version in making people think it *is* the Bible. To question it is to question God. Yet we must question it and look at it for what it is. *(Exploration Into God, pp. 26-7).*

The only question at issue is *how* the Biblical doctrine is to be given expression today, in a non-supranaturalistic world-view. For the New Testament writers the conviction of the personal character of God as gracious, holy, self-giving love was expressed unquestioningly in the representation of him as *a* Being, a supreme Person. This was the only available projection, and to say that Jesus used it is in itself to say no more than he was genuinely a man of the first century. The question is whether the reality of the experience which Jesus knew—and to which Christians have testified ever since—is tied to this projection: for if it is, I fear for its ability to *become* a reality for many in our generation. ("The Debate Continues," p. 262)

The "death of God" is no doubt an unhappy slogan—certainly if it is taken as in any sense referring to a metaphysical event. Yet it has had its value in drawing attention to a phenomenon which I believe *is* more than the absence, silence, or eclipse of God. It is registering the fact that for millions today the living God has been replaced, not by atheism in the sense of a positive denial of God, nor by agnosticism in the nineteenth-century sense, but precisely by a dead God. The reality of God has simply gone dead on contemporary man in a way that has never quite happened before. *(Exploration Into God, pp. 47-8).*

Most of us today are practical atheists. The 'god-hypothesis' is as irrelevant for running an economy or coping with the population explosion as it was for Laplace's system. As a factor you must take into account in the practical business of living, God is 'out'—and no amount of religious manipulation can force him back in. He is peripheral, redundant, incredible—and therefore *as God* displaced: in Julian Huxley's words, 'not a ruler, but the last fading smile of a cosmic Cheshire Cat'. *(The New Reformation? p. 109).*

Is not the situation of many of us today that we feel we *must* be atheists, and yet we *cannot* be atheists? God as we have been led to posit him *is* intellectually superfluous, *is* emotionally dispensable, *is* morally intolerable—and yet, in grace and demand, he will not let us go. The hound of heaven still dogs us, the 'beyond in our midst' still encounters us, when all the images, all the projections, even all the words, for God have been broken. *(The New Reformation? p. 115).*

The simplistic representation of God as a Person is the source or at any rate the occasion of great stumbling—as well as, still, of great comfort and faith. It produces in many sheer unbelief. Such beings, it is held, simply do not exist (or at least there is no evidence for them), and the reality of the God-relationship is quickly made to turn on quite extraneous arguments and proofs. In an age of science and technology the image of an invisible Superman personally creating phenomena as a potter makes a pot strikes more people as incredible than helpful. And in an age of planning a cosmic planner who cannot or does not prevent disasters merely appears supremely incompetent or grossly culpable.

On more and more occasions it is positively imperative to sit loose to the image—or even to discard it—if the truth it is intended to represent is to be maintained. And I am profoundly convinced that the truth does remain. For this reason I believe it is more important to insist on the continuity of belief in God as personal—and to retain the word "God" however loaded—than to give it up. The reality of being surrounded, sustained, claimed abides—even though there is a healthy process of detachment going on from certain childish notions of dependence which religion has often fostered (contrary to everything in the New Testament's equation of "sonship" with the maturity and freedom of man come of age). And the need to speak in some way of "God" represents the conviction that this encompassing reality, the element in which man lives and moves and has his being, is not merely materialistic or even humanistic. The question is *how* one gives expression to this conviction.   *(Exploration Into God, pp. 149-150).*

2. The Sources of Theology

Different assessments of the place of theology in faith reflect different assumptions about the sources of theology. These different assumptions revolve around whether theology's content is disclosed from God or discovered by man. Often the question of sources is discussed by drawing a line between revelation and reason. For such discussions, the entire content of theology must be either revealed by God or reasoned out by man. But this conventional way of specifying the rival data upon which theological systems claim to rest is misleading. In actuality, very few theological traditions completely separate revelation and reason.

The rival sources of theology may be classified more accurately by distinguishing between *special* and *general* revelation. The more familiar divison between revelation and reason too easily lends itself to charges of irrationalism in theologies invoking revelation and to accusations of egoism in theologies appealing to reason. Actually, revealed theologies employ reason in giving an account of the content of revelation, and natural theologies generally draw inferences about realities beyond the physical world and human consciousness. In short, both approaches employ reason in understanding a given subject matter. The real issue is the kind of data and the mode of reasoning involved in theology. So-called "revealed theologies" appeal to a *special* revelation for their subject matter and approach. Man must have supernatural help since human finitude and sinfulness prevent him from discovering any ultimate and saving truth for himself. Thus, theological reasoning deals with the data of a supernatural revelation under a supernatural guidance. In contrast, so-called "natural theologies" rest on a *general* revelation. The basis and implications of authentic religion can be inferred from certain permanent features of the natural environment and human experience. Man needs no outside help since he is capable of discovering the religious truth about himself and his ultimate environment through his own capacities. Thus, theological reasoning works on the data of a general revelation under the tutelage of a rational norm. Finally, then, theological systems variously claim to be based on special revelation, on general revelation or on some combination of both kinds of revelation.

Orthodoxy bases theology primarily on a special revelation of saving truths. As we have seen in our discussion of fideism, both Protestant and Catholic forms of this theological orientation recognize that some knowledge of God's will and work can be gained from general revelation. But this natural theology can never furnish saving knowledge. Salvation requires knowledge of God's superrational nature, of Christ's supernatural accomplishments and of history's supertemporal consummation. Such knowledge comes only through a special revelation, supernaturally given by God and supernaturally appropriated by believers. But, since the Bible contains the whole counsel of God necessary for salvation, Orthodox theologies actually rest on two *levels* of special revelation. The primary revelation of God's saving truths to man was to the writers of the Scriptures. The consequent revelation of God is through the biblical writings. In other words, God has specially revealed himself in two distinct ways. To prophets and apostles, he directly and immediately communicated his saving truths. Orthodox theologians disagree over whether God inspired the very words or the total message found in Scripture. But they all agree that the biblical revelation rests upon supernatural inspiration. To all except those who enjoyed this direct and immediate communication, God reveals himself through the Scriptures interpreted under the leadership of his Spirit. Therefore, Orthodox theologies ground all saving truth in the Bible's miraculously given and received revelation. Indeed, theology is nothing more than deductively unfolding and systematically arranging the truths of the Bible.

Liberalism appeals primarily to a general revelation of God at work in the world and particularly at work in the spiritual life of man. Unlike Orthodoxy, Liberalism does not limit or locate God in special revelations of truth, miraculous interruptions of nature or unique incarnations in history. The whole natural and human process reveals God's nature and will. Not all men are equally gifted in discovering God nor equally dedicated in serving God. The Bible clearly reflects man's disparate but progressive struggle through the ages for religious understanding and fidelity. But, for most Liberals, Jesus represents history's clearest illustration of God's will and work and of man's nature and destiny. Jesus has an enduring significance for Christian faith and human history by virtue of fulfilling more completely than any other man the potentialities of all men to be sons of God and brothers to one another. Hence, Christians are called to emulate the faith of Jesus rather than accept beliefs about Jesus.

Faith means serving God and loving man in one's own time and place in the spirit of Jesus. Theology seeks to clarify and inspire such living faith. Therefore, liberal theologies are based upon the faithful experience of contemporary believers. Since this experience involves the whole range of knowing and doing, scientific and humanistic studies as well as political and economic life contribute to theology's vision. More important than these 'non-religious' sources, the biblical writings and past theological systems offer valuable clues to the present work of God and duty of man. Above all, Jesus furnishes the greatest inspiration and deepest insights for faith in every generation. But, while making important use of these religious clues and catalysts, liberal theologies strive to account for the living faith of contemporary believers rather than transmitting the belief systems of some distant past.

Neo-orthodoxy bases theology wholly on special revelation. While acknowledging that revelation is a personal and present experience, Neo-orthodoxy scores Liberalism for offering an inadequate account of God's sovereignty and man's limitations. God is not universally available as a facet or support of human pursuits, nor can man think rightly about God through finite and sinful reasoning. God is present and knowable only when and where he chooses. Liberalism too easily identifies God with human concerns and concepts. This categorical denial of general revelation and natural theology leaves Neo-orthodoxy completely dependent upon special revelation. Yet Neo-orthodoxy is unwilling to equate the Bible with revelation as does Orthodoxy. A *living* God must reveal himself to men in the concreteness of present events rather than simply through information about past events. Neo-orthodoxy finds God present and knowable in the concrete events of personal and corporate existence. But the ground and norm of all present revelatory events is the unsurpassable Event of Jesus Christ. Whenever and wherever God acts and speaks today, he is known and served in and through his past Deed and Word. Jesus Christ performs this mediatorial function through Christian preaching based on Holy Scripture. God's present involvement in historical events is apprehended through recollecting his past Deed and Word as witnessed in the Bible. Such recollection is the medium through which God enlivens faith to his own concrete will and work in present events. Since theology furnishes the substance and scope of preaching, neo-orthodox theologies base theology on God's unsurpassable revelation in Jesus Christ. Theology must pay attention to new advances in knowledge and to new structures in society since preaching must awaken faith to God's present reality. But man's changing knowledge and society's changing shapes affect only theology's verbal forms and social strategies. The content of theology must be wholly derived from God's self-disclosure in Jesus Christ.

PAUL M. VAN BUREN

A basic decision must be made by anyone who feels himself claimed by the Christian Gospel. Either "being a Christian" is something "religious" and quite distinct from secular affairs, or Christian faith is a human posture conceivable for a man who is part of his secular culture. What a Christian thinks about a given situation, the conclusions to which he comes, and the actions

78

which he performs, may differ from those of one who is not a Christian. Whether they always will do so remains to be seen. The question is whether a Christian is to be distinguished from an "unbeliever" by a different logic or thinking. Bonhoeffer contended that to separate Christian faith and secular life in the world is to reject the very heart of the Gospel, and we shall conduct this study on the assumption that "being a Christian" does not deny one's involvement in the secular world and its way of thinking. This assumption will govern our attempt to understand the Christian conviction that "Jesus is Lord." With the philosophical method of linguistic analysis already reflecting so clearly the way in which we think, speak, and understand today, it seems promising to try it as an interpretative tool. We have fundamentally nothing more to suggest than a certain "arrangement," as Wittgenstein put it, of what is already known, but it is our hope that by a fresh juxtaposition of the various elements of the problem, we shall suggest a fruitful line of development and contribute to the accomplishment of the theological task for our time. *(The Secular Meaning Of The Gospel, pp. 17-8).*

A certain "arrangement" may help dissolve some of the dilemmas which beset contemporary theology, and it will also suggest a method for the constructive task which remains: to develop the consequences of this arrangement and the resulting method in sufficient detail to make clear their possibilities and limitations. As a point of departure, the relationship between the Gospel and the life, words, and death of Jesus is a matter that calls for careful linguistic analysis. *(The Secular Meaning Of The Gospel, p. 19).*

When the language of the Gospel is analyzed so as to reveal its logical meaning or function, the history of Jesus of Nazareth proves to be indispensable to it; if this history is pushed into the background, faith may be a perspective, but it is either not historical at all, or it is grounded in some other piece of history. *(The Secular Meaning Of The Gospel, p. 196).*

The Gospel...is the good news of a free man who has set other men free, first proclaimed by those to whom this had happened. And it has happened again and again during nineteen centuries that, in the context of hearing this apostolic proclamation, men have been liberated. Their response, which the New Testament calls "faith," consists in acknowledging that this has happened by accepting the liberator, Jesus of Nazareth, as the man who defines for them what it means to be a man and as the point of orientation for their lives. They are "in Christ," which is to say that their understanding of themselves and their lives and all things is determined by their understanding of Jesus. They are a "new creation" in that this orientation to the whole world is new for them. (*The Secular Meaning Of The Gospel, p. 138*).

Those who first said, "Jesus is Lord," expressed a particular perspective upon life and history. This confession, ascribing universality to a particular man, indicated that faith constituted a certain understanding of self, man, history, and the whole world, and that this universal perspective had its norm in the history of Jesus of Nazareth and Easter. This perspective upon life and the world was understood not as a point of view selected by the believer, but as a "blik" by which the believer was "grasped" and "held." The perspective of faith was spoken of as a response "drawn from" the believer. (*The Secular Meaning Of The Gospel, p. 140*).

This perspective arises in connection with hearing the Gospel concerning Jesus of Nazareth and it looks back to him continually as its historical point of orientation. To affirm the Gospel is to express this historical perspective. The man who says, "Jesus is Lord," is saying that the history of Jesus and of what happened on Easter has exercised a liberating effect upon him, and that he has been so grasped by it that it has become the historical norm of his perspective upon life. His confession is a notification of this perspective and a recommendation to his listener to see Jesus, the world, and himself in this same way and to act accordingly. (*The Secular Meaning Of the Gospel, p. 141*).

This interpretation of Christian faith is related to Hare's concept of "blik." The language of faith expressed in the Gospel may be understood if it is seen to express, define, or commend a basic presupposition by which a man lives and acts in the world of men. That is why we call it a historical perspective. . . . The "blik" of the Christian finds its adequate expression in the Gospel, however, and it is related always, if sometimes indirectly, to the history of Jesus of Nazareth. This is why we call this perspective *historical.* (*The Secular Meaning Of The Gospel, p. 143*).

Ramsey has suggested how a "blik" arises. It comes out of what he calls a situation of discernment or disclosure, a situation which is seen suddenly in a new way demanding a commitment of the viewer. The languages of revelation, Easter, the "illumination of the Holy Spirit," and conversion reflect just such a situation. The decisive discernment situation for Christianity is Easter and the

Easter proclamation concerning Jesus of Nazareth. Men may come to Christian faith in all sorts of ways, of course. A man may have begun to be a Christian from reading the book of Genesis, or he may have come through a more distant point of entry. When he has "arrived," however, when he has heard and accepted the whole of what the Gospel has to say, the norm of his perspective will always be the history of Jesus and Easter. *(The Secular Meaning Of The Gospel, pp. 143-4).*

Finally, Braithwaite has taken religious statements to be assertions of an intention to act in a certain way, together with the entertainment of certain stories. As far as it goes, this analysis agrees with our interpretation. We would clarify the "intention" with such words as "discernment" and "commitment," and we would define the "certain way" as a response to and a reflection of the way of Jesus of Nazareth. It is a way characterized by a freedom "caught" from him. We would go further than this, however. In order to live in the "freedom for which Christ has set us free," we need indeed to "entertain" again and again that piece of history, for it does not just provide an encouragement to walk in the way of freedom; it is the context in which the light dawns anew and in which that freedom proves again to be contagious for us. *(The Secular Meaning Of The Gospel, p. 145).*

The argument of my book suffers from two major limitations, or at least there are two problems which beg for fuller and more careful development. One has to do with metaphysical assumptions...The second problem lies in the dependence of my interpretation on the past, on the history of Jesus and of Easter. It may be argued, however, that one feature of contemporary secular culture is its almost exclusive concern with contemporaneity: the past is not of great moment to most of us most of the time. Moreover, does not Christian faith qualify an interest in the past, leading us to say, in various ways, that the past is of no avail unless it becomes *'somehow'* contemporaneous with the believer? It would have been more honest to the tradition and also to contemporary thought if I had argued that in fact it is not the historical event which becomes an occasion for *'discernment'* for the believer, but rather the *story* of the event, or even the image of Jesus which is portrayed by the contemporary church in its preaching and worship. ("Christian Education *Post Mortem Dei,*" pp. 4-6)

An analysis of the function of the language of biblical Christology discloses the meaning of the Gospel and clarifies the issue between Christian faith and unbelief in terms which the contemporary Christian can understand. The New Testament points to Jesus as a man singularly free for other men, and as a man whose freedom became contagious. Its documents were written by men who had received, together with this freedom, a new perspective upon all of life, a perspective which looked to the history of this one man as its norm. They proclaimed the good news of this contagious freedom and of the character and consequences of this perspective, however, in the form of cosmological assertions about the world and the human situation which are meaningless to secular men. To affirm these assertions is to deny the character and tendency of modern thought, which believers share with the rest of their society. What is more important, to affirm them is to affirm only the form and not the intention of the apostolic message.   *(The Secular Meaning Of The Gospel, p. 157)*.

When we ask after the meaning of the Gospel in this secular age, we are asking after the function of the apostolic message, not its form. We are asking why these things were said, what was intended, what was their use. The function of the language of the Gospel has been demonstrated. It expresses, defines, and commends the historical perspective described. Faith is thereby shown to be the holding of this perspective under its historical norm, rather than a special religious way of knowing arcane information about the cosmos or the human situation. Loyalty to the intention of the apostolic message, therefore, demands our willingness to transform the assertion of the apostolic preaching; indeed, it has demanded this same willingness in every age.   *(The Secular Meaning Of The Gospel, p. 158)*.

WILLIAM HAMILTON

My starting point may be said to have two parts, one negative, the other positive.

The negative part is the perception..of the deterioration of the portrait of the God-man relation as found in biblical theology and the neo-orthodox tradition. This theological tradition was able to portray a striking and even heroic faith, a sort of holding on by the fingernails to the cliff of faith, a standing terrified before the enemy-God, present to man as terror or threat, comforting only in that he kept us from the worse terrors of life without him. This God, we used to say, will never let us go. But he has, or we have him, or something, and in any case this whole picture has lost its power to persuade some in our time.

But our negations are never very important or interesting. There is a positive affirmation or starting point by which I enter into the country inhabited by the death of God settlers. It has to do with the problem of the Reformation or being a Protestant today...

Today we may need to look at the Reformation in a[new]sense, no more or less true than the earlier approaches, but perhaps needing special emphasis just now and fitting new experiences in both church and world. This approach is more ethical than psychological or theological, and its focus is not on the free personality or on justification by faith, but on the movement from the cloister to the world. Of course, there is no specific event in Luther's life that can be so described, but the movement is there in his life nonetheless, and it is a movement we need to study. From cloister to world means from church, from place of protection and security, of order and beauty, to the bustling middle-class world of the new university, of politics, princes and peasants. Far more important than any particular ethical teaching of Luther is this fundamental ethical movement...

This view of the Reformation, along with my preliminary negative comment, does allow a kind of picture of faith. It is not, this time, holding on by the fingernails, and it is not a terror-struck confession before the enemy God. It is not even a means of apprehending God at all. This faith is more like a place, a being with or standing beside the neighbor. Faith has almost collapsed into love, and the Protestant is no longer defined as the forgiven sinner, the *simul justus et peccator,* but as the one beside the neighbor, beside the enemy, at the disposal of the man in need. ("The Death of God Theologies Today," pp.35-7)

There is no question about it: "death of God" is a striking, rhetorical and offensive phrase. We death-of-God theologians do not call ourselves that in order to give offense. We mean "death." Traditional religious thought has spoken about the "disappearance" or "absence" or "eclipse" or "silence" of God. It means, by these words, that men do not permanently enjoy the experience of faith or the presence of God. The presence is, from time to time, withdrawn, and men cannot count on the timing or character of its return. This is a common enough religious affirmation in our time, but it is not what we death-of-God people are talking about. We are talking about a real loss, a real doing without, and—whatever we do expect of the future— we do not expect the return of the Christian God, open or disguised.

There is, incidentally, a practical advantage in the shocking character of the phrase "death of God." It is just not something that conventional religious people or bishops or officials can pick up and use in their own way saying, "Why, we've been saying that all along." There are those who feature this kind of complacency, but it is tough to do it with "death of God." The phrase is, you might say, nonsoluble in holy water, even when uttered with extreme unction.

The affirmation of the death of God is Christian in two senses. It is, for the most part, made by Christian theologians. (Not entirely, however, and a dialog between Christians and Jews around this idea is coming into being that seems most promising and exciting.) And it is made by us in order to affirm the possibility of thinking and living as Christians. To say "death of God," then, is somehow to move toward and not away from Christianity. Thus it should be clear that we theologians are not trying to reduce the Christain faith to a bland and noncontroversial minimum so that it can be accepted by scientists, rationalists and freethinkers. We are not particularly anxious about relevance or communication. It is not because we long to slip something into the mind of "modern man" that we do what we do. It is because something has happened to us, and because we suspect that it may have happened to others, that we are talking about the death of God. ("The Death of God," p. 84).

Question: In radical theology, is it required that one have had a concrete experience of the loss of God? A deconversion experience, one might say?

I would hope not, for this would mean one could not come into the radical position from ordinary unbelief or secularism. But it is true that the contemporary development of what is called the radical or "death of God" theology is tied up with the breakdown of the biblical-neo-orthodox theological position, and thus radical theology has been, in its first stages, characterized by the theme of the loss of transcendence. My answer to the question would be, I think, that the loss of transcendence is a possible way in, but it is not necessary. What is necessary is, with or without the personal experience of the "death of God," a feeling for and participation in the "death of God" as a historical-cultural event in Europe and America over the last two hundred years. That historical story must somehow become the individual's story, whatever the texture of his personal religious or irreligious life might have been. Deconversion experiences help, but do not define the radical theology. ("Questions and Answers on the Radical Theology," pp.236-7).

Question: ...Would you excuse a personal question and tell me what is the special character of your experience of the "death of God"? Or would you object to the phrase "experience of the death of God"?

No, I think the phrase makes some sort of sense. The experience is for me a complex one, made up of a number of strands, each inconclusive in itself. It does not entail a discovery of a new way of knowing (van Buren's book), or a reflection on the significance of the seventeenth-century scientific revolution (Wren Lewis) or a simple statement of the irrelevance of God to modern man (Braun). There are perhaps five points that can be mentioned without expansion.

1. The Bonhoeffer theme. Here I would put my development of Bonhoeffer's idea of man come of age, the end of religion, the breakdown of the idea of God as problem solver and need meeter. God is not needed, even on the boundary or in the depths, to do things the world cannot do.

2. The Dostoevsky-Camus theme. The problem of suffering as written about by such writers, and as lived out in the 20th century, has put an end, I think, to classical doctrines of Providence, and thus to the very center of the biblical doctrine of God. A God to whom could be ascribed the death of the six million Jews in our time would be a monster.

3. The theological theme. Part of the "death of God" theology is a very conventional witness to the breakdown of the Barthian-neo-orthodox theological period in Protestantism. (Perhaps, as Michael Novak's recent *Belief and Unbelief* suggests, neo-orthodoxy is now ready to be taken up by the younger Catholics.) It is at the point of its solution to the problem of knowledge of God that its breakdown has been most tellingly felt—the doctrine of revelation. "We cannot know God," the traditional formulation of the doctrine of revelation went, and we would still agree. "But he has made himself known in Jesus Christ," they went on; and we would confess that we no longer have any means of making connections with this confession of a knowledge being given. (Incidentally, another witness to the end of the Barthian interlude is the recovery of interest in natural theology among some of the younger theologians. A lot has been promised, but little produced, one should note.) A passage from Paul Tillich will clarify my point. "So the paradox got hold of me that he who seriously denies God, affirms him. Without it I could not have remained a theologian." *(The Protestant Era, pp. xiv-xv).* This came with liberating force to a whole generation of American Christians, and still does, I presume. It takes the experience of denial of God and names it "faith." It seems to make not having a god, unfaith, impossible, since all the experiences that might count against God become in effect further content for the very idea of faith itself. It is just this confusion of having and not having, of saying yes with saying no, this paradox that kept the young Tillich a theologian, that has collapsed. And one might add: without rejecting this paradox, I could not have remained a theologian.

4. A fourth element might be described as an affirmation of a change in the way man stands before his world. Certain kinds of experiences of dependence, wonder, awe, are no longer available to man, and thus not available as experiences on which to base an understanding of God.

5. Finally, the "death of God" means that there is an increased confidence in those nontheistic forms of explanation of man's experiences of moral obligation, need of judgment, longing for healing or community that the arts and the sciences provide us. The "death of God" does not imply the disappearance of the mystery, richness, complexity of life; but is does say that God can no longer be a word, a name, or a concept appropriate to explain these things. ("Questions and Answers on the Radical Theology," pp. 216-8).

As Protestants, we push the movement from church to world as far as it can go and become frankly worldly men. And in this world, as we have seen, there is no need for religion and no need for God. This means that we refuse to consent to that traditional interpretation of the world as a shadow-screen of unreality, masking or concealing the eternal which is the only true reality. This refusal is made inevitable by the scientific revolution of the seventeenth century, and it is this refusal that stands as a troublesome shadow between ourselves and the Reformation of the sixteenth. The world of experience is real, and it is necessary and right to be actively engaged in changing its patterns and structures.

This concentration on the concrete and the worldly says something about the expected context of theology in America today. It means that the theological work that is to be truly helpful — at least for a while — is more likely to come from worldly contexts than ecclesiastical ones, more likely to come from participation in the Negro revolution than from the work of faith and order. But this is no surprise, for ever since the Civil War, ever since the Second Inaugural of Lincoln, the really creative American theological expressions have been worldly rather than ecclesiastical: the work of Walter Rauschenbusch and the work of Reinhold Niebuhr are surely evidence for this. ("The Death of God Theologies Today," pp. 47-8).

By way of a provisional summary: the death of God must be affirmed; the confidence with which we thought we could speak of God is gone, and our faith, belief, experience of him are very poor things indeed. Along with this goes a sharp attack on religion which we have defined as any system using God to meet a need or to solve a problem, even the problem of not having a God. ("The Death of God Theologies Today," p.41)

GABRIEL VAHANIAN

Both religion and literature may be said—in spite of their distortions, their failures, even their meretricious tendencies—to be what ultimately opposes, loudly or faintly, the question mark against all the achievements, material as well as spiritual, by which a given culture deceives itself into its own ethnolatrous counterfeit, and religion into an acculturated phenomenon. In other terms, although literature and religion may vary in their respective purposes, they both are, at bottom, an attempt to formulate the image of an imageless reality, i.e., the verbal and ultimately irreducible nature of the human reality; and this explains why, when this aspect is neglected or violated, existence is encumbered either with clichés and slogans or with dogmatism and superstition.

Expressive of the verbal nature of the human reality, literature and religion alike, or any similarly imaginative or metaphoric function, will always question man's deed, and will question it as long as word and deed do not coincide. And as long as word and deed do not coincide, man will always be able at least to speak this word and thus to manifest his resistance to every form of objectification, whether religious or secular. Doubtless, man is what he does—or, for that matter, what he eats—but he is also defined by something more, something else: call it the weakness of his strength or the greatness of his misery, it is what I call a "word"... *(No Other God, pp. 41-2).*

Constituting man as history, the word is the agent which in the last analysis forbids or frustrates the identification of man with his works, in order to transcend, even in a last breath, their ultimate incapacity to signify anything. Indeed, to name a thing means to transcend it; and to speak is to be irreducible to, though simultaneously inalienable from, any aspect, however humble and frail, of the human experience. *(No Other God, pp. 44-5).*

The word is an icon—not a graven image, and not a static or logical symbol. And the word is an icon only when it is iconoclastic. *(No Other God, p. 58).*

It is no accident that as a sign the word means what it signifies only in an arbitrary way. This is not because the ideal always denounces the shortcomings of the real, or because the real always belies the ideal. It is because the *real* always transcends and puts into question our realizations. I do not simply mean that an actual table is only an approximation of table-ness, or that there is incongruity between the word and what is names; I mean that the inadequacy of the word to what it names is not only a negative but also a positive factor. More precisely this inadequacy is at once negative and positive, and actually points to the fact that the word is an icon, the image of an imageless reality, which it can equally reveal and conceal, the way to which it can open or obstruct. (The iconostasis in a Greek Orthodox church is indeed what separates the holy of holies from the rest of the sanctuary.) But the word can open or obstruct the way only if it is *iconoclastic*—if it rebels against freezing reality into an image, a cliché, a slogan, or a dogma—even to the point where the word can partially if desperately recover its iconoclastic function only by sinking into a nihilistic, ultimate refusal of meaning, quite beyond the simple refusal to consider meaning as inherent in the thing which is named. *(No Other God, pp. 42-3).*

What then is the word? Something that means something but does not accomplish anything. And this remains true even when it is made to convey propaganda, whether religious or political. The time always comes when the vanity of the word lays bare all our pretensions, our idolatrous proclivity as well as our natural inclination toward self-apotheosis, or toward the apotheosis of our cultural achievements and our religious securities, or toward ethnolatry or idolatry. Though the word, more exactly through the vanity of the word, the world is recognized as world and the flesh as flesh, and life is affirmed as a gift, as a mandate. Our systems of thought, theological, philosophical, aesthetic, or otherwise, our political dreams and our social programs suddenly appear as the unwarranted amplification of an overconfidence in the power of the word, in the process of which its inherent weakness, its vanity is overlooked. Indeed, the history of the word, of literature— religious and otherwise—is the history of man's adaptation to the world, of his adoption of the world, and also of his refusal to surrender to exigencies of objectification with which his adoption of the world necessarily confronts him. Through the word, culture thus expresses man's legitimate refusal of adaptation, and becomes also, as Ricoeur points out, that which disadapts man and holds him ready and open for the future, for the other. This is what we call the iconoclastic function of the word: it enables man to conceive his being as a project but prevents him ultimately from identifying it with the realization of this project, from being saved by his works as if "eternal life" were "a phenomenon of this life," though "in a certain sense it is already present" in this life. The word provides man with a home and a city, and tells him at the same time that here is no abiding city. It is by faith that Abraham "sojourned in the land of promise, as in a foreign land" (Heb. 11/9). As Auden puts it, in a somewhat laconic fashion:

Life is fleeting and full of sorrow and no words can prevent the brave and beautiful from dying or annihilate a grief. What poetry can do is transform the real world into an imaginary one which is god-like in its permanence and beauty, providing a picture of life which is worthy of imitations as far as it is possible. It is not possible, of course, but without the attempt the real world would get even worse. *(No Other God, pp. 55-6).*

The metaphoric power of the word, the transference of the name of one object to another does not mean that the properties of one are transferred to the other; nor does it mean that the new world which is then brought about becomes the property of my word, any more than the Word of God—that supreme metaphor of the meaningfulness of human speech—becomes the property of the word of man: "My thoughts are not your thoughts, neither are your ways my ways, says the Lord" (Isa. 55/8). Otherwise, the metaphor clots into a cliché or a dogma as the case is when the Word of God becomes identified with a certain human form of speech, and faith with certain standards of belief or practices. *(No Other God, p. 57).*

Whether spiritual or secular, the word of man hence constitutes a parable of his transcendental nature: not even his works can reduce him to a cultural or religious particularism. On the other hand, because "every civilization and every culture is thus a tower of Babel," man can never speak the last, the ultimate word, any more than he can be defeated by the unessential vacuity of his words or of his works: such is, as an empirical phenomenon, the meaning of Pentecost, of the Word of God. Nor does this seem so far fetched if one reflects on it as a consequence of the biblical view of the "humanity" of God. To put it crudely, the Bible speaks of the transcendence of God almost always as though it were an "empirical" phenomenon. Is this not, in fact, also the meaning of the New Testament's insistence on the necessity of Jesus Christ for God's accessibility to man? The word of man is man's access to the Word of God: no man can speak of it, nor does any man speak who does not speak the Word. *(No Other God, p. 40)*.

Thus, what prevents me from becoming an object among other objects, from identifying authentic, i.e., eschatological, existence with a series of empirical data, is the word; or rather, it *should be* the word. For the word can prevent me from that only when it is itself freed by the Word of God, only because the Word of God belongs to the word of man: man's word is the flesh of God's Word. As human speech, literature can hence be said genuinely to aim at transfiguring the world and depicting man's situation "before God." *(No Other God, p. 54)*.

Though the preceding comments no doubt need to be further clarified, they may suffice to permit us to deny that there is any valid dichotomy between the sphere of religion and the sphere of literature. *(No Other God, p. 48)*.

HARVEY COX

The "death-of-God" syndrome signals the collapse of the static orders and fixed categories by which men have understood themselves in the past. It opens the future in a new and radical way. Prophecy calls man to move into this future with a confidence informed by the tradition but transformed by the present. Theology helps prophecy guide the community of faith in its proper role as the avant-garde of humanity. ("The Death of God and the Future of Theology," pp. 388-9).

The starting point for any theology of the church today must be a theology of social change. The church is first of all a responding community, a people whose task it is to discern the action of God in the world and to join in His work. The action of God occurs through what theologians have sometimes called "historical events" but what might better be termed "social

90

change." This means that the church must respond constantly to social change, but it is hampered from doing so by doctrines of the church deriving from the frayed-out period of classical Christendom and infected with the ideology of preservation and permanence. They are almost entirely past-oriented, taking their authority from one or another classical period, from an alleged resemblance to some earlier form of church life, or from a theory of historical continuity. But this will no longer do. A church whose life is defined and shaped by what God is *now* doing in the world cannot be imprisoned in such antiquated specifications. It must allow itself to be broken and reshaped continuously by God's continuous action. *(The Secular City, p. 91).*

Our perception of reality is highly conditioned. It is influenced by our personal careers, our social location, the job we hold, and the web of meanings arising from all of these by which the ideas and experiences we encounter are screened and selected. Hence our perception of reality can be changed only as these conditions themselves are changed.

This is an immensely important fact for any theology of social change, any revolutionary theology, to take into consideration. It implies that people simply cannot be expected to see or react responsibly to emerging social and political problems merely by hearing sermons or reading articles. Something else has to change first. The summons they hear must occur within the matrix of a new social situation, a new objective context which provides the basis for a changed perception of reality. *(The Secular City, pp. 104-5).*

The coming of the secular city supplies the new occasion. In face of its coming, attitudes which have been brought along from yesterday must be discarded, and a new orientation which is in keeping with the new social reality must be initiated. Today, the Gospel summons man to frame with his neighbor a common life suitable to the secular city. He responds by leaving behind familiar patterns of life that are no longer apropos and by setting out to invent new patterns.

The summons in no sense requires a thoughtless novelism, a scurrying after the new simply because it is new. It means rather that antiquity is no longer *per se* a mark of authenticity. Old ideas and practices must compete on an equal basis with new ones. What one has accepted must be constantly tested in the light of a world which never stops changing. Thus the past is celebrated and appreciated, but it can never be allowed to determine the present or the future.

The coming of the secular city is a historical process which removes adolescent illusions. Freed from these fantasies man is expected to assume the status of sonship, maturity, and responsible stewardship. His response to the call must include a willingness to participate in the constant improvisation of social and cultural arrangements which will be changed again and again in the future. The acceptance of provisionality is part of maturity. So is the need to exert one's own originality. No one supplies the steward with a handbook in which to look up procedures by which to cope with every problem in the garden. He must be original. No one provides secular man with surefire solutions to the ever-new problems thrown up by the tireless historical process. He must devise them himself. His maturity lies in his sensing the vast ambience of his assignment, in his willingness to let go of obsolescent patterns, and in his readiness to evolve ways of dealing with the emerging realities of history.   *(The Secular City, p. 105).*

One of the most frequently repeated criticisms of theologians such as myself who dispense with otherwordliness and Christian ecclesiology is that we allegedly lose any dimension of transcendence and become absorbed without remainder in the natural world as such. Some critics claim we fritter away that indispensable point of leverage from which the present world may be judged and transformed, that we become "me-too" theologians. Where is the point of critical leverage in a viable theology of the secular? ("Why Christianity Must Be Secularized, " p. 19)

What *is* a transcendence "in and through the secular"? We cannot sacralize the past. The "overhead" is gone. The "depth" language of Tillich turns out to be no more than a new spatial imagery with the same problems the "overhead" once had. What then in our existence within history does point us toward the transcendent? At what place in his life is man touched by something which acosts him, calls him to accountability, is not subject to his manipulative control?

Theologians today have begun to answer that question with the term "future." The disappearing instant where all that was and is stands before what is to be—this is the point where the transcendent touches secular man. There he senses infinite possibility, the need for choice, the reality of hope and mystery. In this respect, as in many others, modern secular man, whose horizon of intention is history itself, has more in common with biblical man than with "classical Christian man." The Jewish scriptures refer to God variously as "He That Cometh," the "God of Promise," and "the one who goes before." Early Christianity had a radically future-directed orientation: the point of leverage for the young church was not a sacral past but a *coming* Kingdom.

Likewise for theologians of the secular today, history is seen as unconditionally open-ended, transcendence becomes temporal rather than spatial, and the church is viewed as that part of the world which lives already in the reality of that which is hoped for. As the writer of the *Epistle to the Hebrews* says, "Faith is the substance of things hoped for." ("Why Christianity Must Be Secularized," p. 20).

We need a no-nonsense "leveling" in theological discourse. I think that if we can affirm anything real which also transcends history, it will be the future as it lives in man's imagination, nutured by his memory and actualized by his responsiblity. ("The Death of God and the Future of Theology," p. 385).

A serious effort to think systematically about the future and to hold the future open for man will eventually stretch some of our existing canons of thought to the snapping point. But this enterprise may also result in a valuable rediscovery of certain neglected elements in the biblical heritage. It will prove beneficial, however, only if we go into it fully conscious of the colossal challenge it represents to many of our accepted ways of thinking and only if we become aware of the historical roots of this present effort to make the future rather than the past normative for social ethics and political theory.   *(On Not Leaving It To The Snake, p. 32).*

Thus the question of whether we can develop a viable secular theology today depends on whether theologians can reappropriate eschatology and make it once again as central to the life of the church as it was in the beginning of that life. Eschatology has to do with "the last things" or with the future. It is usually dealt with by theologians in a peripheral way. But Roman Catholic theologian Karl Rahner now calls Christianity "the religion of the absolute future," and Protestant theologian Gerhard Sauter argues that the "ontological priority of the future" is the unique component of biblical faith. My conviction, too, is that eschatology must be utterly central to theology, that all doctrines must be seen in the light of faith's awareness of an unconditionally open secular future for which man is unreservedly accountable. When all the dogmas and institutions of the church are seen in this light, our task as theologians becomes clearer. It is neither to prune nor preserve the faith but to interpret and reinterpret it for succeeding epochs of men. ("Why Christianity Must Be Secularized," pp. 20-1).

If God works in the world of secular events, and if it is the responsiblity of his people to discern his action, this requires a theology *of the secular.* If the Incarnation suggests a worldly focus for theological work, then we need to think in *secular terms.* If the significance of the classical doctrines is not eternally fixed but open to interpretations that illuminate new concerns in history, this requires *a secular theology.* ("Why Christianity Must Be Secularized," p. 15).

THOMAS J. J. ALTIZER

Perhaps the deepest obstacle to the realization of this new vocation of theology is the priestly conviction that the canon of Scripture is closed, revelation is finished and complete, the Word of God has already been fully and finally spoken. Later we shall raise the question as to whether this belief is possible for the Christian; but already Paul could only establish his apostleship by insisting upon his own immediate communion with the Word, and Paul's Word, like the radical Christian's, demands an annulment of the old convenant of Sinai and the Torah of Israel's priestly and legal traditions. The radical Christian also inherits both the ancient prophetic belief that revelation continues in history and the eschatological belief of the tradition following Joachim of Floris. This tradition maintains that we are now living in the third and final age of the Spirit, that a new revelation is breaking into this age, and that this revelation will differ as much from the New Testament as the New Testament itself does from its Old Testament counterpart. Of course, the great Christian revolutionaries of the nineteenth century went far beyond their spiritual predecessors. But we can learn from earlier radical Christians the root radical principle that the movement of the Spirit has passed beyond the revelation of the canonical Bible and is now revealing itself in such a way as to demand a whole new form of faith. To refuse such a new revelation of the Spirit would be to repudiate the activity of the Word which is present and to bind oneself to a now empty and lifeless form of the Word. Nor can we expect the new revelation to be in apparent continuity with the old. Now that historical scholarship has demonstrated the chasm existing between the Old Testament and the Christian visions of Paul and the Gospel of John, might we not expect a comparable chasm to exist between the New Testament and a new revelation? Yet this should by no means persuade us that no new revelation has occurred. We can only judge by the fruits of the Spirit, and if a new vision has arisen recording a universal and eschatological form of the Word, a form of the Word pointing to a total redemption of history and the cosmos, then we should be prepared to greet it with the full acceptance of faith. *(The Gospel Of Christian Atheism, pp. 27-8).*

I'm very much concerned with the Bible...but I have to say several things here. First of all, if we accept the proposition that God Himself is an evolving process, that He has *become* Christ and then that Christ has continued to be active and real in history and experience, why, then we have to maintain that revelation continues and that it is not confined to Biblical revelation. That's a critical principle to me. We have in the Bible most fundamentally, from the point of view of faith, the record of the original revelation to His chosen people. The Bible is of course a human document, although I believe it embodies revelation. As a human document, it is not literally true and more important, it's not *finally* true.

The Bible records the history of revelation and, perhaps more important, records the fundamental direction and process both of revelation itself and of the *movement* of God. Today, the Christian can have faith in the Bible as God's Word, and the Word of Christ, but not believe it is His *final* Word or His *total* Word, but that it records the initial, provisional form of revelation. We can understand what I would believe to be later forms of revelation by their ground in the Bible, their relation to the Bible, test them with the Biblical form of revelation. ("Can We Manage Without God?" p. 61).

From the perspective of a forward-moving and evolving Church it must be said that all images of God are limited and provisional, even the biblical images, for to give a final authority to any given image of God is to turn away from the forward and evolving movement of God Himself. ("Catholic Philosophy and the Death of God," p. 275).

Thus neither the Bible nor church history can be accepted as containing more than a provisional or temporary series of expressions of the Christian Word. If the Word is a living Word it cannot be confined to a moment of the past just as it cannot be awaited as a revelation of the future. ("Creative Negation in Theology," p. 867).

So far from continuing to find its ground in the finality of Biblical revelation, theology must seek contemporary expressions of the Word of faith, opening itself to the address of a Word that has become fully actual in the present, an incarnate Word that has ceased to be meaningful and real in its original or initial expression. *(The Gospel Of Christian Atheism, p. 77).*

Once we are liberated from the root idea that the biblical and apostolic images of God have an absolute and eternal authority, then we can become open to the possibility that everything which orthodox Christianity has known as God is but a particular stage of God's self-manifestation, and must in turn be transcended by the forward movement of God Himself. If the Christian God is truly an evolving God, then we must understand that he evolves to new forms or manifestations by negating His past expressions, by leaving them behind as empty and lifeless shells, as His energy wholly and completely moves forward to a redemptive and apocalyptic goal. An evolutionary understanding of God will understand God as evolving by means of a gradual series of self-transformations, thereby leading to a realization that God cannot fully and forever be identified with any one of His manifestations, nor even with a particular series of such manifestations, but rather must be known as a forward-moving process which is continually transcending and thus moving beyond each one of His particular epiphanies or expressions. ("Catholic Philosophy and the Death of God," p. 278).

Moreover, as the idea of organic development is thought through to its theological conclusion, it will surely become obvious that any genuine evolutionary understanding is incompatible with the idea of an original deposit of faith which is absolute and given or unchanging and immobile. Already New Testament scholarship has demonstrated that there are a variety of "original" forms of faith present in the beginning of Christianity, at least as these can be ascertained by historical investigation. Nor can I even imagine a modern historian maintaining that there is no substantial dogmatic distinction between the faith of a Paul or a Peter and the faith of an Ignatius or Irenaeus, to say nothing of an Augustine or a Thomas Aquinas. Among other things to think historically is to recognize a transformation in consciousness in accordance with the movements of history, and such thinking leaves no room for the naive supposition that historical or organic development is simply the progressive enlargement of an original and never changing form. I am given to understand that conservative Catholics today are crying: development, yes, but transformation, no. Yet this is at bottom a refusal of both the modern and the Catholic idea of development: there can be no organic or historical development apart from transformation. ("Catholic Philosophy and the Death of God," p. 275).

No, if the Christian faith has undergone an historical transformation then the theologian cannot truly maintain that God Himself remains unchanged. For the Christian believes that God has fully revealed Himself in Jesus Christ, and that that revelation is present in the Bible and in the Church's original deposit of faith. Thus the theologian cannot look upon the historical transformation of faith as the product of a simple growth or coming to maturity of faith. If faith itself is passing through an evolutionary transformation, then we must regard that transformation as a consequence of the evolutionary movement of God. ("Catholic Philosophy and the Death of God," p. 276).

If modern thinking has reached a new understanding of the evolutionary movement of nature and the cosmos, and likewise a new understanding of the historicity or integral reality of the various situations and conditons of man, then we are faced with the challenge of reaching a new conception of the relation between cosmic evolution and the historical movement of humanity or human consciousness, a challenge which has at least partially been met by Whitehead and Teilhard de Chardin. This challenge would seem to be peculiarly open to the Catholic thinker, for Catholicism grounds its anthropology in ontology, its understanding of man in a prior understanding of being itself, thereby leading to the necessity of natural or philosophical theology as the foundation of theological thinking. At no other point has Protestant theology reacted so negatively to Catholicism, for most Protestant theologians have insisted that to understand God by way of His analogical relation to that meaning of being which is present in consciousness is to subordinate the God of revelation to a purely human thinking, and thus to make of the God of faith a demonic idol. In part such Protestant critics are questioning the integral or open presence of God in the world, confining the meaning of God to that meaning which is present in the special revelation of the Bible; hence they refuse any kind of general revelation which is present in nature or history. Precisely because the Catholic thinker is open to such general revelation he must take with ultimate seriousness the movement of history and the cosmos, and foreswear every temptation to erect a chasm between the God of faith and the God who is manifest in nature and consciousness. ("Catholic Philosophy and the Death of God," p. 273).

Therefore, Christian theology is a thinking response to the Word that is present upon the horizon of faith: but that horizon does not lie in the past, it lies in that future which extends into the present. Accordingly, a theology that merely speaks a word of the past is not engaged in the true task of Christian theology. Only a theology unveiling a new form of the Word, a form that is present or dawning in the immediate and contemporary life of faith, can be judged to be uniquely and authentically Christian. *(The Gospel Of Christian Atheism, p. 18).*

JOHN A. T. ROBINSON

Traditional Christian theology has been based upon the proofs for the existence of God. The presupposition of these proofs, psychologically if not logically, is that God might or might not exist. They argue from something which everyone admits exists (the world) to a Being beyond it who could or could not be there. The purpose of the argument is to show that he must be there, that his being is 'necessary'; but the presupposition behind it is that there is an entity of being 'out there' whose existence is problematic and has to be demonstrated. Now such an entity, even if it could be proved beyond dispute, would not be God: it would merely be a further piece of existence, that might conceivably not have been there—or a demonstration would not have been required.

Rather, we must start the other way round. God is, by definition, ultimate reality. And one cannot argue whether ultimate reality *exists.* One can only ask what ultimate reality is like—whether, for instance, in the last analysis what lies at the heart of things and governs their working is to be described in personal or impersonal categories. Thus, the fundamental theological question consists not in establishing the 'existence' of God as a separate entity but in pressing through in ultimate concern to what Tillich calls 'the ground of our being.' *(Honest To God, p. 29).*

Integral to any God-statement, at any rate in the Judaeo-Christian tradition, is the consciousness of being encountered, seized, held by a prevenient reality, undeniable in its objectivity, which seeks one out in grace and demand and under the constraint of which a man finds himself judged and accepted for what he truly is. In traditional categories, while the reality is immanent, in that it speaks to him from within his own deepest being, it is also transcendent, in that it is not his to command: it comes, as it were, from beyond him with an unconditional claim upon his life. The fact that life is conceived as a relationship of openness, response, obedience to this overmastering reality is what distinguishes the man who is constrained to use the word "God" from the nonbelieving humanist. *(Exploration Into God, p . 66).*

Our experience of God *is* distinctively and characteristically an awareness of the transcendent, the numinous, the unconditional. Yet that is a feature of *all* our experience– *in depth.* Statements about God are acknowledgements of the transcendent, unconditional element in all our relationships, and supremely in our relationships with other persons. Theological statements are indeed affirmations about human existence–but they are affirmations about the ultimate ground and depth of that existence. *(Honest To God, p. 52).*

But for the Bible 'the deep things of God' cannot be plumbed, the transcendence of God cannot be understood, simply by searching the depths of the individual soul. God, since he is Love, is encountered in his fullness only *'between* man and man'. And this is the burden of the whole Prophetic tradition–that it is only in response and obedience to the neighbour that the claims of God can be met and known. This message is focused in a passage to which I constantly find myself returning in the book of Jeremiah, where the prophet is addressing Jehoiakim, the son of Josiah:

Did not your father eat and drink and do justice and righteousness? Then it was well with him. He judged the cause of the poor and needy; then it was well. *Is not this to know me? says the Lord.* God, the unconditional, is to be found only in, with *and under* the conditioned relationships of this life: for. he *is* their depth and ultimate significance. *(Honest To God, p. 60).*

Theological statements are not a description of 'the highest Being' but an analysis of the depths of personal relationships–or, rather, an analysis of the depths of *all* experience 'interpreted by love'. Theology, as Tillich insists, is about 'that which concerns us ultimately'. A statement is 'theological' not because it relates to a particular Being called 'God', but because it asks *ultimate* questions about the meaning of existence: it asks what, at the level of *theos,* at the level of its deepest mystery, is the reality and significance of our life. A view of the world which affirms this reality and significance in personal categories is *ipso facto* making an affirmation about the *ultimacy* of personal relationships: it is saying that *God,* the final truth and reality 'deep down things', *is* love. And the specifically Christian view of the world is asserting that the final definition of this reality, from which 'nothing can separate us', since it is the very ground of our being, is 'the love of God in Christ Jesus our Lord'. *(Honest To God, pp. 49-50).*

Julian Huxley, in his persuasive book of that title, argues that the end of supernaturalism means 'religion *without revelation'.* The discrediting of 'the god hypothesis' throws him back upon a religion of Evolutionary Humanism. 'My faith', he says in his closing sentence, 'is in the possibilities of man.'

But it is precisely the thesis of this book that this is not the only alternative. I am convinced, as I have said, that we should follow Huxley, who is here at one with Bonhoeffer, in discarding the supranaturalist framework. But whereas Huxley does it in the interest of religion without revelation, Bonhoeffer does it in the interest of Christianity without religion—not, of course, that Bonhoeffer desires to abolish religion the way that Huxley wants to dispense with revelation: he simply wishes to free Christianity from any necessary dependence upon 'the religious premise'.

The essential difference can perhaps best be brought out by reverting to the distinction between the apparently similar affirmations that 'God is love' and that 'love is God'. For the humanist, to believe in a 'religion of love' is to affirm the conviction that love *ought to be* the last word about life, and to dedicate oneself to seeing that it everywhere prevails. Thus Professor R. B. Braithwaite maintains that to assert that God is love *(agape)* is to declare one's 'intention to follow an *agapeistic* way of life'. Belief is the avowal of a policy, the declaration that love is the supremely valuable quality. And such belief, of course, requires no revelation.

But the Christian affirmation is not simply that love *ought to be* the last word about life, but that, despite all appearance, it *is*. It is the conviction, again, that 'there is nothing . . . in the world as it is or the world as it shall be . . . that can separate us from the love of God in Christ Jesus our Lord'. And that takes an almost impossible amount of believing. It is frankly incredible *unless* the love revealed in Jesus is indeed the nature of ultimate reality, unless he is a window through the surface of things into *God*.

100

Christianity stands or falls by revelation, by Christ as the disclosure of the final truth not merely about human nature (that we might accept relatively easily) but about all nature and all reality. The Christian's faith cannot rest in the capacities of man. Indeed, it strikes him as astonishing that someone of Huxley's honesty and intelligence should be able to reissue his book in 1957 without a single reference to the possibility, not to say probability, that there might not, within his frame of reference, be any prospects for humanity at all. No, the Christian's faith is in Christ as the revelation, the laying bare, of the very heart and being of ultimate reality. And that is why, in the categories of traditional theology, it was so necessary to insist that he was *homousios,* of one substance, with the Father. For unless the *ousia,* the being of things deep down *is* Love, of the quality disclosed in the life, death and resurrection of Jesus Christ, then the Christian could have little confidence in affirming the ultimate personal character of reality. And this — not his religiosity, nor his belief in the existence of a Person in heaven — is what finally distinguishes him from the humanist and the atheist. *(Honest To God, pp. 127-9).*

3. The Criteria of Theology

What are the criteria by which theological statements or systems can be judged true or false? As we have already discovered, disagreements among theologians abound. Such disagreements pose no problem for Christian laymen as long as they remain ignorant of theological diversity or blithely reject all theological views but their own as erroneous. But the modern world has undermined such ignorant and dogmatic bliss. Theological disagreements have become a problem to theologians and laymen alike.

The problem of theological disagreement can be ignored only by reducing all theological judgments to subjective statements. If religious beliefs and moral mandates merely express the way persons or cultures feel about things, then unresolvable disagreements over these matters are unavoidable. And as our discussion of Relativism pointed out, a great many people have reached the conclusion that religion and morality are subjectively relative. But most theologians and laymen stubbornly believe that man's religious and moral life is grounded in and answerable to objective reality. If this be correct, men need not completely agree in their theory or practice of faith any more than scientific theory and practice have everywhere and everytime been the same. But faith no less than science seems to require an objective basis in reality to warrant the importance and concern men vest in religion and morality.

The question of criteria for the truth or falsity of theological statements is raised most sharply by asking how theologians settle their disagreements rather than by asking how they support their claims. Every theological system rests on evidence and makes claims on truth. But are there criteria for resolving differences between theological systems? Many contemporary philosophers insist that knowledge is objective only if established by criteria which both support claims and eliminate rival claims. For example, people certainly disagree in their interpretations of scientific phenomena and even sensory experience. Any reading of science, history and law reveals how often men disagree over how to describe and explain even *observable* phenomena. But these disagreements over observable phenomena are never considered insoluable in principle. Certain methods of investigation and verification have been developed to dispel disagreements among skilled and unbiased observers. Science in particular has made great strides and enjoys great prestige because criteria have been developed for establishing scientific knowledge and resolving scientific disagreements. Scientists on occasion disagree about the truth of specific scientific statements but they all agree on the methods for establishing the truth of any scientific statement. But are there comparable criteria in theology? Are theological criteria more or less exacting than scientific criteria? How do theologians support their claims and reconcile their differences?

Unfortunately, no universal agreement over criteria prevails in theology as a whole to date. Differing conceptions of theology's importance and sources lead to divergent views of how theological claims are tested for truth and error. Theories of verification usually correspond to the distinction between special and general revelation made earlier. Theologies based on special revelation appeal to supernatural verification. In one way or another, the truth of theological statements is judged and established by God. On the other hand, theologies based primarily on general revelation make no such appeals to supernatural guarantees. Theological opinions must be tested by human beings employing rational tests. But, within this broad divison between supernatural and natural criteria, various accounts of the grounds for accepting theological statements are possible.

Orthodoxy predictably derives its criteria for the truth of theology from the Bible. Drawing truth norms from a source other than the Bible would elevate that source *above* the Bible. Orthodoxy recognizes the Bible alone as God's supernaturally given and guaranteed revelation. The Scriptures furnish both the content of theology and the criteria by which that content is judged true. Within this general commitment, however, a variety of biblically derived criteria for truth prevail. Verbal inspirationists usually assume that all verses in the Bible are equally inspired and hence uniformly normative. Of course, not all verses are equally clear so the true and full sense of obscure passages must be searched and known by other places that speak more clearly. But every verse ideally is known to be true when clearly understood. Other orthodox theologians, while still maintaining the infallibility and inspiration of the entire Bible, find diverse forms and even levels of revelation in the Bible. For them, proper interpretation of this multiformity requires selective biblical criteria. The true sense of Scripture may rest on some broad norm like Martin Luther's dictum that only Scripture which witnesses to Christ is revelatory and true. More often, the vagueness of such broad norms prompts more explicit tests for true biblical understanding. A system of interlocking tests may be required to establish the true sense of Scripture. For example, some orthodox theologians interpret the Old Testament in light of the New Testament, the Gospels in light of the Epistles, the incidental passages in light of the systematic, the local passages in light of the universal and the symbolic material in light of the didactic. But, despite this variety of specific criteria, Orthodoxy is characterized as a whole by its exclusive appeal to the Bible for the content and the credentials of belief.

Liberalism invokes human experience as the court of appeal for theological statements and systems. Since God is at work in the whole natural and human process, all knowledge claims and truth tests must manifest a fundamental continuity and unity. Orthodoxy seems to agree in its claim that revelation transcends but does not contradict reason. Revelation and reason are portrayed as separate but complementary ways to discover and establish truth. But Liberalism argues that Orthodoxy's separation of revelation and reason dooms theology to irrationalism and irrelevance. By deriving the criteria of truth from revelation, Orthodoxy has no surefire way for deciding between conflicting claims of revelation. Its dogmatic biblicism offers no real protection against multiple and even fantastic interpretations of the Bible. Furthermore, by equating the content of Scripture with revelation, Orthodoxy can never harmonize belief with modern thought and life. Men can no longer conceive or experience God in the miraculous way portrayed in Scriptures when taken literally. Therefore, Liberalism shifts the burden of theological proof from God to man. Theological judgments can be tested only in the laboratory of human experience. But liberal theologians differ widely in their accounts of how religious beliefs are *empirically* confirmed. Attempts have been made in some circles to emulate the experimental methods of science. Theology is portrayed as a system of principles based on certain "constants" in man's religious and moral experience. When these principles are acted upon consistently and wholeheartedly, predictable consequences follow which scientifically confirm these religious and moral claims. But most liberal theologies mean something other than the experimental methods of science when references are made to 'empirical confirmation.' Theology, unlike science, does not deal with phenomena which can be quantifiably measured or experimentally controlled. Theology's subject matter manifests no invariable regularites or even statistical probabilities. For this reason, theology can never achieve the exact precision and observable confirmation of scientific proofs. But religious and moral beliefs can be proved in a *broadly* rational and experiential way. Belief systems which satisfy such logical criteria as consistency within the system of theological claims and compatibility with extra-theological knowledge are rationally supported. More important, theological claims which measure up to pragmatic tests like explanatory power, social utility and personal fulfillment are experientially confirmed. The claims of a religious outlook are rationally and experientially verified if they cohere with other bodies of knowledge and illumine all domains of life and activity. Therefore, while admitting a variety of specific criteria, Liberalism appeals to human reason and experience when separating truth from error in theology.

Neo-orthodoxy claims that the truth of theology can only be established by God as revealed in and through Jesus Christ. Neo-orthodoxy and Liberalism alike reject Orthodoxy's treatment of the Bible as God's only infallible and normative revelation, but for different reasons and with different results. Neo-orthodoxy argues that a direct equation of revelation with the Bible imprisons

God in past history and places revelation at human disposal. Orthodoxy's Biblicism makes no allowance for God's self-disclosure in current events and establishes few checks against mis-interpreting the Bible. But Neo-orthodoxy charges that Liberalism's appeal to general revelation confirmed by human experience invites an even more dangerous compromise of God's truth. Testing man's understanding of God by some standard other than the will and work of God subjects God to that standard. And, when that standard consists of rational and pragmatic considerations, God can easily be confused with egoistic projections of human interests and ideas. Liberalism's empiricism minimizes man's stubborn egoism and self-deception and thus opens the door to confusing God with idolatrous concepts and concerns. Therefore, Neo-orthodoxy insists that since God is known only in sovereign and free self-disclosure such revelation furnishes the criteria of its own truth. None other than God can confirm a given word or deed as truly revelatory. Furthermore, since revelation discloses and establishes a *personal* relation to God, man can never possess completely nor prove conclusively such revelation. The intimacies of personal relations offer no such objective guarantees. Revelation always requires a personal response of committed truth and love. Such risk is surely justified when God gives himself to trusting and loving faith. But, as we have seen previously, God only gives himself as he gave himself in Jesus Christ. God's unsurpassable Word and Deed in Jesus Christ is the norm of every other word and deed which mediates his presence and power. And, since Jesus Christ is known only through preaching based on Scripture, theology's ultimate criterion is God's self-disclosure in Jesus Christ through the medium of Scripture. Theology truly understands revelation only when God speaks *through* the Bible. No other criteria can establish *when* God speaks through the Bible. God speaks when he speaks and man can only await and acknowledge such miraculous self-disclosure in humble trust and love.

PAUL M. VAN BUREN

Christian faith finds expression in language. It is expressed in other ways as well, but with respect to faith, as with respect to so many of man's concerns and activities, language is one of the principle ways in which we communicate with one another. Believers, when speaking as believers, have said all sorts of peculiar things. They have said "Jesus is Lord," "Glory to God in the

Highest," and "I believe in the Holy Spirit and eternal life." But believers have spoken as ordinary men, in ways which do not seem particularly to express Christian faith, in saying such things as "Johnson is President," "Three cheers for the Yankees," and "I believe in the graduated income tax and old age pensions." There seem to be no important relations between these two sets of sentences. Is it because the second set are about concrete things and persons which all of us or many of us care about, whereas the former set have to do with another world? Or put the question another way. I know that Johnson is President. Do I know that Jesus is Lord? In each case, how? In each case, what sort of knowing am I talking about? ("Christian Education *Post Mortem Dei,*" pp. 7-8).

In turning to the method of linguistic analysis for assistance in finding the *meaning* of the Gospel, we shall be taking a somewhat different tack from most of those who have worked on the problem of Christian faith in a world "come of age." We do not reject the insights which existentialism has contributed, but we cannot forget that our English-speaking culture has an empirical tradition and that the world today is increasingly being formed by technology and the whole industrial process. Whether this is to be regretted or applauded, it is nevertheless the case. The language of existentialist theologians seems strange to the man whose job, community, and daily life are set in the context of the pragmatic and empirical thinking of industry and science, except perhaps in moments of exceptional personal crisis. In his daily life, the thinking of such a man—and we are all more or less this man—reflects the culture in which he lives. He thinks empirically and pragmatically. *(The Secular Meaning Of The Gospel, p. 17).*

The argument of my book rests on the acceptance of what could be called the metaphysics of "So what?", a way of seeing the world and of understanding how things are, which seems to be operative for most of us in the West most of the time. When we ask "so what?", in response to something said to us, we are asking for the implications or consequences of that which has been said, or of that which is said to be the case. The kinds of responses which we take to be answers to our questions, as opposed to those which strike us as evasions or nonsense, reveal our operative understandings of the way things are, of what is 'real' and what matters to us. This configuration or network of understandings I take to be the 'going' metaphysical assumption of our culture.

If asked for more precision about the character of this

metaphysics, I am willing to answer that it is somewhat empirical, somewhat pragmatic, somewhat relativistic, somewhat naturalistic, but also somewhat aesthetic and somewhat personalistic. My answer is intentionally vague, in order to make clear that the metaphysics in the terms of which I have developed my interpretation of faith is meant to be descriptive. I wish neither to defend nor attack this way of seeing the world and ourselves in it. I do suggest that it is possible to clarify a descriptive metaphysics which is characteristic of our age, and if I have misrepresented it, I should glad *(sic)* to be corrected. In any case, it is in the terms provided by this framework that I have tried to develop my interpretation of the language of faith. ("Christian Education *Post Mortem Dei,"* pp. 4-5).

Whether the pattern and presuppositions of our daily thinking ought to be what they seem to be is not a question I have argued. I have assumed that we do see the world in certain ways, that our culture has what can be called a loose metaphysics, and for the purposes of doing theology today, I have proposed that we explore the possibilities of standing on this common ground. ("Christian Education *Post Mortem Dei,"* p. 5).

The disdainful remark that the common sense of today is only the poor leavings of the best thinking of yesterday and beneath the dignity of philosophical investigation, which I have heard from several philosophers, bothers me a bit. After all, the common sense of today is the pattern of thinking in which we do our major arguing and debating of the great issues of our society. ("The Dissolution of the Absolute," p.337).

The verification principle shows that theological statements which are meaningless in a secular age when they are taken as straightforward empirical assertions about the world, nevertheless prove to have a use and a meaning as the expressions of a historical perspective with far-reaching empirical consequences in a man's life. *(The Secular Meaning Of The Gospel, p. 199).*

Logical Positivism judged all theological statements to be meaningless because they could not meet the verification principle of that philosophy: that, apart from the assertions of logic and mathematics, only those statements which can be verified or falsified empirically are meaningful statements. Statements having to do with an invisible, ineffable God, a transcendent "absolute," and the whole field of classical metaphysics in general could be neither proved nor disproved. Having no empirical function, they could not be called true or false, and they were consequently regarded as meaningless. During the past quarter of a century, however, there has been a shift toward a more flexible conception of language. The verification principle has continued to be important, but it has another function in contemporary linguistic analysis. There are a variety of "language-games," activities with their appropriate languages, and a modified verification principle is now used to ask what sort of things would count for an assertion and what sort of things would count against it. If we know that, we can say in which "language-game" the assertion is "at home." It is now recognized that different kinds of language are appropriate to different situations. The language of love is not that of biology, nor is the language of politics that of physics. The word "cause," for example, has different functions in the disciplines of physics, economics, and history. There is no reason why one should look for the same sort of evidence for a biologist's statement concerning a certain experiment and a statement of love by a lover. The modified verification principle can help us to sort out the pieces of our language, lest we try to understand the language of love in terms of biology or the language of politics in terms of physics. *(The Secular Meaning Of The Gospel, pp. 14-15).*

When human knowledge was conceived of hierarchically—say on the model of a Gothic arch—it made sense to build comprehensive systems, and there could also be one queen of the sciences. But since the Gothic arch has been displaced by the marketplace as a model for human understanding, comprehensive systems have become strangely out of place, just as royalty finds itself out of a job in the context of the marketplace.

Pluralism means that we have granted that there are many ways of looking and seeing, many points of orientation, and that attempts to pull these all together into one grand scheme do not bring us closer to understanding how things are. The generalist has been displaced by the specialist in our society, in area after area of our common life.

Relativism means that we appear to be coming more and more to a consensus that there is more than one way to look at any matter, and that what is said can be called true or false only in the terms provided by the particular point of reference. The student of art, for example, is encouraged to look at a given work of art in the light of the problems which the artist set for himself or were set for him by his situation. It is not a serious question for the student of art to ask what is the single greatest painting of all time.

Pluralism and relativism do not mean, however, that there are no distinctions to be made. One may have reasons for preferring one scale of values to another, one way of looking at a problem to another. But it is, I think we should agree, a mark of education and good sense to refrain from dogmatic statements which necessarily deny all merit to all other positions and points of view. One can hold serious commitments without universalizing them and without insisting that all who disagree are either knaves or fools. If relativism has an unpleasant sound, then let us call it tolerance. By whatever name, it is an important feature of the (secular) spirit of our age; and when we run into its denial, as in McCarthyism or Goldwaterism, most of us are at least uncomfortable. Somehow extremism has lost status, and if at moments it seems to make headway again, I think most us regard this as a step backward, as a betrayal of what little progress civilization has made. ("The Dissolution of the Absolute," p. 341).

There is no arguing about "bliks." Another man may find some other piece of history to be his key to the understanding of life and history: that of the Buddha or Mary Baker Eddy. Or his perspective might be informed by some idea or ideology. It might be a dialectic of history and the Communist Manifesto, an eighteenth-century Declaration of Independence, or the economic theory of Adam Smith. He who has his freedom from Jesus will not agree, however, with those who would say that all sources of freedom are the same. The fact remains that the history of Jesus is not the same as the history of the Buddha, the Communist Revolution, or Henry Ford. It is one thing to say that Christians have always taken the history of Jesus to be indispensable and definitive for their faith, but it is quite another to think that this "uniqueness" can somehow be proved. Chrisitans have never been able, however (and when they were at their best have not tried), to *prove* the "superiority" of their historical perspective over other perspectives. *(The Secular Meaning Of The Gospel, p. 155).*

The meaning of the Gospel is its use on the lips of those who proclaim it. The Christian has seen a man of remarkable and particular freedom, and this freedom has become contagious for him, as it was for the apostles on Easter. The history of this man and of Easter has become a situation of discernment, reorienting his perspective upon the world. If he should have occasion to tell that story, therefore, he can only do so to express, define, or commend this historical perspective, for this is the secular meaning of that Gospel. *(The Secular Meaning Of The Gospel, p. 155).*

In the last analysis, a tree is known by its fruit. While much may still be unknown about the dynamics of freedom and of the effect of a liberated man upon other men, enough is known of this effect to indicate what the Christian means when he says that he sees all of life in the light of the Easter proclamation concerning Jesus. *(The Secular Meaning Of The Gospel, p. 199).*

From Peter's confrontation with Cornelius and the debate concerning the entry of the Gentiles into the all-Jewish early church, down through the history of Christian thought and life, there has been more than one way of expressing the substance of the Gospel. We might also observe that Christians were once called atheists by a misunderstanding, but religious, culture. If there are some who feel that our interpretation is too radical, they should remember that only certain alternatives are available in our time. The other choices are even less attractive, whether they are a sectarian secularism which ignores essential elements of the Gospel, giving us a faith without Christ or a Christ without Jesus, or a very orthodox but meaningless faith which refuses to enter the secular world. The way which we have followed is admittedly conditioned by the particular attitudes with which we began this investigation, but it has led us to an interpretation which may claim for a secular Christianity the full tradition of the faith. *(The Secular Meaning Of The Gospel, p. 200).*

WILLIAM HAMILTON

Professor Gilkey has listed five marks of the death of God tradition, and they should perhaps be set down: (1) the problematic character of God and of man's relation to him today, (2) the acceptance of the secular world as normative intellectually and ethically good, (3) the restriction of theological statements to what one can actually affirm oneself, and with this the rejection of certain traditional ideas of tradition and authority, (4) the centrality of Jesus as one who calls us into the world to serve him there, (5) uneasiness with mythological, super-historical, eschatological, supernatural entities or categories. ("The Death of God Theologies Today," p. 46).

Radical theology is, in terms of its content, clearly "reduced," when compared to various old and new orthodoxies. But it is not self-reduced for strategic reasons: to appeal to modern man, or to attract people influenced by science or Oxford philosophy or despair. It has no interest in contemporaneity or relevance, for their own sakes. It is not that we want to appeal to something—secularism, say—that is out there; but because something has happened to us which we are bound to accept and, accepting it we want to see what this entails for the Christian profession. ("Questions and Answers on the Radical Theology," p. 225).

I certainly don't want to trivialize the idea of the "death of God" by claiming merely that this thing has happened to me and perhaps a few friends. We are not describing a psychological shift. The "death of God" is not merely private, subjective, psychological. It points to something that has taken place in the world of reality. This side of our claim is the one that seems pushy and arrogant. There is one way to neutralize that arrogance, in part. And that is to note that the radical theologians, along with a good many others in the Western world today, have really accepted the relativistic spiritual and intellectual situation in which we live. No one—no Christian, no non-Christian—has either a handicap or a head start in the intellectual free-for-all. No one of us, religious or nonreligious, can claim that we contain something that makes allegiance to us necessary, inevitable, by definition superior to all other allegiances. None of us bears anything necessary; only something possible. Our theology of mission consists, therefore, not of proofs that we make better liberal democrats, whole persons, facers of tragedy than anyone else, but just the demand that we, along with others, be tested by the quality of personal and corporate lives we elicit. By their fruits, and not their apologetic theologies, shall you know them and decide whether they merit your free choice. ("Questions and Answers on the Radical Theology," p. 219).

The plea for a religionless Christianity is thus a plea to give up all claims for the necessity of religion generally. Christianity—as would be true of any religion and any irreligion—is not necessary. It is merely one of the possibilities available to man in a competitive and pluralistic spiritual situation today. Christians are perfectly free to offer their wares to the world come of age, the religionless world. But they have no head starts, ontological or psychological. This in turn implies no clergy deductions, no tax exemption and no preferential treatment of any kind. Finally, when men say "no" to Christianity, it is a real "no," and not a deeply concealed "yes" masked under a protest against false religion. There are those, Bonhoeffer says, who can make it today without God and without despair and guilt. And their success is just as real as the fulfillment of those who live happily and have a God.

We can begin to see what Bonhoeffer is doing and persuading us to do. He is undermining the traditional Christian confidence in language, argument, debate; in short, our assurance that we can persuade an indifferent world that it really needs God. He is forcing us to shift our center of attention from theology, apologetics, criticism of culture, the problem of communication, and even from hermeneutics, to the shape and quality of our lives. He has enabled us to note, in Protestantism, perhaps he has even brought about, the end of theological confidence, and the beginning of a time of confusion between theology and ethics. The communication of the Christian in our world is likely to be, at least for a time, essentially ethical and nonverbal. Christians themselves, at work in the world of the twentieth century, saying their "yes" to it as vigorously as possible, provide the dynamic evidence for the truth or falsity of their message. ("Dietrich Bonhoeffer," pp. 117-8).

GABRIEL VAHANIAN

The question whether or not theology is an autonomous, ecclesiastical science is a false question. Theology is truly ecclesiastical only to the extent that it is open to and assumes the world and its wisdom, only to the extent that it asserts the worldliness of that world of which, for want of the Church, God is always the contemporary. In Christ eternity itself, so to speak, becomes dated, the word becomes flesh. Even the Bible, unless it be idolatrously equated with the Word of God, does not witness to, or proclaim this Word otherwise than through human words as well as in spite of them. Clearly, the Bible itself points as much to the theologian's intellectual dependence on the wisdom of the world as to his independence from it. The more theology is biblical, the more it will take seriously the twin exigency of homogeneity and heterogeneity in relation to any given situation in which it must operate. Theology is no sacred science: it used to be the channel through which the world understood itself as church and through which the Church asserted the reality of the world. Rather, theology is that critical and self-critical task of faith in terms of which the world understands itself as church and the Church manifests the reality of the world. What prevents theology from dissolving itself into an immanentist ideology is precisely what the tradition called, in the strict sense, theo-logy. *(No Other God, pp. 67-8).*

Indeed, "with God word and deed are one: his speaking is the way of his acting." God speaks and the thing happens (Ps. 33/9). "...So shall my word be that goes forth from my mouth; it shall not return to me empty, but it shall accomplish that which I purpose, and prosper in the thing for which I sent it" (Isa. 55/11). "All things were made through (the word), and without him was not anything made that was made" (John 1/3). "By faith we understand that the world was created by the word of God, so that what is seen was made out of things which do not appear" (Heb.11/3). By contrast, the word of man "cannot make one hair black or white" (Matt. 5/36); for this reason, Jesus adds: "Let what you say be simply 'Yes' or 'No'; anything more than this comes from evil" (Matt. 5/37; cf. James 5/12). Hence the language of man at the least is "an ambigous blend of Yes and No" (II Cor.1/18), like an icon, like a symbol which both points to and is not that which is symbolized.

But a symbol which does not hark back to, or assert, empirical reality is a convention. Likewise, when language becomes a mere convention of signs and sounds, it robs the human reality of its verbal nature, of its charismatic power to be with others and never to be without God. Language, therefore, is symbolic and can communicate only where there is communion. Communication, communion, being-with-others—being is ultimately the text of which language is the expression, the translation, the ambiguous Yes and No. Instead, we have today become "accustomed to think of words chiefly as bearers of a definite sense, of a content of ideas." Consequently, we too easily overlook the fact that the real power and significance of words lie in their effecting something, aiming at something, even when it is just a matter of "information," and quite certainly in the mode in which more than information is communicated, when one communicates himself to another, and so by means of words there takes place a "having together with the other." Meeting in the deepest sense is not something that takes place apart and separated from words, but it happens in the event of speech.

But language is also an "abstraction in that it does not manifest reality," though it may signify it, "in and through truth," in and through being. Language is an abstraction in the sense that it produces nothing, except its meaning and even then there is something "gratuitous" about it, as Ricoeur remarks. "It can state, question, invoke, and at the same time say nothing, or lie and deceive, or babble. Hamlet dies saying: Words! Words! Words!" Is it any wonder, then, that a contemporary writer should identify literature an an *activite de mort* inasmuch as literature "succeeds only because it results in books, but fails because it can do nothing for or against the real"? A strange way, is it not, of ultimately denying literature in the very name of literature?

Because the real is verbal, both realism and formalism (like antonomy and heteronomy) are bound to flounder, inasmuch as they both tame, in one way or, another, the iconoclastic function of the word. *(No Other God, pp. 51-2).*

Though the Word of God and the word of man may coincide, the former "never becomes so incarnate in the word of man that they are one and the same." The Word of God is the expression for the phenomenon of being able to speak the word of man, which word cannot establish itself and may not do so without either eliminating the Word of God or simply contradicting the very nature of the word, or, what amounts to the same thing, without violating the infinite qualitative difference between God and man. *(No Other God, p. 38-9).*

God as the Word is not a necessary part of human speech, is not essential to it; or else the reality of God could not be apprehended as an empirical phenomenon. Nor could the Word become flesh. And it becomes flesh neither by adding to nor subtracting from man's word some kind of dimension whereby this word will recover the iconoclastic vocation of its authenticating power: "There is no other light shining in Jesus than has always already shined in the creation." Accordingly, to confess that *"Christ* is revelation and that revelation is the *word"* also implies that God's Word lies in man's word and, on the other hand, that revelation is "an *occurrence,* and not a communication of supernatural knowledge"; that is to say, "revelation does not mediate a worldview," an objective quantification of the word, like culture in general and literature in particular and like moral achievement in the contemplation of which "we really only discover ourselves, or at best, an image of what we ought to be and can be." *(No Other God, pp. 53-4).*

From the theological distinction between the Word of God and the word of man one can only draw the following conclusion, namely: the concept itself of a sacred Scripture could not hold unless there were no such thing as a sacred language, a sacred

114

word: just this we may take to be the meaning of the biblical canon. The Word of God does not communicate a worldview, a body of supernatural knowledge, but addresses me in my own words—and of course it is not possible even to make such a statement without the mediation of some "sacred" revelation, whether the latter is a body of scripture or tradition. The Bible itself is not the Word of God; it contains that Word. It does not create but witnesses to the Word of God; it preaches the Word of God in spite of itself, not because it is sacred. In and of itself it cannot make this happen.

Now then, what is the Word of God, since it does not "designate a complex of statements that can be found and understood with respect to their 'content'?"

To raise this kind of question means to think of God's reality in terms of some objectifying conceptuality according to which this reality would be something up there, or out there, or within me, i. e., a natural phenomenon of this world. The Word of God is what happens when God speaks and the thing happens, when the creation points to the infinite qualitative difference between itself and the creator, when "the word, the word of God, which we ourselves shall never speak, has put on our weakness and unprofitableness so that *our* word *in* its very weakness and unprofitableness has become capable at least of becoming the mortal frame, the earthen vessel, of the word of God." When this happens, the Word of God is not what the word of man is lacking, any more than the reality of God is the missing link of the human reality, but what affirms man; that is, the possibility of saying what the Word of God is, of hearing the Word of God, is itself the Word of God, and this is what is meant by confessing Christ as the Word of God incarnate. *(No Other God, pp. 62-3).*

Through the word, the Word of God becomes a phenomenon of the world, as was Jesus himself *qua* historical figure. Consequently, nothing is more contrary to the spirit of the gospel than the idolization of Jesus or of the Bible, and it follows that the Word of God will not be heard through the word of man, except where the latter is established, nor Jesus become the Christ except where man is also asserted through that act of faith by which alone he can legitimately assume his contingency. *(No Other God, p. 40).*

HARVEY COX

We come to the "truth question" today *through* the ethical

question. In fact, it is precisely here that the whole issue of what "truth" means and what it means to "believe" comes into focus. For theologians, mired in a scholastic conception of reality, truth is a quality belonging to statements which correspond to an objective essence. For the secular mentality, truth is valency, weight, experiential significance. The Gospel is true if it is dependable. To be a Christian is not to attach credence to propositions but to be among a people whose memories and hopes illuminate human experience and provide a sense of direction. I would submit that this latter view of truth, far from being a crass betrayal of the faith, actually comes much closer to the Hebrew notion of truth, *amath,* than does some abstract correspondence view of what it means for something to be true. ("Why Christianity Must Be Secularized," pp. 17-8).

Urban-secular man is pragmatic. In the dictionary sense of the word, this means he concerns himself with "practical or material affairs" and is interested in the "actual working out of an idea in experience." He devotes himself to tackling specific problems and is interested in what will work to get something done. *(The Secular City, p. 54).*

To say that technopolitan man is pragmatic means that he is a kind of modern ascetic. He disciplines himself to give up certain things. He approaches problems by isolating them from irrelevant considerations, by bringing to bear the knowledge of different specialists, and by getting ready to grapple with a new series of problems when these have been provisionally solved. Life for him is a set of problems, not an unfathomable mystery. He brackets off the things that cannot be dealt with and deals with those that can. He wastes little time thinking about "ultimate" or "religious" questions. And he can live with highly provisional solutions. *(The Secular City, p. 55).*

In the functional era, corresponding to technopolis, things become things to do. "The nouns of the ontological era," says [CornelisA.]van Peursen, "become the verbs of the functional era." We are concerned with thinking rather than with thought, with acting justly rather than with justice, with the "art of loving" rather than with love. To sum up the whole sequence, van Peursen says: In the period of myth, the main issue was *that* something is; in the period of ontological thinking, it was *what* something is; in the period of functional thinking, it is *how* something is, how it functions.

Clearly, van Peursen has described in philosophical terms what we mean here by pragmatism. The question remains, however, whether the functional-pragmatic view of truth contradicts the biblical tradition. Must pragmatic man discard the Bible?

Van Peursen does not think so. He believes quite strongly not only that the view of truth emerging in the functional era does *not* depart from the Bible, but that it actually coheres much better with the Bible than did the mythical or ontological definitions it displaces. He demonstrates his case by a careful study of how the Hebrew word *'emeth,* usually translated "truth," is used in the Old Testament. The word designates something that can be counted on, something that is found to be dependable. It is used to refer to a vine which bears fruit, as expected, in the fall. God is spoken of as true because He does what He says He will do. He delivers the slaves from captivity and is thus true to His people. Performance is the yardstick of truth. *(The Secular City, pp. 56-7).*

So understood, pragmatic truth does not seem such a sheer contradiction to biblical categories. We may begin to see why the New Testament word for truth, *aletheia,* constantly appears in syntactical contexts we once found jarring. Jesus says he *is* the truth and that his followers should *do* the truth. He constantly gauged truth by what people did rather than what they said. *(The Secular City, p. 58).*

But pragmatism as a style and a method should never be allowed to degenerate into pragmatism as a new ontology. The danger of functional thinking is that it narrows into "operationalism." This hazard arises when, having isolated some particular aspect of a phenomenon for special attention, we then forget that there *are* other aspects. It results from taking a helpfully restricted view of something and then deciding there is nothing more to it—the age-old temptation to forget that there are an infinite number of ways to look at the same blackbird. *(The Secular City, p. 58).*

The awareness that his own point of view is relative and conditoned has become for secular man an inescapable component of that point of view. His consciousness has been relativized. He knows that not only his language, his customs, and his clothing style, but also his science, his values, and his very way of perceiving reality are conditioned by his personal biography and the history of his group. In our time the Copernican revolution has reached out to incorporate everything into its sweep. All things are relative. Everything "depends on how you look at it."

The persistent protest against idols and icons which runs

through the history of biblical faith provides the basis for a constructive relativism. It makes possible a stance by which the national, racial, and cultural idolatries of the age can be put in their place. It allows secular man to note the transience and relativity of all cultural creations and of every value system without sinking into an abyss of nihilism. He can confess the subjectivity of his perception while insisting that the object of that perception is nonetheless real.   *(The Secular City, p. 27-8).*

Changing times often jar us into noticing aspects of the Bible and the traditional faith that previous periods had kept obscured. We live in a time in which the close coexistence and consequent relativization of divergent worldviews has begun to produce a personality that can sit loose to all worldviews. Gollwitzer has called him the "areligious man." His is a psyche with a high level of tolerance for uncertainty and provisionality. His faith does not provide him with a total scheme by which he categorizes and files life's infinitely variegated experiences. Rather his faith enables him to live with joy and confidence without such a scheme. He still requires what Daniel Callahan calls an "identity." This identity will be mediated through a culture. But if culture itself *provides* this identity it will tend to be a precarious thing, subject to the injurious buffeting of cultural dislocation. For the man of faith the ultimate source of his identity is not the culture, but God. He appropriates his identity through a faith which though it partakes of various cultures is never wholly identified with them. In this way, the self will be able, as Callahan says, to " . . . find ways of responding intelligently to the very uncertainty which life is bound to throw before him." ("Response to Critics," p. 113).

The ability to live with uncertainty, provisional answers, undefined situations and unclassifiable experiences without seeking to press them into a mold identifies the mature man, not the neurotic. Too often a personal worldview, reinforced by constant ritual repetition, becomes an obstacle to expanded and enriched experience rather than a bridge to such experience. Yet we have constantly tried to pander the Gospel to modern man as just this kind of handy vehicle for total meaning. We have scolded him for the complex and multi-faceted character of his life, forgetting that this is precisely what makes him a modern secular man rather than a simple tribesman. We have interpreted the Gospel as a call away from this complexity and back to some kind of simple "eternal verities." We have pictured the church as somehow an antidote to the accelerating differentiation and interdependent specialization of our new technological epoch.

118

If the church is to speak and be heard in the secular world of today it cannot continue to beckon man back to simpler styles of social organization and personality integration. Even more importantly, if the church is to preach the Gospel and not some obsolescent religious advice, it must be clear that, as God told Job, it is he alone and not man who knows how all the fragments fit together. ("Secularization and the Secular Mentality," p. 86).

There is, of course, no high court before which those who affirm God's reality and hiddenness can press their case against those who suspect, as Kafka did, that there is No One There at all. But the difference is real. It is both pointless and patronizing to try to suggest to nontheists that they are really Christians who don't know any better, that the problem is just semantic or conceptual. Nontheists deserve to be taken seriously, not treated as children. In fact, only when we do take them seriously, as they understand themselves, can any real dialogue begin, and they do have much to offer us. Because the experience of the *deus absconditus* and that of the no-god-at-all are so similar, because we share the common discomposure of those who live in a dissonant and exhilarating time, we need the nontheists. But we need them as they are, not as we would like them to be.

The difference between men of biblical faith and serious nontheists is not that we do not encounter the same reality. The difference is that we give that reality a different *name,* and in naming it differently, we differ seriously in the way we respond. *(The Secular City, p. 227-8).*

THOMAS J. J. ALTIZER

Today a new theologian is speaking in America, a theologian who is not so confident of the truth or certainty of faith, yet a theologian who is willing to discuss the meaning of faith. From the perspective of the theology of our century, the strangest thing about this new theologian is his conviction that faith should be meaningful and meaningful in the context of our world. Indeed, the very conviction that faith is eternally given or wholly autonomous is forcefully being challenged. Having come to the realization that Christian theology cannot survive apart from a dialogue with the world, it is increasingly being recognized that dialogue is a mutual encounter: faith cannot speak to the world unless it is prepared to be affected by that world with which it speaks. Moreover, the new theologian is confessing that the Word has ceased to be truly or decisively present in the established and traditional forms of faith. Certainly the older forms of faith have little meaning in our world, yet if we as Christians believe in an actually incarnate Word, then either the Word has perished or it has undergone a radical transformation. Refusing either to deny the Word or to affirm it in its traditional form, a modern and radical Christian is seeking a totally incarnate Word. When the Christian Word appears in this, its most radical form,then not only is it truly and actually present in the world, but it is present in such a way as to be real and active nowhere else. No longer can faith and the world exist in mutual isolation, neither can now be conceived as existing independently of the other; thus the radical Christian condemns all forms of faith that are disengaged with the world. A given and autonomous faith here reveals itself to be nonincarnate—and is judged to be a retreat from the life, the movement, and the process of history—with the result that faith must now abandon all claims to be isolated and autonomous, possessing a meaning or reality transcending the actuality of the world, and become instead wholly and inseparably embedded in the world. *(The Gospel Of Christian Atheism, pp. 16-17).*

Does God lie at the center of Christian faith and proclamation? Is the Christian Word forever inseparable from its historic ground in the existence and the power of God? Must Christian witness inevitably speak of the glory and the sovereignty of God? These are questions which faith itself is now posing to the Christian and they are questions that must be met by the Christian who dares to accept the contemporary challenge of faith. It is the thesis of this book that the Christian, and the Christian alone, can speak of God in our time; but the message the Christian is now called to proclaim is the gospel, the good news or the glad tidings, of the death of God. Few Christians have thus far been able to embrace the death of God as a redemptive event, but an acceptance of his death looms ever larger in contemporary Christian thinking, and it is unquestionably true that the greatest modern Christian revolutionaries willed the death of God with all the passion of faith. Christian theology, however, has yet to learn the language of the death of God. Yet this should not persuade us that we are here meeting an anti-Christian rebellion which is foreign to the reality of faith: for theology is a thinking response to the witness of faith, and it appears only after and not before the epiphany or the movement of the Christian Word. *(The Gospel Of Christian Atheism, p. 15).*

Contemporary radical theologians inherit the nineteenth-century Catholic and Protestant theological conceptions of the evolutionary development of Christianity, but recognizing that the forward historical movement of Christianity has led to the eclipse or silence of God, they call for a radical break from the God who was once manifest and real in faith, and hence for a renunciation or negation of the sovereign and transcendent God of the Christian tradition. Indeed, radical theologians have discovered that genuinely contemporary forms of faith are already freed from everything which the Bible and Christianity have known as the sole or autonomous *deity* of God. Thus a death of God theology is a theology grounded in the death or dissolution of the Christian God; at the very least it demands an abolition of all God language in the positive expressions of both faith and theology, which means that it will admit nothing of what either the Bible or the Christian tradition has known as the God apart from Jesus Christ.   *(Toward A New Christianity, p. 12).*

Significant though the work of new schools of theology may be, it is necessary to insist that many if not most of the important theological developments are taking place outside the academic precincts of theology, even outside ecclesiastical and public circles of faith; and all radical theologians are influenced as much or more by these developments as they are by forces within the professional theological world. The common charge that radical theologians are simply in quest of the modern at any cost fails to take account of this fact. For these theologians are persuaded that the witness of faith is present wherever there is life and energy, and in a world come of age the primary duty of the theologian is to listen to the world. What should be noted in these radicals is above all their conviction that the life and energy of Christ is present wherever the world is most active and real.   *(Toward A New Christianity, pp. 13-14).*

Christianity is a historical faith, not simply because it is grounded in a sacred history of the past, but more deeply because it celebrates the human reality of history as an epiphany of the Word. An incarnate Word embodying a real transfiguration of Spirit into flesh cannot be sought in a heavenly beyond, nor can it be reached by a backward movement to primordial time; it is only in the actual and contingent processes of history that Spirit fully becomes flesh. Here, Spirit never truly appears in a pure or eternal form, nor does it simply appear as Spirit, except insofar as it is known apart from its movement into flesh. Moreover, it is only a regressive and religious form of Christianity that would confine the Word to its Biblical and past historical expressions. When the Incarnation is known as a dynamic process of forward movement, then it must be conceived as a progressive movement of Spirit into flesh, even if it should succeed in evoking a religious reversal of its own movement and process. Each historical expression of the Word will bear its own peculiar and distinct reality, and while no clear path may be seen to lie between one and another, faith must ever seek that particular form of the Word which acts in its own present.   *(The Gospel Of Christian Atheism, pp. 45-46).*

JOHN A. T. ROBINSON

The conception of God as *a* Being, a Person—like ourselves but supremely above or beyond ourselves—will, I believe, come to be seen as a human projection. (Most people already recognize this in the case of the Devil.) It is a way of making real and vivid to the imagination, by personification, the conviction that reality at its deepest is to be interpreted not simply at the level of its impersonal, mathematical regularities but in categories like love and trust, freedom, responsibility, and purpose. The real question of God is not the *existence* of a Being whom we visualize as embodying these in his Person. It is whether this conviction about the ultimate nature and meaning of things is true. *(Exploration Into God, p. 29).*

Doctrine is the definition of the experience; the revelation discloses itself as the depth and meaning of the relationship. To ask men to believe in the doctrine or to accept the revelation before they see it for themselves as the definition of their experience and the depth of their relationship, is to ask what to this generation, with its schooling in an empirical approach to everything, seems increasingly hollow.   *(The New Reformation? p. 40).*

It is not the Church that puts *its* question and waits to hear *its* answers returned to it. It is the world that puts the questions—and refuses to accept any prefabricated answers. The only authority it acknowledges is that which authenticates itself as such in the search for truth. *(The New Reformation? p. 81).*

Any presentation of Christianity with a hope of speaking outside the religious in-group must be genuinely and gladly secular. This will doubtless seem merely quixotic to most churchmen, who still speak and write as though 'the Christian mind' and 'the secular mind' were simply antithetical. 'Secular*ism*', like 'scient*ism*', and indeed human*ism*, as a self-contained philosophy, may be a great enemy. But I believe it is of the utmost importance to recognize that secularization itself represents a shift in man's whole way of looking at the world (such as marked the transition between the Middle Ages and the Renaissance) towards which the Christian faith as such is neutral—if indeed, like the scientific revolution, it is not an actual fruit of the Gospel. In any case, it must be respected and welcomed as the God-given frame of reference within which the Christ has to be made flesh for our day. *(The New Reformation? pp. 51-2).*

Secularism rejects a *supranaturalistic* world-view. This does not mean that it rejects God: that would be to beg the whole question at issue. What it does reject is *a picture of the world in which the* reality *of God is represented by the existence of gods or of a God in some other order or realm of being 'above' or 'beyond' the world in which we live.* ("The Debate Continues," p. 256).

The process of secularization, with its distrust of any proposition going beyond the empirical evidence, is forcing the Church to strip down its statements and be rigorously honest about what it can claim. In this I believe we have nothing ultimately to lose: indeed, there is a natural reticence in the Biblical tradition about 'naming' God or making any pronouncements about him as he is in himself. God is known through his effects. And what theology analyses and describes is the existential relationship in which those effects are known. It is no more speaking of something outside human experience than are comparable analyses of mother-love as an essential constituent of the child's existence as a person. Theology is concerned with the fact that in this relationship of mother-love, as in every other relationship or commitment of life, there are also elements of 'the beyond', claims of the unconditional, which bespeak a depth of reality in which all human love and indeed everything else is grounded. This is the reality which the Christian revelation interprets and defines in terms of the love and grace and fellowship of the Trinity. ("The Debate Continues,"pp. 253-4).

There is a sense in which the new crisis is simply driving theology back to what it has always known and witnessed to, namely, that God is "ineffable," that there is literally nothing that can be said about him without falsification—except that something must be said. All language, all definition is impossible: yet it is necessary that something be said, as Augustine put it of the

Trinity, *ne taceretur*-lest by silence the reality should appear to be denied and therefore equally falsified. From one point of view, the meaningless monosyllable "God" simply stands for an "*x*," an asterisk over all human language, signifying that which cannot be expressed yet cannot be eliminated. *(Exploration Into God, p. 52).*

To affirm belief in God is indeed to assert a faith in "how things are." But it is to make an affirmation not of something beyond our experience or in another world, but of something given in our relationships in this world. It is to say that "deepest down things" (in Gerard Manley Hopkins' phrase) we can trust the universe not only at the level of certain mathematical regularities but at the level of utterly personal reliability that Jesus indicated by the word "*Abba*, Father!" It is the faith that this is as true and objective a picture of reality as that described by the natural sciences, and more fundamental. The "promise to pay" which it presupposes is not only that of my own commitment. Faith is the trust that what is unconditional for my life, namely (in Christian terms), "the love of God in Christ Jesus our Lord," cannot be conditioned by anything, that nothing in all creation is able to separate from it.

God-statements are statements about the veracity of this relationship. They cannot finally be proved or disproved, any more than human trust or love can finally be proved or disproved. *(Exploration Into God, pp. 67-8).*

All *we* can describe or designate is the grace and claim of the *Thou* from the side of the relationship in which we find ourselves held. In this reserve of utterance the believer is not being subjectivist in the sense of regarding God merely as a function of human existence. On the contrary, he knows that human existence is but a function of this utterly gracious, disturbing, all-encompassing reality to which his life is the response—or this reality cannot properly be given the name of "God" at all. *(Exploration Into God, pp. 72-3).*

The question of God is the question whether, for instance, Jesus' relationship to the reality he could only address as 'Abba! Father!' is veridical or not. Is the constitution of the universe such that it justifies the trust, 'Father, into thy hands I commend my spirit'? Is reality ultimately gracious, or is it in the last analysis impersonal or neutral? Can love, the *agape* of the Cross, be the last word about it? The man who believes in God, as defined in Christ, believes that in the unconditional constraint of love he encounters something that speaks to him not simply of his own deepest self, nor of what he would like to make true, but of what most

124

profoundly is true of Being itself. Reality itself has this character: it can be trusted at this level of personal commitment, and not merely at the level of its mathematical reliabilities. To make this response, this act of trust, is the meaning of faith. What distinguishes the believer from the atheist is this utterly personal, gracious and unconditional relationship in which he knows himself held. ("Comment," pp. 230-1).

II. WHAT IS FAITH'S FRAMEWORK?

The second group of queries that must be addressed to the radicals concerns faith's framework of beliefs. Just as basic principles interlock to form distinct and distinguishable theological foundations, so specific beliefs fit together to form a coherent account of faith's realities and relationships. We must now investigate the various frameworks of belief which prevail among the radicals. As in the preceding section, summary statements of orthodox, liberal and neo-orthodox theologies will furnish a historical and theological context for representative selections from the writings of the radicals.

As we have seen in the preceding section, the relationship between faith and belief is conceived differently by the approaches vying for theological supremacy in the Church today. Certainly every theological tradition recognizes that living faith means more than intellectual assent to religious beliefs. Vital faith involves realities and relationships which are more than the ideas and ideologies which describe them. But theological traditions part company over whether belief systems are prior conditions or simply accompanying features of living faith. Making allowances for distinctive emphases, Orthodoxy and Neo-orthodoxy basically agree that certain beliefs establish living faith while liberal and radical theologians claim that belief systems merely illumine faith's ultimate ground and life style.

But, in any case, the only way of investigating radical faith against the background of more venerable options is through their respective theological accounts of faith's realities and relationships. Actual entities and living experiences can be analyzed and compared only when they are objectified in the form of intellectual concepts. Therefore, in this section of our inquiry into the meaning of radical Christianity, we will trace out the major doctrinal elements of these competing belief systems.

From Christianity's beginnings, the dominant frameworks of belief have been variations on three themes. The doctrines of God, Man and Christ have constituted the warp and woof of Christian thought. The whole range of Christian beliefs about the realities and relationships involved in faith intersect at these three points. In most classical theological systems these doctrinal coordinates are discussed under headings of the existence and attributes of God, the nature and destiny of man and the person and work of Christ. Our investigation will follow this classical scheme but employ the more contemporary nomenclature of the reality of God, the meaning of existence and the function of Christ.

1. The Reality of God

Like many truisms, the claim that Christianity centers in the reality of God is easily misleading. Christian theologians have always grounded faith in some reality which is usually called "God." But simply saying that Christianity is a theocentric faith obscures the differing concepts of the reality denoted by the word or name "God." The overwhelming majority of Christian theologians have conceived of God as a personal Being who is universally powerful, everywhere present and personally interested in human affairs. But such personal theism, along with its crude anthropomorphic caricatures among believers and non-believers alike, has often been rejected in favor of more impersonal or less voluntaristic views of faith's ultimate ground. And, even among those who view God as possessing intelligence, exercising will and accomplishing effects, varied renderings of divine knowledge, volition and action prevail. Hence, the word or the name "God" carries different meanings in differing systematic accounts of the Christian faith.

Classical discussions of God's relation to the natural cosmos and human experience were couched in terms of the polarities of transcendence and immanence. Until recently, these polar concepts have always carried spatial and temporal as well as metaphysical connotations. Primarily, they have expressed judgments about the metaphysical relationship between God and the world. Divine transcendence is a way of saying God is more than the world and creator of the world. Divine immanence claims an intimate relationship between God and the world's being and value. But, in all classical debates over the reality of God prior to this century, these metaphysical connotations were firmly tied to spatial and temporal meanings as well. Divine transcendence also meant God is "beyond" and "before" the world while divine immanence located God "within" and "alongside" the world.

Three distinct patterns of God's relation to the natural process emerged from these classical debates. *Theism* views God as an eternal Being transcending the world yet somehow immanent in the world. God completely transcends the world in his own existence and fulness. But, though self-existent and self-fulfilling, God brings and holds the universe in being through his creative power and overflowing goodness. Theism further portrays God's creative and sustaining work coming from "beyond" yet present "within" the universe. Various analogies are employed for conceiving the mode of God's immanence. God may be portrayed as being 'in' the world like a craftsman in his handiwork, like a king in an ambassador or like a spirit in a body. But running through these different analogies, theism finds an enduring place for immanence within transcendence. By contrast, *pantheism* simply equates God with the totality of all things. Calling God the Creator and Sustainer of the universe is simply another way of saying that each existent has its being and value by belonging to the Whole. Some pantheists think of the Whole as conscious and dynamic, others as impersonal and static. But all explain religious experience without recourse to a supernatural being or realm. Man's religious needs are fully met by gaining a vision of the individual's place in the totality of nature and history. Compared to theism, pantheism views God in terms of immanence without transcendence. *Deism* draws a radical distinction between God and the world. God created the world but he wholly transcends categories of human thought and processes of worldly occurrence. At most, God can be rationally inferred as the Cause beyond and behind the world. But God can never be personally experienced as a power within or alongside the world. Deism, in contrast to theism and pantheism, portrays God in terms of transcendence without immanence.

But, while still illumining dominant emphases in alternative views of God, this classical trilogy is no longer exhaustive or adequate for the contemporary debate about God. Of course, traditional theism which places God in heaven and earth, in eternity and time remains the prevailing concept of God for most Christians. Pantheism endures as a philosophical alternative to traditional theism's remote God and other-worldly piety. And a kind of deism flourishes among educated and alienated church members as a rival to traditional theism's appeal to miraculous and dogmatic revelations. But, during the past hundred years, new alternatives to traditional theism have arisen which do not fall under the rubrics of pantheism or deism.

These new alternatives have emerged from fresh scientific studies and philosophical accounts of religious phenomena and are usually associated with new styles of liberal theology or with the pioneering statements of radical theology. One new approach to the reality of God retains the dual relation of transcendence and immanence but rejects all spatial and temporal connotations for these terms. Thus, God and the world are distinguishable but not separable. God 'transcends' the world as the creative ground of the world and 'indwells' the world as the purposive fulfillment of the world. This account may be called *panentheism* since all things have their being and value in God, yet God is not simply the sum total of all things. A second new way of conceiving God which fails to fit the older tripartite typology may be labeled *projectionism*. According to this view, God is not a Being apart from the world (theism or deism), not the Totality of the world (pantheism), nor the metaphysical structure of the world (panentheism). God is a projection of human imagination which helps men resolve psychological needs, preserve social institutions, or envision moral precepts. Even so, religious experience plays a vital role in human life and should not be considered an illusory or dispensable expression of human imagination. Religion's imaginative constructs vivify understanding, elicit feeling and reinforce will in the vital psychological, social and moral dimensions of life. Beliefs about God become misleading and destructive only when men forget that these beliefs are really parables of human experience rather than descriptions of a divine being.

In short, the contemporary theological scene embraces a wide range of subtle but significant differences in how the reality of God is conceived. We must be alert to *which* concept of God is affirmed or rejected in the comparisons that follow.

Orthodoxy holds to a theistic view of God as the one and only omnipotent, onmipresent, omniscient and omniperfect Being. Although God is separate from the cosmos, he created it in the beginning, sustains it through time and will complete it in eternity. God exercises his control over the cosmos indirectly through the operation of order and law built into nature, history and consciousness. But God also directly intervenes in natural process, historical occurrence and human consciousness when it serves his overall purposes. These ultimate purposes are supernaturally revealed through certain miraculous events which play a vital role in the eternal deliverance and completion of God's elect. The doctrine of the Trinity, which is supernaturally revealed from God, binds all of these qualities and acitvities of God into a unity. Orthodox theologians seek to avoid treating the three 'persons' of the Godhead as three separate beings by claiming that each 'person' shares in all the activities of the others. But, at the level of preaching and piety, the trinitarian formula of Father, Son and Spirit usually corresponds to temporally distinct operations of creation, redemption and sanctification. Orthodoxy then views God as the one unsurpassable and unchangeable Being who originally fashioned a good universe, who once reclaimed his fallen creatures and who will perfect his responsive children.

Liberalism also conceives of God theistically but emphasizes far more than Orthodoxy the personal and immanental character of God. This stress on the universal benevolence and immediacy of God invites charges of pantheism and humanism against Liberalism. And, in fact, a minority voice within the liberal movement does interpret the Christian faith in essentially pantheistic or humanistic terms. Yet for all of its stress on divine immanence Liberalism as a whole affirms the transcendence of God. God as personal and purposive Spirit is more than his cosmic embodiment. But Liberalism believes Orthodoxy's stress on transcendence leads to a distorted view of God's reality and faith's substance. Orthodoxy's rendering of transcendence restricts God's presence to a few spectacular events, limits God's grace to a few select believers, reduces Christian faith to beliefs about these saving events and orients Christian life toward otherworldly concerns. In contrast, Liberalism claims that God is at work creating, sustaining and fulfilling his creation in *every* place and time through *ordinary* processes and persons. Stressing divine immanence magnifies this universal presence of God and preserves the experiential nature of faith. Furthermore, since theology merely articulates faithful experience, the doctrine of the Trinity is nothing more than one human way of describing the simultaneous presence and uniform activity of God in nature, history and consciousness. But the fundamental category for describing the whole of the divine will and work is "fatherhood." Liberalism views God as the universe's fatherly source and support and as man's fatherly champion and companion.

Neo-orthodoxy develops a theistic view of God which countermands the immanental and humanitarian God of liberal theology. Liberalism's rejection of the remote God and otherworldly piety of Orthodoxy is fully warranted. But neo-orthodox theologians charge that the liberals lose sight of the distance between God and man. By conceiving of God as universally immediate, benevolent and knowable, Liberalism too easily identifies God with human concepts and concerns. In order to protect against such idolatries, Neo-orthodoxy reasserts a doctrine of radical transcendence. God is "wholly other" than any natural process, historical occurrence or human thought. But joined with this stress on God's total separation from the world is the paradoxical claim that God works immanently in the world. Precisely this paradox of God's distance and nearness sets Neo-orthodoxy apart from Orthodoxy. As we have seen, transcendence and immanence carry spatial and temporal connotations in Orthodoxy. When God is conceived in this way, his direct presence and activity in the world must be miraculous and occasional. But Neo-orthodoxy rejects this way of portraying God's redemptive and revelatory activity. God is present and active in events which may be apprehended and explained on two distinct levels. Every redemptive and revelatory event, even the unsurpassable event of Jesus Christ, is simultaneously but unconfusedly a natural occurrence *and* a supernatural presence. The 'outer surface' of the event can be fully known and explained in natural terms. But the 'inner depth' of the same event can be encountered only through faith and explained only in supernatural terms. Neo-orthodoxy claims that this redefinition of the paradox of God's transcendence and immanence eliminates the conflict between scientific and theological explanations of the same event, preserves the personal character of God's presence and faith's response, and protects God's unabridgable sovereignty and freedom. Thus, Neo-orthodoxy views God as the Wholly Other Person who gives himself in ordinary events and persons by hiding himself from all but the eyes and the ears of faith.

PAUL M. VAN BUREN

The foregoing interpretation of the history of Jesus, Easter, and of the Gospel provides a logical account of the language of Christian faith without resort to a misleading use of words. The word "God" has been avoided because it equivocates and misleads. It seems to be a proper name, calling up the image of a divine entity, but it refuses to function as any other proper name does. Circumlocutions such as "transcendence," "being," and "absolute" only evade but do not overcome the difficulty. *(The Secular Meaning Of The Gospel, p. 145)*.

The empiricist in us finds the heart of the difficulty not in what is said about God, but in the very talking about God at all. We do

130

not know "what" God is, and we cannot understand how the word "God" is being used. It seems to function as a name, yet theologians tell us that we cannot use it as we do other names, to refer to something quite specific. If it is meant to refer to an "existential encounter," a point of view, or the speaker's self-understanding, surely a more appropriate expression could be found. The problem is not solved, moreover, by substituting other words for the word *God:* one could supply the letter *X...* and the problem would remain, for the difficulty has to do with how X functions. *(The Secular Meaning Of The Gospel, p. 84).*

Today, we cannot even understand the Nietzschian cry that "God is dead!" for if it were so, how could we know? No, the problem now is that the *word* "God" is dead. *(The Secular Meaning Of The Gospel, p. 103).*

Simple literal theism is wrong and qualified literal theism is meaningless. The first of these assertions is another way of making Bultmann's point that myth is no longer tenable; the idea of the empirical intervention of a supernatural "God" in the world of men has been ruled out by the influence of modern science on our thinking. In making such statements, we reveal our own commitments to modern science, and we would only add that modern thought tends to grant the validity of the findings of the natural sciences. For those holding these commitments, thunderbolts can no longer be explained as weapons of the wrath of an invisible God, and the phrase "God did this," therefore, cannot logically mean what it says. If we begin to qualify this phrase, however, we find one qualification calling for another until nothing is left of the original assertion. *(The Secular Meaning Of The Gospel, p. 100).*

In the frank recognition that the lot of oblique language about God is no better, and in some ways worse, than that of simple literal theism, we come face to face with our real problem of understanding the Gospel today: the difficulty of finding any meaningful way to speak of God. *(The Secular Meaning Of The Gospel, p. 102).*

I think we can say something about what has gone wrong here. There was a time when the Absolute, God, was taken to be the cause of a great deal of what we would today call quite real phenomena, from rain and hail to death and disease. God was part of what people took to be the network of forces and factors of everyday existence, as real and as objective as the thunderbolts he produced. But today we no longer have the same reference for the word "reality." ("The Dissolution of the Absolute," p. 339).

The world in which I live, and apparently not alone, is a world which I would like to describe as following upon, or in the late stages of, a major socio-psychological shift in our culture, which I shall label "The Dissolution of the Absolute." It seems to have been the case, prior to this shift, that thoughful men spoke not infrequently, and as though they had no thought of not being understood by their peers, of the Absolute, the HighestGood,or of Reality (with a capital R). This characteristic of language and thought has become increasingly difficult to maintain or recapture. The change has come about, so far as I can see, not as a result of a frontal assault on the idea of the Absolute, but by a process of dissolution or decay. The Absolute was not murdered, *Zarathustra* not withstanding; it died of neglect. ("The Dissolution of the Absolute," p.335).

Few have taken as little account of this shift as have the theologically inclined, although it should be evident that religion and theology are as much or more touched by the dissolution of the Absolute as any area of human activity. One consequence of failing to see this change that has taken place has been a certain degree of linguistic and logical confusion, resulting from attempting to operate in a world without absolutes while using ideas and languages drawn from a world in which the idea of the Absolute had an important place. The confusion is not unlike that of the substitute player in a football game rushing onto the field firmly clutching a baseball bat. ("The Dissolution of the Absolute," p. 337).

To ask theology and religion to accept the dissolution of the Absolute, to open their eyes to the world in which they live, is admittedly to ask much. It means that religion must not only become much more guarded in speaking of God (if not give this up altogether); it means also that more care be exercised in speaking of "unique revelation," "absolute commitment," and some single "ultimate concern."It is to ask of the life of faith that it be lived as a certain posture, involving commitments, but held in balance with many other commitments; a certain willingness to see things in a certain way without feeling obliged to say that this is the only way in which they can be seen. The question may fairly be asked whether theology and faith can survive this shift of focus; whether Christianity, for example, which has for so long proclaimed a monistic view of the universe, a single and unique point of reference as the only valid one, with a single and unique revelation

132

of this truth, can learn to live in a world from which the Absolute has been dissolved. However one may choose to answer this in theory, we are in fact in the actual process of finding this out, for living when we do and as we are is not exactly a matter of choice. ("The Dissolution of the Absolute," p.342).

I too am aware of the historical fact that "the fundamental contention of Christian theology" has ordinarily, if not always, been expressed by the doctrine of God, but the point that I should like to explore is whether it must be so, whether in an age of the dissolution of the absolute Christianity has an alternative course to that of nursing a monistic hangover. I do not know where such an alternative road will take us, and I too have my moments of existential anxiety about this, but I do not wish to give up the quest until I know more about it. ("Straw Men and the Monistic Hangover," p. 42).

If the choice is between "God," however subtly hidden in oblique language, and the man Jesus of Nazareth, the empirically-minded, secular "believer" can only choose the latter, for he does not know what to do with Theology. Analogical as well as literal language about God makes no sense to him. *(The Secular Meaning Of The Gospel, p. 79).*

The assertion that Jesus is "in" the Father and the Father "in" Jesus suggests just this transposition of the question concerning "God," which lies deep in the Christology of the New Testament. Whatever can be known concerning "God" has been answered by the knowledge of Jesus made available in the event of Easter. Whatever "God" means—as the goal of human existence, as the truth about man and the world, or as the key to the meaning of life—"he" is to be found in Jesus, the "way, the truth, and the life." *(The Secular Meaning Of The Gospel, p. 147).*

The Nicaean Creed, however, was written to resolve a problem in Christology: the relationship between Jesus of Nazareth and God. This fact suggests that its authors were defining the basis of their historical perspective. When the confession is understood in this sense, its trinitarian structure is significant. First, Christian faith consists of a single, complete orientation to the whole world. Second, this orientation is that of a life lived in freedom and love for men, which has its norm in the history of Jesus of Nazareth. Third (and here we include the later development of the third article, concerning the Holy Spirit), the Christian acquires this orientation by being "grasped" by its norm. When this happens to him, he becomes free to acknowledge this norm and to live accordingly.

It may be objected that we have discussed only the language of the doctrine of the "economic Trinity" (the way in which the triune God is related to creation) and said nothing about the "essential Trinity" (the way God is "in himself"). The assertion that God is "essentially" and not just "economically" triune, however, is the declaration of faith that God really is as he has shown himself to be, that his self-revelation is to be trusted. If the doctrine of the essential Trinity has a function, it is to define faith as a "blik," in contradistinction to an "opinion" which might be held in a provisional way. Of course a man may be converted out of one perspective into another, but as long as he has a particular "blik," the world he sees through it is for him the world as it "really" is. *(The Secular Meaning Of The Gospel, p. 161).*

There are "many 'gods' and many 'lords' " but for those for whom the freedom of Jesus is contagious, who have been so touched and claimed by him that he has become the criterion of their understanding of themselves, other men, and the world, there is but one "Lord": Jesus of Nazareth. Since there is no "Father" to be found apart from him, and since his "Father" can only be found in him, the New Testament...gives its answer to the question about "God" by pointing to the man Jesus. Whatever men were looking for in looking for "God" is to be found by finding Jesus of Nazareth. *(The Secular Meaning Of The Gospel, p. 147).*

WILLIAM HAMILTON

The death of God radical theologians, recently given far more visibility than they either desired or deserved, are men without God who do not anticipate his return. But it is not a simple not-having, for there is an experience of loss. Painful for some, not so for others, it is loss nonetheless. The loss is not of the idols, or of the God of theism, but of the God of the Christian tradition. And this group persists, in the face of both bewilderment and fury, in calling itself Christian. ("American Theology, Radicalism, and the Death of God," p. 6).

"Death of God" raises a host of questions and problems that we are just beginning to sort out and investigate. For example: just what kind of statement is this phrase "death of God"? For Hegel it was little more than a symbolic way of stating the inner meaning of the crucifixion. For Nietzsche it was an actual event in the space

134

and time of 19th century Europe that only a few perceived. For Sartre today it seems to mean merely that the European intellectual cannot, unfortunately, believe in God any more. Does "death of God" refer to an event? If so, when did it happen? Out there, as part of some historical or ontological reality; or within, in that part of the self that does the believing? Or perhaps in our language? Questions like this are being asked, and taken seriously. ("The Shape of a Radical Theology," p. 1220).

What does it mean to say that God is dead? Is this any more than a rather romantic way of pointing to the traditional difficulty of speaking about the holy God in human terms? Is it any more than a warning against all idols, all divinities fashioned out of human need, human ideologies? Does it perhaps not just mean that "existence is not an appropriate word to ascribe to God, that therefore he cannot be said to exist, and he is in that sense dead"? It surely means all this, and more. The hypothetical meanings suggested still all lie within the safe boundaries of the neo-orthodox or biblical-theology tradition, and the death of God group wants clearly to break away from that. It used to live rather comfortably there, and does so no longer. Perhaps we can put it this way; the neo-orthodox reconstruction of the Christian doctrine of revelation seems to have broken down for some. It used to be possible to say: we cannot know God but he has made himself known to us, and at that point analogies from the world of personal relations would enter the scene and help us. But somehow, the situation has deteriorated; as before, we cannot know, but now it seems that he does not make himself known, even as enemy. This is more than the old protest against natural theology or metaphysics; more than the usual assurance that before the holy God all our language gets broken and diffracted into paradox. It is really that we do not know, do not adore, do not possess, do not believe in God. It is not just that a capacity has dried up within us; we do not take all this as merely a statement about our frail psyches, we take it as a statement about the nature of the world and we try to convince others. God is dead. We are not talking about the absence of the experience of God, but about the experience of the absence of God. Yet the death of God theologians claim to be theologians, to be Christians, to be speaking out of a community to a community. They do not grant that their view is really a complicated sort of atheism dressed in a new spring bonnet. ("The Death of God Theologies Today," pp. 26-8).

Question: If "death of God" is somehow an event, then

presumably it is an event that may be said to have happened sometime. When?

As long as you see that "death of God" is a complex event, one that cannot be simply pointed to, then the "when" question can be accepted. There are three parts to my answer of the question:

1. The coming of Jesus as the self-emptying of God is part of the "death of God." Here is God taking on sin, suffering, and mortality. Here is the end not only of religion, and transcendent gods of power and sovereignty, but the beginning of the disappearance of the Christian God himself.

2. If the incarnation is, so to speak, the enabling part of the event of the death of God , the nineteenth century is that time when the death itself is predicted, believed in, lived out. The Christian God, in Europe and America, is dying by departing wholly from the world (deism) or collapsing into the world (romanticism, Marx, Ibsen) between 1789 and 1914. The first date suggests the problem of the relation of regicide and deicide, and the second reminds us of D. H. Lawrence's comment that God died in 1914. One of the immediate tasks of radical theology is a thorough interpretation of the idea of the "death of God" in the nineteenth century. We need a wholly different nineteenth century than the one traditional Protestant theology bequeathed to us.

3. But there is a third part of the "when" answer, and that is now, here, mid-twentieth-century America. In a way, Nietzsche's madman (himself) was right in saying that he had come too soon. There is something about our time and place that is making the event prepared by the incarnation and analyzed by the nineteenth century come home. The twentieth century is proving to be a time when the "death of God" can be affirmed without guilt, fear, or sadness. It was Wallace Stevens who wrote: "To see the gods dispelled in mid-air and dissolve like clouds is one of the great human experiences. It is not as if they had gone over the horizon to disappear for a time; nor as if they had been overcome by other gods of greater power and profounder knowledge. It is simply that they came to nothing." ("Questions and Answers on the Radical Theology," pp. 215-6).

If God is dead, as we say, what do we put in his place? What does the work in this godless Christian vision that God used to do in the classical tradition? Have we, it might be asked, taken the full measure of the terrible cry of Ivan Karamazov, If there is no

God, then everything is permitted? Are people really strong enough to lose not only the fear of hell and the consolations of the next life, but also the reality of God?

There are two answers, or two forms of the same answer, to the question about the replacement of God. In one sense the answer must be "the human community" and in another sense it must be "Jesus." Let us distinguish between two kinds of meaning or function classically ascribed to God. If by God you mean the means by which forgiveness is mediated, or consolation in time of sorrow or despair, or judge of my arrogance and my idolatry–then we say that these functions, as central for us as they ever were in classical Christianity, must be taken over by the human community. We must learn to forgive each other with the radical unconditioned grace men used to ascribe to God...We must learn to comfort each other, and we must learn to judge, check and rebuke one another in the communities within which we are wounded and in which we are healed. If these things cannot now be done by the human communities in the world, then these communities must be altered until they can perform these tasks and whatever others, once ascribed to God, that need to be done in this new context. In this sense the death of God leads to politics, to social change, and even to the foolishness of utopias.

But it would be misleading to pass over to what we are calling the human community every task once given to God. There is another kind of meaning attached to the classical idea of God that needs another kind of surrogate. If by God you mean the focus of obedience, the object of trust and loyalty, the meaning I give to love, my center, my meaning–then these meanings are given not to men in general but to Jesus, the *man*, in his life, his way with others and his death. We death-of-God theologians thus stake out a claim to be able to make it as Christians not merely because we speak of the death of the Chrisitian God, but because we see as the center of the Christian faith a relation of obedience and trust directed to Jesus...

The human community in general not as it is, but as it might be altered to become—and that particular instance of the human community, Jesus of Nazareth, thus take over the work, the action, the deeds, once ascribed to the Christian God. ("The Death of God," p. 139).

GABRIEL VAHANIAN

God is a word, the word that our words do not speak unless they are shocked both out of their literal and out of their symbolic meaning. *(No Other God, p. 61)*.

Today our words are either symbolic or literal: either way their form is their content—a definition which stands in flagrant contradiction with my definition of the word as an icon. Such aesthetic reductionism is merely another instance of the general surrender to immanentism which is characteristic of our time, and results either from the divorce between the literal and the symbolic or from their conflation, their confusion. Religious symbolism makes no sense today precisely because it cannot be communicated except with words and images that have lost their metaphoric power, or that have been severed from the metaphoric power of the word of man. A faith which has been drained of its iconoclastic vocation can only wallow in words and images that cheat man into idolatry instead of confirming him as an iconoclast. *(No Other God, p. 61)*.

True iconoclasm begins with oneself, with the smashing of one's own idols, *i.e.*, of one's superannuated conception of God, of faith and religious allegiance. *(Wait Without Idols, p. 243)*.

Modern man is not so much intent on inventing God, in case he does not exist, as he is on inventing concepts which, considering that they are only substitutes, are doing God's job as best they can.

Some of these concepts are plainly weird. God is referred to as a "Co-pilot" or a "Porter." Sometimes he is conceived as a Cosmic Pal. But all the time he is the nicest fellow one can ever dream of meeting. All those concepts have a common denominator: they all are anthropomorphic and they all originate in the inflationary imagination of sentimentalism. But whatever the theological or philosophical connotations may be, this anthropomorphism means that men worship the God they deserve. Men create God in their image. Their concepts of God represent but a hypertrophy of their self-understanding, and sometimes a pharisaic or moralistic sanction of their aspirations. Man's understanding of the deity is dependent on his highest values, and these are often created by his environment. God becomes no more than the ideal man. *(The Death Of God, p. 75)*

In the Bible itself, God is referred to as a shield, as one who is "mighty in battle" and "teaches" the soldier's hand to war. He is paternal, even maternal, a shepherd, a friend, a bridegroom, a

138

husband.

Why is it, then, that the modern ways in which popular religiosity designates God make one shudder? What is wrong with designations for God as a "Porter" or the "Man Upstairs"? Why are such expressions more objectionable than certain Biblical ones which are no less down-to-earth and just as fragile?

It is not the modern phrase which can (or must) be objected to so much as the understanding it expresses of the self and its relation to other selves and the world, and to God. By contrast with the Biblical instances, these modern, popular appellations suggest that the deity is a missing link in man's unsuccessful attempts to grasp the meaning of his self and of the world. The deity becomes just a global hypothesis, a mere cog of an intricate machine, whether friendly or formidable. Thus the conception of God as the Cosmic Pal is but another step in the development of universal anthropocentrism, away from the original theocentrism of the Bible. *(The Death Of God, pp. 77-8).*

The problem of God today is thus the primary problem of theology, not so much because that would be consonant with the tradition as because that is the only way of saying "no" to an idolatrous religiosity which would preserve of its heritage only its cultural aspects. *(No Other God, p. xii).*

What I have denounced elsewhere as the charter of an incipient post-Christian idolatry is now proclaimed as the first article of an immanentist religiosity. So-called "Christian atheism" glories precisely in what I deplored when I first used the term "death of God"; and it can do so, furthermore, only by appealing to the disaffected, though still residually Christian, religiosity of Western man. *(No Other God, p. xi).*

It was bad enough to inherit a God-based concept which had lost all concrete meaning. It is incomparably worse to attenuate and in fact deny the reality of the death of God by sublimating it into a new fangled soteriological concept. The death of God makes sense and is indeed a liberating event only when it is considered as a cultural phenomenon. But to argue that a historical fact as such (personally I prefer to call it a cultural phenomenon) totally and exclusively lays claim to my whole existence amounts to making it a new absolute, an idol hailed at the front door with all the red carpet treatment while God is whisked out through the back door. *(No Other God, pp. 4-5).*

Indeed, to admit that the biblical worldview is no longer valid need not prevent our recognition that the reality of God was affirmed not because of but in spite of that worldview, however transcendental or sacral it was considered. Consequently, although the Bible was written in terms of a given worldview we can still claim that it neither has nor is a worldview in itself, and that consequently no worldview, immanentist or otherwise, *ipso facto* invalidates theology or faith in God. As a matter of fact, an immanentist worldview might yet help us to grasp and live more concretely the meaning of faith as eschatological existence: for the first time in twenty centuries God is not a crutch, God is not "reasons." *(No Other God, p. 7).*

There is no other God than the wholly other God whose reality can be attested by no graven images, no frozen or absolute metaphors, for the simple reason, indeed, that his reality is given with "the actualization of language," with the fact of existence, even the empirical irreducibility of the human phenomenon. Indeed what is a graven image but the symbolic reduction of the metaphoric power of the word, the denial of the iconoclastic instrumentality of human existence as word?   *(No Other God, pp. 57-8).*

The line of demarcation between God and the idol is a thin one. Rationally, God cannot be distinguished from the idol, just as in theological language we would affirm that the believer is not justified by his faith. From this it follows that idolatry is but a caricature of faith in God and that, similarly, man often is but a caricature of himself, even to the extent of being nothing other than such a caricature. *(Wait Without Idols, pp. xi-xii).*

The Biblical tradition has generally maintained that man is created in the image of God, but in such a way that God nonetheless remains imageless. God is not the sum total or the result of man's imagination. There is always a qualitative difference between God and man, as *intimate* as it is infinite. *(The Death Of God, p. 70).*

To conclude, the Christian era has bequeathed us the "death of God," but not without teaching us a lesson. God is not necessary. That is to say, he cannot be taken for granted. He cannot be used merely as a hypothesis, whether epistemological, scientific, or existential, unless we should draw the degrading conclusion that "God is reasons." But if we cannot any longer assume that God is, we may once again realize that he *must* be. God is not necessary, but he is inevitable. He is wholly other and wholly present. Faith in him, the conversion of our human reality culturally and existentially, is the demand he still makes upon us, the choice he confronts us with. ("Beyond the Death of God," pp. 11-2)

HARVEY COX

We now find that the various uses of the word *God*, once conveniently fused, are now coming unstuck. Historical change and social differentiation have combined to make the word the most equivocal term in the English language. Theologians are fond of saying that the word is "empty." Its emptiness, however, is merely the symptom of a much more basic disorder, its equivocality. *(The Secular City, p. 214).*

Modes of religious experience are, as we have noted, shaped by cultural patterns. When social change jars the patterns, conventional ways of experiencing the holy disappear. When the thickly clotted symbol system of a pre-urban society is replaced by a highly differentiated and individuated urban culture, modalities of religious experience shift. When this happens gradually, over a long span of time, the religious symbols have a chance to become adapted to the new cultural patterns. The experience of the death of the gods, or of God, is a consequence of an abrupt transition which causes the traditional symbols to collapse, since they no longer illuminate the shifting social reality.

The "death of God" syndrome can only occur where the controlling symbols of the culture have been more or less uncritically fused with the transcendent God. When a civilization collapses and its gods topple, theological speculation can move either toward a God whose being lies beyond culture (Augustine, Barth), toward some form of millenarianism or toward a religious crisis that takes the form of the "death of God."

In our own period, which is marked by man's historical consciousness reaching out and encompassing everything in sight, the nooks and crannies formerly reserved for the transcendent have all been exposed. Pluralism and radical historicism have become our permanent companions. We know that all doctrines, ideals, institutions and formulations, whether religious or secular, arise within history and must be understood in terms of their historical milieu. How then do we speak of a God who is somehow present in history, yet whose being is not exhausted by the limits of history? How, in short, do we maintain an affirmation of transcendence within the context of a culture whose mood is relentlessly immanentist? ("The Death of God and the Future of Theology," pp. 381-2).

My own response to the dead-end signaled by the "death of

God" mood is to continue to move away from any spatial symbolization of God and from all forms of metaphysical dualism. I am trying to edge cautiously toward a secular theology, a mode of thinking whose horizon is human history and whose idiom is "political" in the widest Aristotelian sense of that term, i.e., the context in which man becomes fully man.

As I move in this direction, there are certain traps I want to try to avoid. First, though it may be satisfactory for some, I want to steer clear of the mystical-atheistic monism of Thomas Altizer. From the perspective of the science of religion, mysticism and atheism have always been similar. Both lack the elements of encounter with an "Other," a confrontation that is characteristic of most forms of theism. In Altizer this structural similarity has come to explicit expression. Second, I want to avoid the uncritical empiricism of Paul van Buren. I think his methodological starting point, derived from contemporary British and American linguistic analysis, is too constrictive. It does not take sufficient account of the nonempirical functions of many modes of human speech, the open and changing character of all languages, and the place of any language within a larger universe of symbolic, metaphorical, and poetic modes of expression. Kenneth Burke, in *The Rhetoric of Religion,* has laid out a type of religious-language analysis which does embrace these larger cultural dimensions, thus offering a corrective to the analysts' presuppositions.

Finally, I want to steer clear of the inverse pietism of William Hamilton, whose perceptive analysis of the cultural mood is sometimes confused with the theological task itself. Since he often deduces the mood of the culture from a description of his own moods and beliefs, the basis of his theology is extremely experiential. This may be good, especially in view of the unjustly severe disparaging of "experience" which was so characteristic of the followers of Karl Barth, but theology cannot become experiential in this sense without courting the danger of becoming subjective. Thus, while I can accept his diagnosis of the cultural *élan,* which is often correct, I decline to enlarge it into a properly theological claim. ("The Death of God and the Future of Theology," pp. 382-3).

I still blithely use the term "God" in an age when some theologians are insisting that he is dead. I use the old appellation, *i.e.,* "God," not because I think it is totally unambiguous but because I think it can be saved from its current ambiguousness and emptiness only if it is employed in markedly altered contexts and in radically new ways. This is the way the meaning of words is changed and renewed.

I think those who feel that "God" is dead have already gone over to the side of traditional theism or classical metaphysics and then merely stood the whole business on its head. They accept an antiquated orthodox definition of who God is, and then merely disagree on the question of whether he is still alive. I would prefer to differ with the orthodox at a more basic level of the argument and insist that the God they say is alive and the others say is dead is just not God. *(God's Revolution And Man's Responsibility, p. 8).*

If the present wake is for the God who *is* (and now *was*), this may clear the decks for the God who *will be.* I cannot say for sure that the opening of such a path will lead anywhere, but the task of opening it would first require a thorough reworking of our major theological categories. We would see Jesus, for example, not as a visitor to earth from some supraterrestrial heaven, but as the one in whom precisely this two-story dualism is abolished for good, and who becomes the pioneer and first sign of the coming New Age. We would see the community of faith as those "on the way" to this promised reality, "forgetting what is behind and reaching out for that which is ahead" (Phil.3:14). Radical theology would have more radical social consequences than the so-called radical theology of the death of God has produced so far.

The doctrine of God would become theology's answer to the seemingly irrefutable fact that history can only be kept open by "anchoring" that openness somewhere outside history itself, in this case not "above" but *ahead.* Faith in God would be recognized, for our time, in that hope for the future Kingdom of Peace that frees men to suffer and sacrifice meaningfully in the present. Still, I would be the worst of imposters if I pretended that in the God of Hope we can immediately affirm the one who will appear when the corpse of the dead God of metaphysical theism is finally interred. He may not appear at all, and our efforts to work out a new and viable doctrine of God for our time may be fated to fail from the beginning. But before any of us throws in the towel, I hope we will exercise the freedom given us by the present *Götterdämmerüng* of the divinities of Christendom, and use this freedom to think as candidly and as rigorously as possible about where we go from here. ("The Death of God and the Future of Theology," pp. 387-8).

I can only concede that the road ahead does seem treacherous and sometimes almost impassable. I refuse, for the moment, to settle for some brand of simple "religious atheism." That seems too easy somehow. But at the same time I find the available "theistic"options equally unattractive. I have no answer. I can only indicate how I am grappling with this conumdrum and where I now hope some new hint of an opening can be found. I am now pursuing the hints, perhaps misleading, of two vagabonds on the periphery of theology, Pierre Teilhard de Chardin and Ernst Bloch...

Both Teilhard the maverick Catholic and Bloch the renegade Marxist saw reality as a radically open-ended process. Teilhard detected in the logic of evolution an ever deepening humanization of man and hominization of the universe. Bloch concerned himself with "Man-as-Promise" and mapped out what he called "the ontology of the not yet." Teilhard roamed through the aeons of geological time and the breathtakingly massive universe and focused on the appearance within them of the phenomenon of man, that point where the cosmos begins to think and to steer itself. Bloch's stage for philosophizing is human history, exhumed from its imprisonment in timelessness and launched on a journey into the future. The hope which makes this future possible, Bloch contends, was introduced into the world by the biblical faith. Both Bloch and Teilhard saw what the Germans now call the *"Impuls der Erwartung."* ("Afterword," pp. 197-9).

In the biblical tradition, we do not speak "about God" at all, either "in a secular fashion" or in any other. When we use the word *God* in the biblical sense, we are not speaking about, but we are "naming," and that is an entirely different matter. To name is to point, to confess, to locate something in terms of our history. We can name something only by using the fund of memories and meanings we carry with us as individuals and as a species. *(The Secular City, pp. 211-12).*

By what name shall we call the one we met both in the life of Jesus and in our present history as the liberator and the hidden one?

Perhaps we should not be anxious about finding a name. Our present fit of tongue-tied verbosity, of empty and ambiguous words, will work itself out in experience, the way it always has. "The story of the word 'God,'" says C. A. van Peursen, " is that it has no given meaning, but acquires a meaning in history..." Naming was the process by which Israel drew more and more reality into history by relating it to the One who had brought them up out of Egypt. First the origin of history, then its

144

consummation were included in this process of "radiation" by which God was named as He was encountered in the world. God manifests Himself to us in and through secular events. The meaning of the word *God* will be altered or a new name will emerge as we encounter that presence in events which draws them into the history of which we are a part, the history of God's liberation of man. Secular talk of God is pointing and naming. As van Peursen says,

...it is in a functional way that man comes into contact with the reality of God, that God acquires a meaning in history...As the Church we have to respond to the world through our acts...transmitting the old message of a Name...which is taking on a new meaning in history, and especially in the functional history of our time.

We cannot simply conjure up a new name. Nor can we arbitrarily discard the old one. God does reveal His name in history, through the clash of historical forces and the faithful efforts of a people to discern His presence and respond to His call. A new name will come when God is ready. A new way of conceptualizing the Other will emerge in the tension between the history which has gone before us and the events which lie ahead. It will emerge as the issues of the urban civilization are drawn into rehearsal of the past, reflection on the present, and responsibility for the future, which *is* history.

This may mean that we shall have to stop talking about "God" for a while, take a moratorium on speech until the new name emerges. Maybe the name that does emerge will not be the three-letter word God, but this should not dismay us. Since naming is a human activity embedded in a particular sociocultural milieu, there is no holy language as such, and the word *God* is not sacred. All languages are historical. They are born and die. Presumably God will continue to live eons after English and all other present languages have been totally forgotten. It is only word magic to believe that there is some integral connection between God and any particular linguistic vocable. *(The Secular City, pp. 232-3).*

THOMAS J. J. ALTIZER

The problem now set for Protestant theology derived from the necessity of reaching a conception of a God who is at once transcendent and immanent, not in the sense that God is simultaneously both transcendent and immanent, but in the sense that transcendence and immanence are fully united or finally indistinguishable in God. *(Toward A New Christianity, p. 10).*

From the point of view of a radical and dialectical Christian theology, the absolutely decisive and fundamental theological principle is that the God of faith so far from being unchanging and unmoving is a perpetual and forward-moving process of self-negation, pure negativity, or kenotic metamorphosis. *(The Gospel Of Christian Atheism, p. 84).*

Everything depends here upon understanding the nature of such movements, of understanding how an evolutionary process could reach its goal by moving beyond its original source, and would moreover be forced to transcend both its beginning and its successive expressions if its own initial momentum is to be carried to its intrinsic resolution. Now it would be false to process or evolutionary thinking to entertain the supposition that because a given form or expression is transcended it is thereby quite simply negated, as though each point or stage in the forward-moving process was isolated and autonomous, or wholly enclosed within itself. No, we must understand that everything is carried forward in this process; or, rather, life itself moves forward, and as it evolves into new forms, it leaves its earlier forms and expressions behind as mere fossils, as its former life is redirected and transfigured by its very expression in new modes. As we can see in our example from Protestant theology, the life and power which were once symbolically evoked by the name of God become present once more in the name of Christ, but they are not the same life and power, they have assumed a yet more immanent, yet more incarnate expression, and as a consequence the name of God now points to a darkened and emptied transcendence, as the life and energy of an original transcendence has wholly passed into the incarnate immanence of Christ. ("Catholic Philosophy and the Death of God," pp. 277-8).

What can it mean to speak of the Christian God as a dialectical process rather than as an existent Being? First, it means that the Christian God cannot be known as an unchanging, an unmoving, or an impassive Being; nor can he be understood as possessing a common nature or substance that remains eternally the same throughout his revelatory and redemptive acts. If the Christian knows the God who has emptied himself of his original sacrality in actually becoming flesh, then he cannot know a God who remains distinct and self-enclosed in his own primordial Being. The God who acts in the world and history is a God who negates himself, gradually but decisively annihilating his own original Totality. *(The Gospel Of Christian Atheism, p. 89).*

What can it mean to speak of the death of God? Indeed, how is it even possible to speak of the death of God, particularly at a time when the name of God would seem to be unsayable? First, we must recognize that the proclamation of the death of God is a Christian confession of faith. For to know that God is dead is to know the God who died in Jesus Christ. *(The Gospel Of Christian Atheism, p. 102).*

To confess the death of God is to speak of an actual and real event, not perhaps an event occurring in a single moment of time or history, but notwithstanding this reservation an event that has actually happened both in a cosmic and in a historical sense. There should be no confusion deriving from the mistaken assumption that such a confession refers to an eclipse of God or a withdrawal of God from either history or the creation. Rather, an authentic language speaking about the death of God must inevitably be speaking about the death of God himself. The radical Christian proclaims that God has actually died in Christ, that this death is both a historical and a cosmic event, and, as such, it is a final and irrevocable event, which cannot be reversed by a subsequent religious or cosmic movement. *(The Gospel Of Christian Atheism, p. 103).*

What can it mean to say that God has died in Christ? One of my favorite words is the Greek word *kenosis* which in some sense has to do with an emptying process, or a self-emptying process. Now it's true that I use this word in a way which is not, strictly speaking, biblical or scriptural. It has a ground, however, in Paul's letter to the Philippians which I believe is the implicit ground of the original Christian proclamation. We're attempting to say that in Christ, God Himself, the sovereign, transcendent Lord, the source and Ground of all that is, has emptied Himself of His own original plentitude—of His own original transcendent sovereignty, glory, and transcendence—has taken upon Himself the form of a servant, has become man in Jesus Christ. And become man in such a way as to effect an ultimate and final transformation and transfiguration of all things whatsoever. I repudiate the idea that God became man in Christ and then in some sense annulled His humanity by returning to a spiritual realm. I insist instead that the incarnation is a forward movement, an ever increasing forward movement, wherein the original death of God in Christ becomes ever more actual and real in the world. *(The Altizer-Montgomery Dialogue, p. 9).*

I think we are called to understand the death of God as having two full sides, two poles. On the one hand, we affirm in faith that God has died in Jesus Christ, that God has emptied Himself of His divine glory in Christ, therein initiating and effecting in an original and decisive sense the process of redemption. But on the other hand, the process of redemption is an historical process. It's a gradual process. It's a forward-moving process. It's an enlarging process. And it moves in such a way as to carry the life of Christ to all men, to all experience, to all life whatsoever. *(The Altizer-Montgomery Dialogue, pp. 14-5).*

An inevitable objection to this theological project is the question how could God remain in continuity with Himself if He evolves by negating and transcending the particular moments or points of His evolving self-expression? We can attempt to answer this question by realizing that as God moves forward His full life and energy are carried into new forms or expressions so that His energy remains itself even while undergoing transformation. At this point we are touching upon the most difficult problem of contemporary atheistic theology: how can God remain Himself if He passes through an ultimate act or movement of self-negation or self-annihilation? If God dies as God how can He remain God? Or, for that matter, how can He then be known as an eternal process? First, we must note that the biblical tradition, and more particularly Christianity, has a unique understanding of God insofar as it apprehends God as the transcendent Lord who is immanent in His creation. Faith, in its Christian expression, knows God as being at once both radically transcendent and radically immanent, even though the meaning and reality of transcendence and immanence assume different forms in different moments and periods of Christian history. Furthermore, Christianity has always proclaimed that the fullest meaning of God is present in Jesus Christ, that in Christ God has fully and finally become incarnate, and that all things will be made new in the event or process of the Incarnation. It would seem to be inescapable for the Christian to believe that an event of ultimate significance has occurred and is occurring in Christ, and that event has made and is making God present or immanent in an absolutely novel and decisive manner. Indeed, insofar as the Christian believes that the fullness of God is present in Christ, he must believe that here transcendence has passed or is passing into immanence, unless he heretically believes that Christ is not fully flesh. At the very least it would appear that the Christian must believe that in the Incarnation the transcendence of God has undergone a genuine transformation. May we not say that in the Incarnation God empties Himself of His original power and glory, thereby negating and transcending His pre-incarnate Being, so as to make possible a new or apocalyptic union between Himself and the world? ("Catholic Philosophy And The Death Of God," pp.279-80).

JOHN A. T. ROBINSON

The "death of God" theology has made a real contribution in drawing attention to changes that cannot be ignored or reversed. Nevertheless, I am convinced that God-language, however little it may be able to say compared with what it used to be able to say (or may say again), stands for that which by its very nature cannot finally be reduced or translated without remainder into anything else. It stands guard against every attempt to persuade us that this is a closed universe, that the beyond, the unconditional, the radically other—all that Jesus represented by the kingdom of heaven or eternal life—is not as real as, or more real than, that for which we are always prepared to settle.

I do not see how Christians without this dimension (however they express it) can be Christians at all.   *(Exploration Into God, pp. 54-5).*

Our concern is in no way to change the Christian doctrine of God but precisely to see that it does not disappear with this outmoded view. *(Honest To God, p. 44).*

I am convinced that to represent the spiritual reality (in its transcendent aspect) as a Being in another realm is to make it unreal and remote for vast numbers of people today. Not only do they take the projection for the reality and demand "evidence" for the existence of such a Being (often as crudely as Khrushchev's astronauts), but, more importantly, it has the effect of rendering God marginal and peripheral. Men cannot recognize the reality of God in the experienced relationship, because the image which should help to make it vivid locates him in an area in which they no longer *live*. This is the real point I was trying to make in *Honest to God* about the placing of God "up there" or "out there." It is not that people literally believe this and that this is somehow bad. It is that these are "dead" areas. God is banished to the edges of life—to the uncanny (about the only remaining significance for most people of "the supernatural"), to what men still cannot understand or control (so-styled "acts of God"), or to what is revealingly called the "after-life." At the end of their tether men may still turn to the One above—to pray to or to blame; but in the ordinary course of affairs he comes in, if at all, only after the vital connections have been made. Life is completed, for some, by the addition of God. Most others wonder why they should include this extra storey. In any case, the effect is a displacement of him as God. *(Exploration Into God, pp. 31-2).*

The reality of God is not a point within the world. One cannot pin it down like that. Indeed, the word "God" is so slippery and the reality so intangible that many today are questioning whether they have reference to anything that can usefully or meaningfully be talked about. What is it that has got displaced, and what is it that we have to try to recenter? To what reality does the word "God" refer? *(Exploration Into God, p. 42).*

God-language does not describe a Thing-in-Itself or even a Person-in-Himself. And yet it does more than register our commitments. It points to an ultimate relatedness in the very structure of our being from which we cannot get away. It is a way of keeping guard over the irreducible, ineffable mystery at the heart of all experience. *(Exploration Into God, p. 73).*

Nevertheless, one must still ask, what is this elusive reality that God-language is trying, not to capture (because it knows it cannot), but to point to? Can we locate God, not in the sense of pinning him down here but not there, but in the sense of designating the kind of reality we are talking about? To what in human experience does such language have reference? *(Exploration Into God, pp. 59-60).*

To speak of "God" is to refer neither on the one hand to an existence outside one's experience nor on the other simply to one's own way of looking at the world. It is to acknowledge a relationship, a confrontation at the heart of one's very constitution as a human being, of which one is compelled to say, in existential terms, "This is it. This is the *ens realissimum,* that which is ultimately and inescapably true."

God-statements are statements about the reality of this relationship. Of what lies outside it or beyond it we can say nothing meaningful. Hence the reticence of the Bible even to utter the name of God, as though one were presuming to fill in the hole at the center of the wheel. One can only describe the spokes of relationship, the reality which is God-for-us. *(Exploration*

150

Into God, pp. 66-7).

If one had to find a label to replace that of traditional "theism," I would fall back on one that has a respectable pedigree but has never quite succeeded in establishing itself in orthodox Christian circles—namely, "panentheism." This is defined by *The Oxford Dictionary of the Christian Church* as "the belief that the Being of God includes and penetrates the whole universe, so that every part of it exists in him, but (as against pantheism) that his Being is more than, and is not exhausted by, the universe." It is the view that God is in everything and everything is in God. *(Exploration Into God, p. 86-7).*

Panentheism takes its stand against the dualism of theism, moral as well as metaphysical. But it does not side with the indifferentism of pantheism, which has to maintain that evil is in some way illusory or unreal. The evil in the world is indeed terrifyingly real, both at the subpersonal and at the personal level; but it is still part of the face of *God.* That is to say, love is there to be met and to be created through it and out of it. It is not without purpose: meaning can be wrested from it even at the cost of crucifixion. It is not separate from the face of love, and therefore cannot separate from it. That is the saving grace: God is not outside evil any more than he is outside anything else, and the promise is that he *"will* be all in all" *as love.* And that, in Christ, is the ultimate truth of everything *now,* however hidden or obscured. *(Exploration Into God, p. 118).*

This is the vision too, to which the New Testament points, of God as "all in all." This passage is the charter of Christian panentheism. Yet it is, as its context in I Corinthians 15 makes abundantly clear, an eschatological panentheism. This does not mean, for the New Testament, that it is something that will only be true *after* everything else. It is the truth "in Christ" now. As the Epistle to the Hebrews puts it, "We do not yet see everything in subjection" to man – that is, to personal purpose. "But we see Jesus . . . crowned with glory and honor." And it is this, symbolically, that the Christian sees as the first fruits and guarantee of the whole cosmic process. The God who was *in* Christ is the God who is and must be in all. The model of panentheism is essentially an incarnational one. That is why I believe it is fundamentally appropriate to Christianity – in a way that deism or Pantheism or even theism is not – without being exclusively Christian. And, *per contra*, I also believe that the most appropriate model – perhaps the only appropriate model today – for a satisfactory theology of the Incarnation is a panentheistic one. *(Exploration Into God, pp. 160-1).*

Ultimately in speaking of God all words are bound to fail. Yet rather than end in final aposiopesis, there is perhaps one more thing that can be said. One of the insights of our century is that the trans-personal character of God is better expressed not by envisaging him as a bigger and better Individual, nor as a sort of Hobbesian collective Personality incorporating all other persons, but in terms of the interpersonal. This is the result of applying "field" or relational thinking to persons as well as to things. For Buber has taught us that in the beginning—and in the end—is not the individual, the *I* or the *Thou,* but the nexus *I—Thou* And the whole of reality too must ultimately be seen in terms, not of a God, a monarchical Being supreme among individual entities, but of a divine "field" in which the finite *Thous* are constituted what they are in the freedom of a wholly personalizing love. *(Exploration Into God, pp. 159-160).*

What *we* can speak of, from our human situation, is the awareness of being addressed, claimed, and sustained. We can testify to the relationship, utterly personal in its demand and succor, in which we know ourselves held. We can say that however much this awareness seems to come from within, from the gound of our very being, it confronts us also with an otherness to which we can only respond as *I* to *Thou.* *(Exploration Into God, p. 71).*

2. The Meaning of Existence

As we have seen, theology is concerned with more than just the reality of God. Theology seeks to make every aspect of religious faith intelligible. Beliefs about the meaning of existence constitute the second important aspect of every theological system. Like other major doctrinal coordinates, convictions about man influence all the other beliefs which are pieced together to form faith's framework of beliefs. But beliefs about man have a special importance for every theological system by virtue of the universality and inescapability of human existence. Man is the common denominator between the believer and the nonbeliever, the theologian and the scientist, the educated and the unlettered, the ancient and the modern, the Easterner and the Westerner. All men are involved and concerned with the meaning of human existence. Thus, the Church's most strategic conversation piece with non-Christian views and styles of life is a Christian view of man. But, by the same token, the relevance and adequacy of any theological system is most readily tested at the point of its interpretation of human existence. Men recognize and increasingly understand themselves as physiological, psychological, sociological and cultural creatures. Any religious interpretation of human existence must hang together with these other perspectives to be taken seriously or adopted personally. For these reasons, beliefs about the meaning of existence are crucial for any systematic interpretation of Christian faith.

Every Christian interpretation of the meaning of existence offers some account of human life's potentiality, distortion, restoration and consummation. In most classical treatments, these four themes are dealt with under the headings of man's creation, fall, redemption and glorification. Variations in terminology frequently occur in more recent discussions but the four-fold scheme remains the same. Religious accounts in general and Christian interpretations of man in particular seek to deal with the misery and the grandeur, the destruction and the renewal of human nature and destiny.

Theological traditions differ considerably in their views of man's creation, fall, redemption and glorification. These differences are partially reflections of prevailing scientific and philosophical interpretations of human life and behavior. But the theological bases for these differences center in the meaning of man's creation, fall, redemption and glorification. The view of man's created nature and destiny in a given theological system profoundly affects the remaining correlates of its view of man since sin is a falling short of man's ideal potentialities, since salvation is a restoration toward man's ideal potentialities and since eternal life is a consummation of man's ideal potentialities. In other words, the meaning of man's fall, redemption and glorification revolve around a given view of man's created potentialities. But equally important to any systematic account of the meaning of existence is the interrelation between creation, fall, redemption and glorification. Far-reaching consequences follow from whether these are portrayed as discontinuous, overlapping or simultaneous states of human existence. Such important questions as the meaning and relation of man as a natural and spiritual entity, as an individual and social being, as a cultural and religious participant, and as a Christian and non-Christian hinge on the way these states of human existence are juxtaposed. Therefore, we must pay careful attention to the meaning of creation and the relation between creation, fall, redemption and glorification in the comparison that follows.

Orthodoxy treats man's creation, fall, redemption and glorification as serial and separate states, although most orthodox theologians see a kind of overlapping between fall and redemption. Taking the biblical stories of creation quite literally, Orthodoxy claims that all men spring from original progenitors whose fall from their created perfection disrupted natural life and destroyed spiritual existence for all their descendents. In the state of created perfection, man's complementary natural and spiritual endowments were completely free from disorder, debility and dissolution. This hierarchical dualism of nature and spirit was established by God to insure man's spiritual freedom and to develop man's spiritual capacities. But the primordial parents of the human race upset this balance of nature and spirit to the everlasting regret of the whole human race. Orthodox theologians differ over the seriousness of the disruption in natural existence due to the fall, but all agree that sensual bondage, physical suffering, intellectual darkness, social conflict and personal mortality became permanent features of life in the world after the fall. More important, they all believe the fall left nothing more than shattered relics of man's spiritual endowments and relationships. Fallen man is wholly incapable of reestablishing his lost spiritual communion with God and spiritual discipline of life. These dire natural and spiritual consequences came about because of the rebellion of the original parents of the human race and have been transmitted biologically, socially and spiritually to every off-spring since. But Orthodoxy weds this pessimistic view of fallen mankind to a supernatural restoration and other-worldly consummation of human perfection for Christian believers. God has provided the way for man's redemption in this life and glorification in the life to come through Jesus Christ. Redeemed man once again enjoys spiritual communion with God and spiritual discipline of life. For most orthodox theologians, this enjoyment is marked by continual struggle and marred by occasional failure as long as the individual believer lives in his natural and sinful environment. But the break between fallen and redeemed man is already complete in principle if not in fact, in eternity if not in time. Beyond death not only will Christians completely regain the perfection of paradise lost, but the temporary dualism of nature and spirit will also pass away. Man's natural endowments and environment will have served the probationary purpose for which God intended them. All those who learn the meaning of spiritual existence in this natural world will serve God and enjoy him forever in a new life of the spirit. Those who failed will suffer alienation from God and individual torment in an unending death of the spirit.

Liberalism interprets man's creation, fall, redemption and glorification in conscious opposition to Orthodoxy. Liberalism does believe that God wills a temporary dualism of body and spirit to permit freedom and growth to man as a spiritual being. God intends for human beings to share in his own life and purpose by gaining spiritual dominion over their physical nature and material environment. But, unlike Orthodoxy, man's spiritual endowments and relationships are conceived in more natural and this-worldly terms. Man's spiritual nature is constituted by his distinctive but natural capacities for freedom, rationality, morality, reverence and immortality. These spiritual potentialities are not equally or automatically developed among all men, but they are universally given and realizable capacities. Liberalism further modifies Orthodoxy's view of man's creation in the light of new insights into human life. Orthodoxy's belief that man was created complete and perfect in the distant past is contradicted by the scientific discovery that human beings evolved from brutish origins, by the historical discovery that successive civilizations furthered human progress and by the moral discovery that spiritual character develops through personal struggle. In light of these considerations, Liberalism treats man's 'ideal existence' as a future goal toward which men are striving rather than as a past state from which men have fallen. Given this thoroughgoing reinterpretation of Orthodoxy's view of the meaning of man's created nature and destiny, Liberalism's further modifications of the meaning of man's fall, redemption and glorification come as no surprise. Orthodoxy's doctrine of an original fall and inherited depravity is rejected as being incompatible with scientific knowledge of man's evolutionary origins, with moral insight into guilt's individualistic character and with the theological understanding of life's goal-directed essence. This does not mean that liberals are unaware of man's enormous imperfections. They view sin as a falling *short* of man's ideal spiritual potentialities. Men are repeatedly tempted and fall into bondage, irrationality, immorality or irreverence because of their physical natures and social environment, as the biblical parable of man's 'fall' teaches. But Liberalism believes that men can be won from sin by means which God has built into the natural and human process. Man's

155

redemption comes through personal discipline, educational advancement, moral responsibility and inspirational worship. Some men are stronger, wiser, better and nobler than others and such men serve as examples and teachers for their fellowmen. But God's presence and purposes are available to all who exercise and develop their given spiritual capacities. Those who achieve such spirituality in this life already share in an immortality which will continue to be consummated beyond death. For many liberals, such redemption will finally extend to every creature of God. For those who reject universal salvation, death brings total annihilation rather than eternal torment to those who failed to develop their spiritual potentialities sufficiently in this life. But, in any case, everything depends upon living the life of the spirit here and now.

Neo-orthodoxy draws insights from both Liberalism and Orthodoxy in offering still another view of the meaning of existence. Neo-orthodoxy goes further than Liberalism in questioning Orthodoxy's treatment of creation, fall, redemption and glorification as different stages of human existence. All these terms denote simultaneous aspects rather than discontinous states of Christian experience. Similar to Liberalism, Neo-orthodoxy interprets the doctrine of creation in reference to man's present potentialities and concrete experiences. Man's spirituality is a matter of disciplined appetites, rational insight, moral integrity and worshipful reverence. But, unlike Liberalism's dichotomy between body and spirit, Neo-orthodoxy views man as a psychosomatic whole. Accordingly, man's spiritual capacities are delineated less dualistically as free, rational, responsible and trusting relations to God and to neighbor. With respect to the doctrine of the fall of man, Neo-orthodoxy shares Orthodoxy's stress on the thorough sinfulness of man under the actual conditions of existence. Liberalism rightly rejected Orthodoxy's portrayal of sin as a total depravity universally inherited from the fallen progenitors of the human race. But Liberalism's alternative account of sin as a falling short of man's ideal potentialities is judged far too optimistic and sentimental. In rejecting Orthodoxy's literalistic reading of the Bible's story of the fall, Liberalism missed the profound truth in this biblical parable. Sin is both a bondage against which all men are powerless and a corruption for which each man is responsible. Orthodoxy and Liberalism alike fail to tell the whole truth about man's sin because they do not hold both sides of this paradox together. Sin is not necessary because all men possess the potentialities of meaningful existence. But sin is inevitable because no man actualizes these potentialities. Consonant with this essentially pessimistic view of an unbridgable gulf between man's potential and actual existence, Neo-orthodoxy reaffirms Orthodoxy's claim to the wholly supernatural character of redemption. Man is incapable of establishing those authentic relationships to God and neighbor which constitute the true meaning of existence. These relations are established only as God gives himself and empowers his creatures in and through present events as he has before in the past Event of Jesus Christ. But redemption, like creation and fall, is a simultaneous aspect of Christian existence. Redemption is neither a total nor a gradual overcoming of human idolatry and lovelessness. Redemption means continually renewing but never possessing an authentic relation to God and to neighbor. Finally, Neo-orthodoxy completes its multifaceted approach to the meaning of existence by interpreting glorification as a present aspect of Christian existence. Beliefs about the resurrected life are summary expressions of the simultaneous ideal potentialities, recurring disruptions, continual renewal and eternal meaning of Christian existence. Few neo-orthodox theologians explicitly affirm or deny that this "eternal meaning" includes conscious and individual survival beyond death. Faith can speak only of the meaning of existence from its beginning to its end. What went 'before' or lies 'after' remains with God, for God has the first and the last word about human existence.

PAUL M. VAN BUREN

Christian doctrine has not been alone in saying that there is "something wrong" with man, that man is in bondage and in need of freedom. The unique aspect of the Christian perspective, however, is its own definition of what is "wrong" with man and its own measure of the extent or depth of his problem. In the New Testament, man is seen in the light of the free man, Jesus of Nazareth, and compared to him, men are not free; they are bound by fear and anxiety, mistrust and self-concern. The word used to describe this condition, when measured by *this* standard, is "sin." The logical structure of this teaching does not depend on the story of the "Fall," or even on a theory of "inherited guilt." The various traditional forms of the doctrine of "original sin" are not empirical observations about man; they are *comparative* statements of man's condition, measured by the historical standard of Jesus of Nazareth.

Christian doctrine says that sin places man under the judgment of God, the final judge being Christ. This is a development of the idea of man's measurement by the norm of Jesus. To use a norm is to compare and to judge. The connection of language about judgment with language about sin is a logical consequence of the way in which man is seen in the Christian perspective.

The radical language with which the New Testament authors speak of sin ("as in Adam all die, even so in Christ shall all be made alive") becomes meaningful if it is taken as reflecting the way in which a liberated man looks back upon his "slavery." The language about sin is for the Christian a language concerning a problem answered. Orthodox theology does not say that the Christian does not sin, but it sees sin as a problem to which a solution has been given. The Creeds speak of sin in this way: "I believe in...the forgiveness of sins." It is the language of faith and would make no sense in the mouth of one who was not a Christian. The unbeliever may speak of human fear, anxiety, and bondage, but since these conditions are measured against some other norm than Jesus of Nazareth, and since he does not speak of this problem as one who has been liberated by the contagion of Jesus' freedom, he will speak in another way. The word "sin" is peculiar to the historical perspective of Christian faith and it will not retain its biblical meaning apart from this context. Christians are undoubtedly themselves responsible for making themselves incomprehensible to others and to themselves by speaking too much about sin and forgetting too often the context in which the word is logically placed. *(The Secular Meaning Of The Gospel, pp. 178-80).*

What the Gospel finally has to say about sin is that it has been dealt with on the cross once for all, that man has received justification by sheer grace in the event of Easter, and that this gift is to be received and acknowledged in faith. The doctrine of justification by grace through faith expresses the believer's conviction that he has been accepted freely, regardless of his merit, because of Christ. If it is understood empirically, it puts us in a cosmological courtroom which is logically meaningless and morally doubtful. Understood as the expression of the believer's historical perspective, however, it indicates that his freedom is such that he no longer feels the need to "prove" himself to himself or to anyone else. He is free to accept himself, convinced that he is acceptable, for he has been set free by Jesus of Nazareth. His acceptance is simply his trust in the declaration, "Neither do I condemn you," and he acknowledges this word and its speaker, not his own history, as the basis of his perspective. *(The Secular Meaning Of The Gospel, pp. 180-1).*

Considered once more as language expressing the Christian's perspective, the doctrine of sanctification clarifies the nature of his freedom: like the freedom of Jesus himself, it is freedom to be concerned and compassionate, to become involved for the sake of our neighbor in the world about us. As Luther said of the Christian, he is free to become a slave of his neighbor. The relationship between completed justification and the march along the road of sanctification can also be expressed as the relationship between faith and love. Faith is the thankful acknowledgement of liberation and one's liberator. Love is the fruit of this, the exercise of this freedom in serving one's neighbor. In a word, sanctification is love for one's neighbor.

It might be objected that this interpretation ignores the double command of love with which Jesus summarized the Law. Did he not say that love for God was the first commandment and that love for the neighbor was second?...The command to love God first and the command to love the neighbor, when taken together, can only mean that we are to love the neighbor on the model of Jesus and in his freedom. He has set the believer free for the service of the good Samaritan, who came to the man lying by the roadside simply because he was a man in need, and who offered help where it was needed. In hearing this parable, the Christian recognizes that he himself is the man left by the roadside who has been rescued. He recognizes that the key to the parable is the man who first told it, and in the freedom for which he has been set free, he is able to hear the concluding, "Go and do thou likewise," as words of command which point him on his way, the way of love leading toward the neighbor. *(The Secular Meaning Of The Gospel, pp. 182-3).*

Finally, the "eschatological" hope, in this interpretation of the language of the Gospel, is the conviction that the freedom which the believer has seen in Jesus and which has become contagious for him, and the reconciliation which he sees to be associated with this freedom, will prevail on this earth among all men. That is his conviction, not a prediction. To say that this hope is "eschatological" is to say that one would die rather than abandon it. It indicates the unqualified, undebatable aspect of the Christian's historical perspective. *(The Secular Meaning Of The Gospel, pp. 154-5).*

159

The Gospel...is the good news of a free man who has set other men free, first proclaimed by those to whom this had happened. And it has happened again and again during nineteen centuries that, in the context of hearing this apostolic proclamation, men have been liberated. Their response, which the New Testament calls "faith," consists in acknowledging that this has happened by accepting the liberator, Jesus of Nazareth, as the man who defines for them what it means to be a man and as the point of orientation for their lives. They are "in Christ," which is to say that their understanding of themselves and their lives and all things is determined by their understanding of Jesus. They are a "new creation" in that this orientation to the whole world is new for them. *(The Secular Meaning Of The Gospel, p. 138).*

WILLIAM HAMILTON

Radical theology finds that its task is not to be simply described as the avoidance of the word "God." Such an avoidance is fairly common in the modern period; God has become "ground," "depth," "creativity," "love," "the Supremely Worthful," and still managed to do his traditional work. Such renamings are still in the realm of the doctrine of God. For the radical theology the word "God" is gone, and the traditional reality is so substantially altered that no mere new name, word, or phrase will do, but only a thorough and wide-ranging attempt to think through the whole of Christian thought to see what it means to do without the Christian God—not just some of the odder formulations, but everything–from Rom., ch. 8, to last Sunday's prayer of adoration. At some points—eternal life, for example—no reformulation would appear to be possible. Doing without God means doing without eternal life. At other points—forgiveness and the idea of the holy—doing without God does not prove to be too debilitating, and some sort of reformulation can be provided. So we can say that while the word has gone, sometimes the reality behind the word has also gone, and sometimes it hasn't. ("Questions and Answers on the Radical Theology," p. 228).

Let me put this in another way. The death of God means two closely related things: that some of the human experiences to which men have traditionally given the name of God must be redescribed and renamed, and also that some of those experiences are no longer ours. For example, religious men have often pointed to experiences of dependence, awe, reverence, wonder, mystery, tragedy as signs of the incalculable and mysterious character of life, saying of these experiences taken together, "Something like this is what we mean by God." There are, of course, such things about us, and the only point I wish to make here is that one needn't give any of them the name of God. They are real facts of our life, we have human sciences and arts to clarify them, and they point to mystery and wonder, but not to God.

But a second thing is just as true. There are experiences that men have had in the past and which they have traditionally understood as pointing to God that are simply not available to us in the same way today. Take the experiences of dependence, especially in the presence of nature. Listen to a research biologist or doctor or a physicist or a space scientist talk about his work. He is talking about mastery, control and power; not about a sense of his smallness before the universe. This is true of our kids as well. The other night I was out in the back yard with one of my children, who had to identify some constellations for his science homework. When I was young and used to stand under the starry sky, I recall being filled with all the things you were supposed to be filled with: awe, a sense of my own smallness, dependence. But my son is a full citizen of the modern world, and said to me, after he had located the required constellations, "Which are the ones we put up there, Dad?" He was more interested in what he could do up there than in what he could feel down here. He had become a technological man, and this means something religiously. Are there other traditional religious experiences that we're losing touch with? The death of God lives in this kind of world.

It is quite foolish to say that the death-of-God theology wants to reduce life to the scientifically knowable or the immediately relevant. It has no special interest in relevance or in being acceptable to that nonexistent chimera, "modern man". In no sense does it wish to turn its back on the mysterious, the sacred, the holy or the transcendent. It simply will not call such things by the name of God. As a matter of fact, it might be very interesting to work out a way of talking about godless forms of the sacred—ideas and experiences of the sacred that need not include the experience of God. It is doubtless true that some roads to the sacred are ruled out for many of us in our rationalized and technological culture. There probably cannot be, for example, any way to the sacred via holy men, holy books or holy gestures in the usual sense. But even if our way to God is cut off, need it be the case for our experience of the sacred? ("The Death of God," pp. 138-9).

161

If it is true that radical theology has no wish to flatten man's experience of life out to the visible and testable, it is going to have to find some way of interpreting and affirming those elements of wonder, of awe, of reverence, even of the sacred. It just will not use the idea of God in its systems of explanation, but instead whatever in the realm of art, natural science, social science, psychology, that might be most appropriate and illuminating. This means that there might even be such a thing as a godless form of the sacred, experiences of the sacred with a validity apart from any need for a theistic explanation. What would a godless sacred look like? It would certainly involve some kind of experience of the other, the not-self, and it would also have the element of the uncontrollable. It is doubtless true that many roads to the sacred are cut off for modern men in their technological culture; perhaps the way to the sacred via holy men, holy books, holy gestures in the religious sense has become impossible for more and more of us. But may it not be that the experience of sex can become a kind of sacred event for some today? I am not referring to the kind of pseudopious nonsense found among Christians who enjoy being well thought of by Hugh Hefner, but I am referring to the astonishing idea of the sacred in the following passage from *The Scarlet Letter*:

"We are not, Hester, [Dimmesdale is speaking] the worst sinners in the world. There is one worse than even the polluted priest! That old man's revenge has been blacker than sin. He has violated, in cold blood, the sanctity of a human heart. Thou and I, Hester, never did so!" "Never, never," whispered she. "What we did had a consecration of its own. We felt it so! We said so to each other! Hast thou forgotten it?"

Here is an astonishing event—the idea of a sexual relationship, outside of marriage, in the midst of Puritan New England, possessing a sacredness that does not seem to require the idea of God. Perhaps as well death can become a sacred event for some in the time of the death of God. The death of Jesus has always been sacred in a conventional sense for Christianity: pointing uniquely to the character of the divine love and will. For the radical Christian, Jesus' death is sacred in a godless sense: it bears the full meaning of Jesus's own life and work, and it shows the way man is to stand in his world. But apart from the death of Jesus, what would it mean to say that death in general can become a sacred event? What is meant of course is not our actual dying, but our preparation for dying, our living with death. Is not something like this present in the Gettysburg Address when Lincoln declared that neither he nor his hearers could consecrate the ground, not because God alone could, but because "the brave men, living and dead, who struggled here, have consecrated it, far above our poor power to add or detract". However fruitful these particular approaches may be, the radical theologian, having chosen to live as a Christian without God, has a special responsibility for not ignoring the realm of life's mystery, tragedy, wonder, and holiness, and of finding structures and images, even more adequate than the traditional pictures of God, to interpret these dimensions of life. ("Questions and Answers on the Radical Theology," pp. 225-7).

Since the basis for the classic Christian hope is not human immortality but the character of God, the radical theology is simply without a belief in life after death. It must speak of our mortality, our finiteness, without knowing or even believing anything else. This means that radical theology must speak more earnestly of the need, here and now, of facing death, befriending it, withdrawing from it the power to terrify or to make us afraid. "And life is the destiny you are bound to refuse until you have consented to die," Auden has written. Consenting to die, then, becomes a part of affirming life. From this it should be clear that the radical theology can respond deeply to the death of Jesus, but scarcely to the resurrection as abolition of death. ("Questions and Answers on the Radical Theology," pp. 224-5).

This is an optimistic theology. It has a doctrine of sin, but it is not a central doctrine. By optimism I do not mean insensitivity to suffering and tragedy, and I do not mean inevitable progress. Nevertheless, radical theology is both describing and relating itself to a new feeling of hope and optimism in American life today, a conviction that substantive changes in the lives of men can and will be made.

This new optimism is trying to discipline itself to say Yes to the world of rapid change, new technologies, automation, and the mass media. It feels with Bellow's Herzog that we may well be at the end of the Wasteland era, at the end of the time of alienation; that a decisive halt should be called to the pervasive "modern" hostility to technology, speed, and urbanization.

This optimism is found in today's Negro revolution, and the radical theology wishes to learn from and respond to this decisive movement in our natural life. If "Empty Bed Blues," Tennessee Williams, and "Guernica" are the sights and sounds of neo-orthodox theology, perhaps radical theology is closer to "We

Shall Overcome," Saul Bellow, and Robert Rauschenberg. ("The Shape of a Radical Theology," p. 1221-2).

This is not an optimism of grace, but a worldly optimism I am defending. It faces despair not with the conviction that out of it God can bring hope, but with the conviction that the human conditions that created it can be overcome, whether those conditions be poverty, discrimination, or mental illness. It faces death not with the hope for immortality, but with the human confidence that man may befriend death and live with it as a possiblility always alongside.

I think that the new optimism is both a cause and a consequence of the basic theological experience which we today call the death of God. ("The New Optimism," p. 169).

GABRIEL VAHANIAN

In biblical thought human existence is viewed both as nature and as history, as flesh and as spirit, as an empirical, physiological, or biological datum and as spiritual or eschatological reality, meaning thereby that man as spirit coincides with, and is identified *as* but not *with*, man as nature. *(No Other God, p. 33).*

Religious existence is theonomous existence; but the authenticity of religious existence is tested not only by its fruits, but also by its roots. For Biblical thought, the root of authentic religious existence is God. The business of being a Christian depends in a large measure on one's conception of God. This is not merely a matter of academic sophistication, but equally of practical relevance. *(The Death Of God, pp. 74-75).*

Contemporary atheism has come to look at man almost as the Bible itself once did. Hence, instead of rejecting atheism, we should seek to emphasize its contribution to the understanding of faith. *(No Other God, p. 17).*

To claim that faith is inseparable from secularity is not an innovation. Nor is it a reversal of the Christian tradition. It is a renewal, a reaffirmation, of the Biblical doctrine about the nature of this world and the meaning of the believer's presence in it. Essentially the Bible is not otherworldly in its assessment of religious existence. This interpretation fits the Old Testament more adequately than it does the New.But it does not violate the spirit of the New Testament, especially if one is to regard it as the fulfillment, not the negation, of the Old Testament—and one must do this according to the Christian tradition itself.

The Old Testament considers the world as God's creation and asserts that this creation was originally good, despite the fact that it also states (through the myth of the fall) that this goodness can be corrupted. Biblical thought considers the world as man's sphere of action and pre-eminence. Man's responsibility to God and his involvement in the world emerge as polar elements attesting to the original goodness of creation. This polarity never obliterates the possibility that the goodness on which it rests may become self-centered or introverted. The locus of the polarity is at the same time a locus of tension. There is no dichotomy between man's responsibility to God and his involvement in the world, although there is a clear distinction. This distinction does not call for either man's withdrawal from the world or a separation between his religious obligations and his secular tasks. One finds in the Bible an implicit distinction between religious and secular, but the distinction does not involve a radical split between these two spheres. They are distinguished but not split or severed from each other. They complement each other in such a way that, as Martin Buber has said, the secular is not merely secular, but it is not yet holy. The distinction is between the religious and the not yet religious, or the holy and the not yet holy.

Because Christianity conceives of itself as the new Israel, the whole of the New Testament must be regarded in the light of the preceding argument, including those passages which seem otherworldly almost unmistakably. It is beyond the scope of this book to develop the various reasons for making such an assertion. Briefly, however, all religious language is essentially symbolic and not literal, much as fundamentalists and orthodox of all kinds would like it. And to say that it is symbolic implies that allowance is made for the idiosyncrasy of the culture and the class of people in whose language the religious truths are apprehended and expressed. For this reason, the various utterances of the New Testament which are spelled out in otherworldly terms must be interpreted in the light of the implicit coincidence between these terms and the fundamental concepts of the Old Testament to which they essentially refer. In other words, these otherworldly terms are themselves symbolic reinterpretation of the ancient Biblical insight, according to which man's involvement in the world, though not severed from his commitment to God, must not be mistaken for this unconditional commitment.

In the Biblical understanding of man's place in the universe faith, trust in God, and secularity could not be cleft from one another. This is what modern man has possibly discovered in the very ambiguities of his rather lowbrow religious search. *(The Death Of God, pp. 61-3).*

HARVEY COX

The Gospel calls man to maturity, away from a fascinated obsession with his own soul and toward *this* world and this *saeculum* as the appropriate sphere of Christian existence. ("An Exchange of Views," p. 118).

The Gospel does not call man to return to a previous stage of his development. It does not summon man back to dependency, awe, and religiousness. Rather it is a call to imaginative urbanity and mature secularity. It is not a call to man to abandon his interest in the problems of this world, but an invitation to accept the full weight of this world's problems as the gift of its Maker. It is a call to be a man of this technical age, with all that means, seeking to make it a human habitation for all who live within it. *(The Secular City, pp. 72-3).*

Secularization is the liberation of man from religious and metaphysical tutelage, the turning of his attention away from other worlds and toward this one. But how did this emancipation begin? What are its sources?

Secularization, as the German theologian Friedrich Gogarten once remarked, is the legitimate consequence of the impact of biblical faith on history. This is why it is no mere accident that secularization arose first within the culture of the so-called Christian West, in the history within which the biblical religions have made their most telling impact. The rise of natural science, of democratic political institutions, and of cultural pluralism—all developments we normally associate with Western culture—can scarcely be understood without the original impetus of the Bible. Even though the conscious connection has long since been lost sight of, the relationships are still there. Cultural impulses continue to work long after their sources have been forgotten.

There are three pivotal elements in biblical faith which have given rise to one aspect of secularization. Thus, the *disenchantment of nature* begins with the Creation, the *desacralization of politics* with the Exodus, and the *deconsecration of values* with the Sinai Covenant, especially with its prohibition of idols. Far from being something Christians should be against, secularization represents an authentic consequence of biblical faith. Rather than oppose it, the task of

166

Christians should be to support and nourish it.   *(The Secular City, p. 15).*

It is the world, the political world and not the church, which is the arena of God's renewing and liberating activity. The church participates in this liberation only insofar as it participates in the world. To turn our back on the world is to turn our back on the place where God is at work.   *(God's Revolution And Man's Responsibility, p. 24).*

The Bible simply does not know any spiritual realm, any religious realm separate from the carnal realm. The spirit in the Bible is precisely that which enlivens and directs bodily activity. Very early in the Bible, God tips us off to his method of working in the world. He frees the captive people from economic and political bondage. He does not free these people to some kind of inner forbearance or of spiritual liberty... The biblical God recognizes no inner freedom apart from external conditions of f r e e d o m .   *(God's Revolution And Man's Responsibility, p. 29).*

God has given man a thrilling responsibility for this world. But man has not fulfilled his assignment. God has placed the tiller of history in man's hand, but man has gone to his hammock and let the winds and tides sweep his ship along. Man has done things he ought not to have done, but even more importantly he has not done those things he ought to have done. He has refused to live up to the full stature of his manhood and has abdicated his crucial place in the scheme of things. This is what biblical tradition has c a l l e d ''sin.''   *(God's Revolution And Man's Responsibility, p. 39).*

I believe a careful examination of the biblical sources will indicate that man's most debilitating proclivity is *not* pride. It is *not* his attempt to be more than man. Rather it is his sloth, his unwillingness to be everything man was intended to be. His moral discoloration stems only in part from his unwillingness to be sorry for the wrong he has done in the past. It stems even more from his unwillingness to take responsibility for what he will do in the future. *(On Not Leaving It To The Snake, p. ix).*

The world as God makes it, as he gives it to us, and as he places us in it, is not the world as we have taken it from him. We have dislocated and distorted God's world. We created our own cardboard world in which we prefer to live rather than in God's world. God gave man and still gives him dominion over the forces of the world; but, instead of having dominion over the world, we decide to give the world dominion over us. Take, for example, money, political power, sex, work, play—all the things that go into this wonderful world that God has given us, the things he has given us to enjoy and to have in reciprocity with each other. We have made them our little tin masters and ourselves their slaves. Rather than utilizing these things as the God-given means of creating community between man and his fellowman, man and woman, labor and management, nation and nation, we have used them to beat down and to misuse those other human beings through whom God would come to us—the God who is as near to us as the nearest thou. We have rejected the world that God makes and that God gives us. We have fabricated our own little world around our family, our nation, our race, or our class. In so doing we deny the very principle of life as God makes it— interdependence. *(God's Revolution And Man's Responsibility, p. 30).*

It might be useful to add another type of human relationship to Buber's famous pair. Besides I–It relationships, in which the other person is reduced to the status of an object, and in addition to the profound, personally formative I–Thou encounter, why could we not evolve a theology of the I–You relationship? Buber's philosophy suffers from an unnecessary dichotomy. Perhaps between the poles of the two types of human relationship he has elaborated we could designate a third. It would include all those public relationships we so enjoy in the city but which we do not allow to develop into private ones. These contacts can be decidedly human even though they remain somewhat distant. *(The Secular City, pp. 42-3).*

This is a newly evolving mode of human relationships. It is authentically human and more or less unprecedented in previous cultures, but the important thing about this emergent I–You relationship for our purposes is that it is bound to influence our symbolization of God in one way or another. It may be that in addition to the I–Thou relationship with God, and the mystical experience which is already exceedingly rare, contemporary man could meet God as a "you."

Is this so farfetched? Recent discussions of the concept of the covenant in the Old Testament suggest it means that Yahweh was willing to stoop so low as to work in tandem with man, to work on a team, no matter how poorly the human partner was working out. Whether or not this is true, it can certainly be said that in Jesus of Nazareth God did show that He was willing to take man's side of the unfulfilled covenant, to become the junior partner in the asymmetric relationship. It is not demeaning to suggest that the notions of teamwork and partnership need to be explored much more in our conceptualization of God. He who is "high and lifted up" suggests in the life of Jesus that he is willing to put himself in the position of working within a group, of washing his fellows' feet and of needing someone to carry his cross. What seems at first sight irreverence may be closer to the heart of the self-humbling truth of God than we imagine.

The idea of an I—You partnership between God and man is strongly hinted by the language of Galatians 4 which we discussed earlier. In this passage man is viewed as a son and heir. The emphasis is on *son* as opposed to child, and on *heir* as having assumed responsibility. This implies that the strictly vertical relationship which informs a father's relationship to his minor boy is discarded for the adult partnership which obtains between a grown man and his father.

Perhaps in the secular city God calls man to meet Him first of all as a "you." This has far-reaching implications. It suggests that man is not to become fascinated with God himself. Like his relationship to his work partner, man's relationship to God derives from the work they do together. Rather than shutting out the world to delve into each other's depths the way adolescent lovers do, God and man find joy together in doing a common task. Of course this type of relationship will not satisfy the man who is driven by a compulsive interest in "finding" or "experiencing" God. Such people are always dissatisfied by the admittedly sparse revelation of Himself which God has made. It is not the kind of revelation which encourages delving. God wants man to be interested not in Him but in his fellow man. *(The Secular City, pp. 231-2).*

In traditional language, the message of the church is that God has defeated the "principalities and powers" by Jesus and has made it possible for man to become the "heir," the master of the created world. This sounds foreign to us now, but nothing could be closer to the center of human existence in twentieth-century urban society. These "principalities and powers" actually signify all the forces in a culture which cripple and corrupt human freedom...

These principalities and powers, according to the New Testament, were originally intended to be a part of the world, to be dominated and utilized by man. But man's freedom is so complete that he "worshipped and served the creature rather than

169

the Creator" (Romans 1:24). Man thus fell captive to forces over which he was intended to "have dominion." Things he was meant to control controlled him. He had to be extricated. God's action, which goes on all the time but was made known in Jesus of Nazareth, is to call man to freedom *from* the powers and principalities, and to summon him at the same time to responsibility *over* and *for* them.

This is no sequential story. Man is always tempted to surrender his freedom to the powers. God is ever at work making freedom and personhood possible. There is no neutral ground. Man either masters and manages his environment or he is mastered and managed by it. The call to freedom is at the same time a call to responsibility. In terms of modern urban life, this means that we should never seriously ask "Is New York City governable?" or "Can nuclear war be prevented?" or "Can racial justice be achieved?" The fact is that man is placed in an environment of problems which he is called to master. God has not stacked the cards against man the way fate does in Greek tragedy or a Thomas Hardy novel. To believe the kerygma is to believe that man not only *should* but *can* "have dominion over the earth." For the Bible, there are no powers anywhere which are not essentially tameable and ultimately humanizable. To deny this, in word or deed, is to "worship the creature rather than the Creator," to open the door and readmit the banished furies, to genuflect before some faceless Kismet. *(The Secular City, p. 110-2).*

THOMAS J. J. ALTIZER

To speak of the death of God as a final and decisive event is to open oneself to the horizon of our history as the full arena of faith. This has not always been the way of Christian faith. It has only been in the course of a long movement of a particular history, the history of Christendom, that Eternity has been swallowed up by time itself, that a radical finitude has appeared which has dissolved the very meaning of transcendence. Earlier Christians could greet the world as the creation, as a contingent realm deriving its ultimate meaning and reality from a transcendent Creator, even though the primitive Christians looked upon the world as the old creation, an Old Aeon that even now is coming to an end. Scholastic philosophy, as Max Scheler teaches, could know finitude as sheer contingency—*i.e.*, as being wholly dependent upon a reality outside it—because medieval Christendom experienced nature as the creation. When an autonomous nature and an infinite space dawned in the Renaissance, the world was no longer manifest as the creation, and with the subsequent triumph of modern science, contingency in the medieval sense has disappeared from view. The world is no longer meaningful by means of anything which might lie beyond it. ("Word and History," pp. 126-7)

To speak of the death of God is to speak of a movement of God Himself from transcendence to immanence, from Spirit to flesh. It is to speak of a divine process, a forward-moving process with an eschatological or final goal. A process in some sense moving from an original beginning to a final end. And a process which itself initiates, effects, and embodies a total transformation of all reality whatsoever. Now of course in our Christian tradition we have many symbolic ways of speaking of this transformation, for example, the movement of Spirit into flesh, or the movement of Spirit to flesh. But I think we have to understand this in a comprehensive sense. We have to have some sense of an ultimate transfiguration of all things whatsoever, wherein God Himself, who reveals Himself in faith, in the covenant which He established with Israel, to be the Creator and Lord who is an actively and universally redemptive Creator and Lord, is to act in a way which reveals Himself, and reveals Himself in a way which effects a redemption of humanity and indeed of the cosmos itself. And here redemption is not by any means understood in a subjective or pietistic sense, but rather to be understood as a transfiguration, a transformation of all reality whatsoever. Here, as it were, we find a kind of process of reversal. As God in becoming flesh, as the Word in becoming flesh, empties Himself of His own transcendent power and glory — not simply investing the cosmos and history with a new power and a new life, but transforming all reality whatsoever. Thereby the weight of reality or the center of gravity of reality itself now becomes a fullness of life in flesh, in the world, in time, in life, in energy, in movement. *(The Altizer-Montgomery Dialogue, pp. 11-2).*

Precisely at this point lies a new destiny for Christian theology: for with the death of the "Christian God" a wholly new meaning of Creation and Incarnation has dawned! No longer can the Christian believe that his existence here and now is a kind of prologue to his future life in a transcendent Kingdom of God. Nor can he believe that his life in "this world" derives its meaning and reality from an "other world" in the Beyond. Agonizing as this situation may be, the very collapse of the classical theological distinction between "this world" and "that world" has made possible a new epiphany of Christ: a Christ who has not descended from "above," but who is *wholly* and *fully* incarnate in our midst. Finally, only the Christian can greet the radical profane with faith: for only the Christian believes in both Creation and Incarnation, only the Christian believes in a Christ who is in some sense Creator and Redeemer at once. *(Mircea Eliade And The Dialectic Of The Sacred, p. 18).*

I believe that the Christian can rejoice in the death of God. He can rejoice in the loss of transcendence. He can even rejoice in the new chaos, the new darkness into which we have been hurled or thrown by our own destiny. He can rejoice because in a certain sense he can know this chaos as the consummation of God's original movement in Christ. And he can rejoice because he can know that he is liberated from any kind of transcendent ground from any kind of awesome mystery, from any kind of ultimate norm, from any kind of final mystery, from any kind of beyond, and therein is released for a fullness — a totality of life and energy here and now in the world. *(The Altizer—Montgomery Dialogue, p. 17).*

Now that we have reached a point where it is manifest that history itself has moved through the death of God we must celebrate the death of God as an ephiphany of the eschatological Christ. While the Christ who lies upon our horizon no longer appears in his traditional form—indeed, he may never again appear in a form that is in continuity with his previous expressions—as Christians we are called into union with his presence among us even when that presence would seem to negate all that faith once knew as the Word. Yet if the Christ of faith is an eschatological Word, he cannot be fully present in the dark and hidden crevices of a turbulent present, nor can he be fully at hand in the broken body of a suffering humanity. He must instead be present in the fullness of the history before us. ("Word and History," pp. 138-9).

What the Christian knows as redemption is in some sense a gradual process. It's not an event which occurs immediately in one instant of time to effect something that from henceforth is eternally achieved. Rather, Christ Himself is the movement, the embodiment of God's movement into the world. Christ is the forward-moving life and energy which is present in the world and will continue to act until that final day when all things will be reconciled—when all will be manifest as total energy and life. So in a very real sense if we speak of the death of God as a redemptive event, then the death of God has not been consummated so long as redemption itself is not complete. And obviously redemption is not complete. We live in a world of sin, of darkness, of perversity, of injustice, etc. Therefore, if we understand the death of God as a redemptive event, the death of God cannot yet be complete or finally realized and consummated. And the Christian does not believe that it will be consummated until the Apocalypse. *(The Altizer-Montgomery Dialogue, pp. 13-4).*

Yet this process cannot be real apart from an actual transfiguration of flesh and Spirit: flesh must cease to exist as flesh in becoming Spirit, even as Spirit must wholly perish as Spirit in fully becoming flesh. The Incarnation can culminate in a truly apocalyptic or eschatological end only by effecting an absolute negation of the original identities of flesh and Spirit. Thereby the given and intrinsic forms of flesh and Spirit are totally reversed so as to make possible a final movement of each into its respective other. Inevitably, the radical Christian believes that the end of the world, whose immediate coming was proclaimed by Jesus, is the total transfiguration of the fallen form of the world, the end of a flesh that is isolated from Spirit, and so likewise the end of a Spirit that is isolated from flesh. *(The Gospel Of Christian Atheism, p. 47).*

JOHN A. T. ROBINSON

Religion may offer a man a place and purpose in the ultimate scheme of things, but he is not likely to be remotely interested in it, unless he can see it as giving him in the first instance a place and purpose in the immediate setting in which he lives. It is when he sees the Gospel discovering to him social salvation, that is, a position in society in which he really finds himself, where he counts, is of value, and can make a difference, that a man may begin to understand a gospel promising him 'right standing' with God. The content of social salvation—what a man has to become in order to find fulfilment as a member of society—differs from society to society. Christianity must take account of these changes, as in the past it has done, if it is to continue to offer salvation from and to the things that are really relevant. *(On Being The Church In The World, pp. 23-4).*

Our generation, so far from being furthest removed from the outlook of the New Testament, is perhaps in this respect closest to it. The otherworldliness which, from the second century to the nineteenth, placed 'the new world' on the other side of the grave no longer exercises the same pull upon us. We are unable, like our forefathers, to rest everything on immortality or to define the purpose of life as 'making a good death'. Secularism has done its work in detaching us from that idol.   *(On Being The Church In The World, pp. 13-4).*

While the soul of salvation is eternally the same, its body is always changing. The particular ideal of life which in any age translates into a pattern of concrete social relationships the fulfilment of the human spirit in God requires to be redefined with every fundamental change in the structure of society. Salvation becomes disembodied, and therefore irrelevant (for it is through the body alone that men perceive the soul), when this redefinition is not made.   *(On Being The Church In The World, p. 23).*

The man who finds himself compelled to acknowledge the reality of *God*, whatever he may call him or however he may image him, is the man who, through the mathematical regularities and through the functional values, is met by the same grace and the same claim that he recognizes in the I-Thou relation with another person. It may come to him through nature, through the claims of artistic integrity or scientific truth, through the engagements of social justice or of personal communion. Yet always it comes with an overmastering givenness and demand such as no other thing or person has the power to convey or the right to require. Like the child Samuel in the Temple, confusing the call of God with the voice of Eli, he may think at first that it can simply be identified with or contained within the finite relationship by which it is mediated. He may not be able to tell what to make of it, he may find it profoundly disturbing, but he knows it in the end to be inescapable and unconditional. In this relationship, too, he discovers himself known and judged and accepted for what ultimately he is. He finds in it for himself the way, the truth and the life. And if he is a Christian, he recognizes and acknowledges this grace and claim supremely in the person of Jesus Christ, the definition at one and the same time of a genuinely human existence and of this intangible, ineffable reality of 'God'. He agrees, passionately, with the atheist that such a reality cannot be *used* or *needed*. A God like that *is* superfluous, dispensable, intolerable. In fact it is *no God*. And then, when that God is dead, the Lord appears.   *(The New Reformation? pp. 117-8).*

The question of God is the question *whether this depth of being is a reality or an illusion,* not whether *a* Being exists beyond the bright blue sky, or anywhere else. Belief in God is a matter of 'what you take seriously without any reservation', of what for you is *ultimate* reality.

The man who acknowledges the transcendence of God is the man who *in* the conditioned relationships of life recognizes the unconditional and responds to it in unconditional personal relationship. *(Honest To God, p.55).*

To assert that *'God* is love' is to believe that in love one comes into touch with the most fundamental reality in the universe, that Being itself ultimately has this character. It is to say, with Buber, that 'Every particular *Thou* is a glimpse through to the eternal *Thou'*, that it is 'between man and man' that we meet God, not, with Feuerbach, that 'man with man – the unity of *I* and *Thou–* is God'. Nevertheless, as Bonhoeffer insists, 'God is the "beyond" *in the midst';* 'The transcendent is not infinitely remote but close at hand'. For the eternal *Thou* is met only *in, with and under* the finite *Thou,* whether in the encounter with other persons or in the response to the natural order. *(Honest To God, p. 53).*

What essentially the Christian faith is asserting is that in and through all the processes of nature and history there is a personal outcome to be traced and a love to be met which nothing can finally defeat. It does not necessarily imply that these processes are themselves the deliberate expression of willed intention, any more than are the millions of physical and psychological reactions which in human beings form the raw material of personal purpose. It is not that "all things work together for good," or that God deliberately "works" all things thus, by some super-computerized design, but rather that "in everything...he [the Spirit] co-operates for good with those who love God"—that is to say, for those who make the response of love, in every concatenation of circumstance, however pointless and indeed intentionless, there is to be met the graciousness of a *Thou* capable of transforming and liberating even the most baffling and opaque into meaning and purpose. *(Exploration Into God, p. 115).*

It is this union-in-estrangement with the Ground of our being—what Paul Althaus once described as 'inescapable godlessness in inescapable relationship to God'—that we mean by hell. But equally it is the union-in-love with the Ground of our being, such as we see in Jesus Christ, that is the meaning of heaven. And it is the offer of that life, in all its divine depth, to overcome the estrangement and alienation of existence as we know it that the New Testament speaks of as the 'new creation'. This new reality is transcendent, it is 'beyond' us, in the sense that it is not ours to command. Yet we experience it, like the Prodigal, as we 'come to ourselves'. For it is a coming home, or rather a being received home, to everything we are created to be. *(Honest To God, p. 80).*

The relationship to God in which the Christian finds the ultimate meaning and significance of his life *could* not have its unconditional character were it dependent upon the fact that the world does not blow itself up or I am not run over by a bus tomorrow. From his present faith the Christian knows that when the proximate relationships of this life are stripped away, he is left in relationship not to nothing, but to the infinite and eternal love of God, in which even now he is sustained and grounded. Our destiny is to be with him for ever. ("The Debate Continues," p. 265).

3. The Function of Christ

Christology constitutes the third major doctrinal coordinate which determines the warp and woof of faith's framework of beliefs. Jesus Christ performs the distinctive function in most Christian theologies of truly representing and relating God and man. Theological traditions differ widely in their interpretations of this union of true divinity and true humanity in Jesus Christ. As we shall see presently, these differences clearly reflect the views of God and man which prevail in rival theological traditions. But some theory of Christ plays an integral role in every systematic account of the Christian faith.

Classical Christologies make a distinction between the person and the work of Christ. The person of Christ is traditionally explained in terms of the union of distinct divine and human natures in one person. An astonishing variety of ways of defining and relating these two "natures" has characterized Christian thought from the beginning. Even the creedal formula developed by the Council of Chalcedon in A.D. 451 to settle disputes over the person of Christ merely excluded certain inadequate accounts rather than establishing one adequate theory. But, in the last analysis, this variety reduces to a number of subtle distinctions within two broadly different ways of interpreting Jesus Christ as the union of true divinity and true humanity. Jesus Christ is most often portrayed as the union of the substantial essences of God and man. This union formed a unique incarnation of God and actualization of man. As spirit and body are distinctly two though intimately one, so God and man formed one unique whole in Jesus Christ. This interpretation of the person of Christ is known

176

technically as the doctrine of *hypostatic union.* By contrast, the doctrine of the two 'natures' is sometimes interpreted as the union of the concrete wills of God and Jesus. This union formed an unbroken communion of purpose and action between Jesus and God. As male and female become one in marriage while retaining and even enhancing their distinct identities and roles, so God and Jesus formed an unbroken union without diminishing or altering their distinct divine and human identities and roles. This way of handling the two 'natures' of Christ is technically called *prosopic union.* The concept of hypostatic union received the official sanction of the Church in the debates following the Council of Chalcedon and has prevailed as such for centuries. But theories of prosopic union have been advocated by individual theologians throughout Christian history and, beginning with nineteenth century Liberalism, have become increasingly predominant in Protestant treatments of the person of Christ.

Similar to this spectrum of opinions on the person of Christ, rival accounts of the work of Christ exhibit numerous variations within two broad family groups. The predominant group believes that Jesus Christ supernaturally establishes and enables faith. Jesus Christ is a unique demonstration of divine revelation and redemption. Thus, he is the only source of the true knowledge and saving power of God. For the second and much smaller group, Jesus Christ supremely illustrates and inspires faith. Rather than being a unique incarnation of God and actualization of man, Jesus Christ was the pioneer and perfector of a union with God which all men possess completely in potentiality and partially in actuality. Jesus Christ thus exemplifies and inspires the divine sonship which is every man's birthright and authentic destiny.

These distinctive approaches to the work of Christ usually rest on divergent theories of the person of Christ. Theological traditions which portray Christ as supernaturally establishing and enabling faith generally advocate some theory of the hypostatic union of God and man in the person of Christ. On the other hand, theories of a prosopic union between God and Jesus typically support appeals to Jesus as faith's supreme illustration and inspiration. Although these correlations do not hold without fail, theories of *supernatural* person and work and of *exemplary* person and work usually belong together.

But, in the modern era, these classical divisions and parallels have become less firm and serviceable. Most contemporary Protestant theologians find the distinction between the person and the work of Christ misleading if not false. As early as the Reformation, technical discussion concerning the two natures was minimized in favor of a stress on the benefits of Christ. More recently, distinction between the person and work of Christ seldom appear in discussions of Christ's function in Christian life and thought. But, on closer analysis, contemporary Protestant theologians do not so much ignore questions of Christ's identity as eschew explanations in terms of metaphysical essences. Relational or voluntaristic models of the person of Christ are crucial for many contemporary Christologies, even though they are not always explicitly acknowledged or discussed. Therefore, we should remain alert to questions of both who Christ was and what Christ does in the comparisons that follow.

Orthodoxy portrays Jesus Christ as the one and only divine-human Savior of the world. Son of Mary according to the flesh which he shared equally with all men and Son of God according to the Word that dwelled fully in him. Jesus Christ was God's once-for-all revelatory and redemptive entrance into human life. Jesus Christ was a *unique* hypostatic union of true divinity and true humanity. Orthodoxy's account of the unique person of Jesus Christ depends upon the metaphysical assumptions of Greek philosophy. According to ancient Greek thought, physical substance rests on spiritual substance. Thus, man's physical nature is energized and actualized by his spiritual nature. But Jesus Christ was different from all other persons. He was human physically but divine spiritually. The physical nature of Jesus Christ was energized and actualized by none other than the Spirit of God. Put in less technical terminology, God clothed himself in the flesh and blood concreteness of Jesus of Nazareth. God became subject to the physical and psychological conditions of human existence while retaining the moral, rational and spiritual perfections of his divine nature. As the one and only simultaneous incarnation of God and actualization of man, Jesus Christ supernaturally revealed God and redeemed man. This salvatory work of Christ is interpreted in two rather different ways within Orthodoxy as a whole. The *sacramental* strain, typified by Roman Catholicism and Eastern Orthodoxy, conceives of salvation as the deification of man by participation in supernatural grace. This perspective magnifies the divinization of man which occurred in the incarnation as Christ's central accomplishment on man's behalf. The *soteriological* strain more characteristic of Protestantism shifts the emphasis to man's reconciliation to God through reception of

178

divine forgiveness. This approach stresses the atoning work of Christ whereby communion and cooperation with God are restored once more. But these divergent perspectives within Orthodoxy overlap at many points and they agree at the roots that Jesus Christ supernaturally and exclusively reveals God to man and redeems man for God.

Liberalism interprets Jesus Christ as supreme among all the sons of God. Although often retaining the classical formula, Liberalism completely rejects Orthodoxy's interpretation of the two 'natures' of Christ. All Christologies of hypostatic union are judged inadequate for failing to preserve the full humanity and religious relevance of Jesus. By claiming that God is the actualizing and energizing spirit of Jesus, Orthodoxy actually denies the real spiritual, moral and rational humanity of Jesus. In turn, this 'God in a human body' fails to be religiously relevant to ordinary men for two reasons. If Jesus Christ were literally God incarnate, he does not represent authentic humanity because of his unique nature and destiny. More important, he cannot bestow authentic humanity because responsible behavior and spiritual character cannot be imputed. Turning away from Orthodoxy's supernatural person and substitutionary work of Christ, Liberalism stresses the full humanity and representative vocation of Jesus. Jesus was in every way human but, unlike his stumbling brothers in humanity, he lived in accord with God's will and way for men. By virtue of this union, Jesus not only disclosed the true meaning of existence but also the true reality of God. Since God is most clearly present and known in man's moral, rational and spiritual life, the more perfect the man the clearer God's will and work in and through his life. Thus, by stressing both Jesus' union with God and God's revelation through Jesus, liberal theologians claim to interpret correctly the ancient formula of true humanity and true divinity. Consonant with this view of the prosopic union of Jesus and God, most liberals claim that Jesus makes three vital contributions to Christian faith. Jesus illustrates the human life constitutive of faith, symbolizes the divine resources available to faith, and inspires the personal commitment required for faith. These contributions to faith are furnished more by his life than by his death. Jesus' death merely focuses and dramatizes his inspiring and exemplary life. But Jesus can properly illustrate existence, symbolize God and inspire faith only when his real words and deeds are separated from the obscure language and theology of primitive Christianity. Fortunately, according to Liberalism, a

179

trustworthy portrait of how Jesus really lived and died can be achieved through the skills of modern historical scholarship. Numerous differences in detail appear in liberal reconstructions of the life and teachings of Jesus. But the liberal movement as a whole presents a view of Jesus embodying and eliciting faith in the universal fatherhood of God and brotherhood of man.

Neo-orthodoxy once again draws insights from both Liberalism and Orthodoxy in developing a distinctive view of God's unsurpassable self-giving and self-disclosure in Jesus Christ. Similar to Liberalism, Neo-orthodoxy rejects the metaphysical approach of hypostatic union in favor of a kind of prosopic union. Jesus was indeed a thoroughly human and independently existing self in and through whom God was present and knowable. But, echoing Orthodoxy's one-sided stress on the divinity of Christ, Neo-orthodoxy rejects Liberalism's equation of the life of Jesus with the revelation of God. Very few neo-orthodox theologians explain how God worked through Jesus but not as Jesus. But they uniformly base faith on the revelatory and redemptive event of Christ rather than on the exemplary and inspirational life of Jesus. Their sharp distinction if not total separation between the Christ of faith and the Jesus of history rests on three considerations. Liberalism's near identification of the revelation of God with the life of Jesus is judged theologically inadequate, historically impossible and religiously dangerous. Theologically, this intimate relation fails to preserve the uniqueness of God's revelatory and redemptive action in and through Christ. Historically, this close correlation breaks down because the actual words and deeds of Jesus cannot be historically reconstructed from documents which primarily express and convey faith in the God uniquely active in and through Christ. Religiously, this tacit equation too easily reduces God to the human values and concerns which may be unwittingly read back into historical reconstructions of the 'real' Jesus. For these reasons, Neo-orthodoxy treats the human existence of Jesus and the divine presence of God as two distinct and unconfused levels of one historical event. This redefinition of the classical formula of two 'natures' in terms of two 'histories' insures Christ's function in the life and thought of faith. Neo-orthodoxy joins Liberalism in rejecting the idea of Jesus Christ as God's one-and-only revelatory and redemptive incarnation. God is knowable and active in all concrete events and persons. But, again more like Orthodoxy, Neo-orthodoxy finds sinful men completely incapable of encountering or understanding

180

God in their own experience apart from supernatural power and illumination. Such supernatural grace and truth is given anew each time God confronts man. But the ground and the norm of what God is doing and saying in any present moment is his past Deed and Word. God seeks and secures man's reconciliation with the same sovereign freedom, suffering love and transforming power exhibited in and through the life, death and resurrection of Jesus Christ. Thus, Jesus Christ remains the one and only mediator of God's true reality and existence's authentic meaning.

PAUL M. VAN BUREN

The language of Christology is appropriate only to one who himself has discerned what Christians discern, for whom Jesus has become the occasion for a new discernment which has led to a commitment involving his whole perspective. We can summarize by saying that the language of Christology is language about Jesus of Nazareth on the part of those for whom he has been the occasion and remains the definition of their "blik." *(The Secular Meaning Of The Gospel, p. 91).*

The history of Jesus remains a piece of quite ordinary history, open to ordinary historical investigation. It does not become a sort of super-history by virtue of the perspective to which it has given rise, nor is the freedom of Jesus beyond all historical comprehension because it has proved to be contagious for the Christian. However closely they may be bound together, both logically and historically, a perspective is a perspective and history is history. In other words, the history of Jesus remains a piece of human history, and the event of Easter and succeeding occasions of conversion are discernment situations. When an ordinary situation becomes an occasion of discernment for a man, the change lies in the viewing, in what now becomes clear, in the light breaking; it is not an empirical change in the situation. All the physical facts remain the same, even if they can never seem quite the same to him again. This is not a metaphysical paradox; it is the expression of a change in a way of seeing. The change is logically and historically significant, however: it marks the difference between faith and unbelief.   *(The Secular Meaning Of The Gospel, p. 167)*

Jesus of Nazareth was a singular individual. His characteristics seem to have impressed his followers so that he stands out as a remarkably free man in the records of remembered parable,

181

saying, or incident, and in the way in which the early Christian community spoke of him. In describing him with the word "free," however, we would allow that word to take on new connotations from the glimpses of him in the fragments which make up the record. The evangelists themselves indicate this freedom in many ways: they speak, for example, of his "authority," or they point to his openness to friend and foe. Although he is presented as a faithful son of his parents, he is also shown to be free from familial claims. He followed the religious rites and obligations of his people, but he also felt free to disregard them. In miracle stories he is even presented mythologically as being free from the limitations of natural forces.   *(The Secular Meaning Of The Gospel, pp. 121-2).*

If we would define Jesus by his freedom, however, we must emphasize its positive character. He was free from anxiety and the need to establish his own identity, but he was above all free for his neighbor. This was the characteristic which Bonhoeffer, in his last writings, found so impressive. He was free to be compassionate for his neighbor, whoever that neighbor might be, without regard to himself. The tradition reveals the impress of this characteristic with its frequent references to his compassion for those who suffered, his openness to all whom he met, his willingness to associate with those whose company was avoided by respectable people. He was reported to have taught that the greatness of freedom lies in service, and his own freedom was characterized by humble service to others.   *(The Secular Meaning Of The Gospel, p. 123).*

A historical knowledge of Jesus, however, is not faith...When one looks at the sum of Jesus' work with his disciples, considering him either as teacher or example, it must be said that he was a failure. The historical Jesus did not elicit faith, in the sense of the response of the early Christian. His freedom was his alone; at best it was shared only in the most fragmentary and fleeting way by a very few men at certain times. We conclude, therefore, that Christian faith was not, and is not, a direct result of seeing Jesus as a historical figure.   *(The Secular Meaning Of The Gospel, pp. 124-5).*

We arrive at a seeming contradiction when we try to investigate the relationship of faith (or the believer himself) to the historical Jesus. This paradox is a consequence of the event of Easter, which stands between Jesus and the believer, as indeed it stands between Jesus and the New Testament witness to him. If our language poses peculiar problems at this point, they arise from the peculiar character of the Easter event. The fact that what happened on Easter was reported always as a radically new event and yet as concerning Jesus of Nazareth indicates the two sides of an apparent paradox: faith is not based simply on a picture of the historical Jesus, but the historical Jesus is indispensable for faith. In order to achieve greater clarity here, we must turn to the event of Easter and the peculiar problems of the language which was used to speak of what happened.   *(The Secular Meaning Of The Gospel, p. 126).*

Easter faith was a new perspective upon life arising out of a situation of discernment focused on the history of Jesus. The peculiar relationship of this discernment to that history was determined by the peculiar experience which the disciples had on Easter. This was an experience of seeing Jesus in a new way and sharing in the freedom which had been his. One might convey better the tone of the disciples' words if one said that on Easter they found that Jesus had a new power which he had not had, or had not exercised, before: the power to awaken freedom also in them. Bonhoeffer's words are suggestive in this connection: "The experience of transcendence is Jesus' being-for-others. His omnipotence, omniscience and omnipresence arise solely out of his freedom from self, out of his freedom to be for the others even unto death." What happened to the disciples on Easter was that they came to share in this freedom to be for the others. *(The Secular Meaning Of The Gospel, p. 132).*

We might say that, on Easter, the freedom of Jesus began to be *contagious.* The word is used with care. It suffers somewhat from a biological connotation, but we also use it in a figurative way: "He has a contagious smile." In a crowd of people, fear can be "contagious" and produce panic. A child's laugh can be "contagious." It is in this figurative sense that we say that Jesus' freedom from himself and freedom to be for others become contagious on Easter. It carries the sense of our "catching" something from another person, not by our choice, but as something which happens to us.   *(The Secular Meaning Of The Gospel, p. 133).*

There is no empirical ground, however, for the Christian's saying that something of this sort could not happen to a disciple of Socrates. Reading the history of Socrates might conceivably have a liberating effect on a person, who might say that he shared in the freedom of the philosopher. If this were to happen, the Socratic's freedom, presumably, would be defined by the peculiar character

183

of Socrates' freedom. He would acknowledge Socrates as his norm. He would be "in Socrates," let us say, not "in Christ." Perhaps the Socratic, like the Christian, would claim that his was the only valid norm. *(The Secular Meaning Of The Gospel, p. 138-9).*

Jesus of Nazareth may be distinguished, however, from other men who might have a liberating effect upon men. We must grant a "family resemblance" between the language with which we speak of Jesus and the language used to speak of other free men, of course, in order to be able to describe him at all. Nevertheless, we may use a number of the same words in describing two men without denying that the men are actually quite different. When we compare Socrates as portrayed in Plato's *Dialogues,* for example, and Jesus as portrayed in the Gospels, we may say that both men were "free," but we can also see subtle differences. Two different words for "love," *philia* (the attraction of like to like) and *agape* (a love which makes no distinctions and seeks no return on its investment), may serve to indicate something of the difference which we detect between the two descriptions. *(The Secular Meaning Of The Gospel, p. 138).*

WILLIAM HAMILTON

Not all of the radical theologians "dig" Jesus and Christology, but all are aware that some means must be found to stake out our claim to be Christians. Attention to Jesus does this for me. I insist that the time of the death of God is also the time of obedience to Jesus. This entails a claim that the New Testament Jesus can in fact be known, that a figure of sufficient clarity is available to us so that discipleship to him—to his life, his words and his death—is a possible center for Christian faith and life. The Christian is defined, therefore, as the man bound to Jesus, obedient to him and obedient as he was obedient...

At this point, the most pressing question that can be raised against the radical is: "Why have you chosen Jesus as the object of your obedience? Is there some special reason it is he and not Albert Camus, Martin Luther King, or Francis of Assisi? May it not be that radical theology is in fact not theology and not even Christian but at the most a thinly Christianized humanism of a fairly banal variety, and that you have put Jesus in the center of things merely to obscure this fact?"

This question has been put to me—by both friendly and

unfriendly critics. I do not believe the implied charge to be true though I can fully understand how an unfinished theological vision, like that of the radical theology, leaves itself open to this kind of attack. In any case, the question "Why Jesus?" is an important one, and it is not easy to answer. An answer based on the Christian doctrine of revelation is no longer available: "I take Jesus Christ as the center of my understanding both of God and of man because God has made himself known to me, apart from my deserving, wholly in the event of his son." Both this classical doctrine and its more modern confessional version ("the biblical story and my own life story are part of a single story, and in telling the ancient story as part of my own story, I participate in the act of giving God his true name") stand for just that theological world I have had to bid farewell to. Must I then give my answer in purely vocational terms? "I have chosen Jesus because I am called [by whom?] to serve the church by preparing men for the Christian ministry, and therefore I point to Jesus because it is to him that my students must be directed." No, this says too little, just as the doctrine of revelation says too much. Jesus is the one to whom I repair, the one before whom I stand, the one whose way with others is also to be my way because there is something there, in his words, his life, his way with others, his death, that I do not find elsewhere. I am drawn, and I have given my allegiance. There may be powerful teachings elsewhere, more impressive and moving deaths. Yet I have chosen him and my choice is not arbitrary nor is it anxiously made to avert the atheist label. It is a free choice, freely made. ("The Shape of a Radical Theology," p. 1221).

Question: I would have thought you would be more embarrassed than you seem to be about the fact that you say very nice things about Jesus, even make a great deal of him, while at the same time you say no to what was one of his main emphases, the need for absolute trust in God the Father. Can you really maintain a loyalty to Jesus without a loyalty to God?

This is, from my point of view, the most important theological question that can be asked of us. Professor Altizer solves the problem more readily than I by his apocalyptic definition of Jesus, more Blakean than Biblical, as the one who is born out of God's death. I am not yet ready to give up *sola scriptura,* and thus my answer must be more complex and tentative...

I think I would begin my own answer in this way. Early in the nineteenth century, we had to face, under the early impact of historical criticism, both facts that Jesus was firmly committed to demon possession as the meaning of mental and physical illness, and that we were not so committed and needn't be. But obedience to Jesus was not destroyed. Later, at the time of Darwinian controversy, we had to face another instance of Jesus' full participation in the thought forms of his day—the three-story, primitive cosmology. But we do not go to the Bible for science, we were rightly told, and obedience to Jesus was not hurt. At the close of the century we had to face an even more disturbing fact—the fact brought before us by Weiss and Schweitzer that Jesus was completely committed to the apocalyptic views of the Judaism of his day, and that he believed in some sense or other, in an end to the world and in a "coming" associated with that end. He proved, we said carefully, to be wrong about these matters, but not even his commitment to this eschatology proved to be an obstacle to a full Christian loyalty to him. In *Jesus and His Coming,* to be sure, the Bishop of Woolwich tries to exonerate Jesus from these eschatological views, but I do not think his brilliant argument finally convinces. Schweitzer himself showed us one way in which the eschatology, though literally wrong, guaranteed Jesus' eternal relevance to all ages; Bultmann showed us another, according to which the literal forms of the eschatological myths could be translated into tones of moral urgency and radical demand. My point is already made. If Jesus' demonology and cosmology and eschatology were taken as first-century views, appropriate then, not so now, needing re-interpretation and understanding but not literal assent, what is inherently different about Jesus' *theology?* Is there any inherent reason why Jesus' dependence on God as Father—admittedly a central idea to him (but surely no more central than his eschatological expectations)—should not prove to be one of these ideas, central to an understanding of him and his work, but not necessarily transferrable to us? We would have to be able to say what has happened in our time to make that idea, so central to the first century, dispensable today, just as we can now say why the demon theory of disease is inadequate for our medical understanding. I think we can say what has happened, and that is the meaning of the event "death of God" as in part at least an event that is just now taking place in our own time. ("Questions and Answers on the Radical Theology," pp. 221-3).

In Christology, the theologian is sometimes inclined to suspect that Jesus Christ is best understood as neither the object nor the ground of faith, neither as person, event or community, but simply as a place to be, a standpoint. That place is, of course, alongside the neighbor, being for him. This may be the meaning of Jesus' true humanity and it may even be the meaning of his divinity, and thus of divinity itself. ("Thursday's Child," p. 92).

GABRIEL VAHANIAN

Without God no Jesus: this is the corollary of the New Testament's without Jesus no God. *(No Other God, p. xii).*

As Christianity's bequest to modern man, the death of God represents that cultural phenomenon in terms of which a transmutation in the historical texture of our existence makes it impossible for us, from where we stand, to go back to Jesus.

Without God, all that's left is Jesus, a historical figure whose life and work, although it could perhaps be regarded as the life and work of a "man for others," does not adequately account for what the tradition confessed in proclaiming him as the Christ, namely, that in and through this historical figure the God who can reveal himself is only the God who is "God for man." That this binds the reality of God to that of man need not be contested. It also signifies that the human reality is not exhausted by the contingencies of history, any more than it is by the caprices of nature. "If I do not believe in God," Feuerbach argues, "there is no God for me." From a Christian point of view, it would be more appropriate to say: If I do not believe in God, there is no Christ for me; and Jesus becomes a mere historical character, sad and glorious, fierce but impotent, an epitaph of the human consciousness. Indeed, an evanescent Christology can only expose an obsolescent Christianity. *(No Other God, pp. 27-28).*

In the biblical conception of God, the reality of God is ever independent of the cultural frame in which it may be grasped. In other words, our conception of God need not confirm with the biblical concept, externally. The Bible speaks of God in terms of a world view to which it also adheres in other respects. It is consistent with itself. Surely, the least that must be expected from contemporary Christianity is an equal amount of self-consistency. Likewise, the biblical understanding of Christ's person and his work is dependent upon the contemporaneous world view and its cultural setting. The events of Christ's life make this dependence quite plain. But it is equally plain that the presentness of God to man (that is, the incarnation) and the possibility of authentic existence, except conceptually, do not ultimately depend upon man's world view, whether it is mythological or scientific. *(Wait*

Without Idols, p. xii).

In the Gospel of John, the incarnation means the constantly unique event through which destiny is improvised once and for all, and not its objectification. Human existence, because it can never be rehearsed, is not an institution but a necessary improvisation of destiny. Admitedly, institutions too are born of the necessity of improvisation, but they freeze it, they codify it, just as dogmas and religion betray faith by codifying the acts of faith—through which they are improvised—forgetting that existence itself, as a spontaneous act of faith, is an impertinent improvisation on the theme of God's reality, of the presentness of God. *(Wait Without Idols, p. 230).*

"God by himself is not God," writes Barth in *The Word of God and the Word of Man,* "He might be something else. Only the God who reveals himself is God." By himself Jesus is not Christ. Nor, in this connection, is the structure of the Apostles' Creed without significance: Christology forms only the second article, not the first, even though, as the New Testament holds, one must believe in Jesus Christ in order to believe in God. The Christ-event brings to an end man's imaginations about God: "The true light that enlightens every man was coming into the world. He was in the world, and the world was made through him, yet the world knew him not" (John 1/9-11).

Indeed, in the Christ-event God conceals, even forsakes, his divinity. That is, he does not act as a god should according to man's imagination. He does not die; but the Christ-event signifies that the debilities and limitations of the human condition can become the arena of faith, "the victory that overcomes the world" (I John 5/4). Ever since Caesarea of Philippi, if it is not possible to say God without Christ, neither is it possible to confess Christ without God: "Now when Jesus came into the district of Caesarea Philippi, he asked his disciples, 'Who do men say that the Son of man is?' And they said, 'Some say John the Baptist, others say Elijah, and others Jeremiah or one of the prophets.' He said to them, 'But who do you say that I am?' Simon Peter replied,'You are the Christ, the Son of the living God!' And Jesus answered him, 'Blessed are you, Simon Bar-Jona! for flesh and blood has not revealed this to you, but my Father who is in heaven.' "(Matt. 16/13-17).

As flesh and blood alone Jesus is only an ideal man, scarcely the symbol of authority, much less that of faith (Matt. 21/23-27). And in spite of Peter's denials and the cowardice of the other disciples, the story of the passion shows precisely how hopelessly they were committed to Jesus as flesh and blood. Had they not previously idolized Jesus, perhaps they would not have felt forsaken. Indeed all our gods are idols, and above all the god that dies. "Why do you call me good? No one is good but God alone" (Luke 19/18).

Without God, Jesus becomes at best an idol, and ceases to be a man as the title Christ itself implies, or as the early Christological definitions painfully attempted to bring to light, so that not even the attribution of divinity to Christ circumvented his human condition as Jesus. Do we not misunderstand the Fathers of the Church when we fail to realize that a good deal of their talk about the divinity of Christ had to do with the "humanity" of God? Theology, as Vinet says, has more often than not dealt with the tendency to diminish Deity rather than humanity. When all is said and done, one might yet come to the view that on the whole theology has not been concerned so much with a cold speculative concept of God as with the concrete human context in terms of which not only could God be believed in, but without which he could not be believed in. When Isaiah says, "I, I am the Lord and beside me there is no savior. I declared and saved and proclaimed, when there was no strange god among you; and you are my witnesses" (Isa. 43/11-12), Rabbi Simon Bar-Yochai interprets this in the following way: "If you are my witnesses I am God, and if you are not my witnesses I am, so to speak, no longer God."

If there are no witnesses, then there is no God. Or as Paul puts it after listing all the witnesses to the risen Christ: "If the dead are not raised, then Christ has not been raised. If Christ has not been raised your faith is futile..." (I Cor. 15/16-17). The Christ-event, rather than culminating in the death of God, thus implies exactly the opposite: the reality of "the living God," as Peter puts it. And in the cross, it is not God who is being edged out of the world, as Bonhoeffer contends, but our idols. For "there is no other name under heaven given among men by which we must be saved" (Acts 4/12).

Thus, rather than opening the way to Jesus, the death of God obstructs it, hermetically. If there are no witnesses to God, then "Christ has not been raised" and "faith is in vain"(I Cor. 15/14), and Jesus is a miscarriage of history. Rather than liberating Jesus from mythological and supernatural fetters, the death of God delivers him up to historical anonymity and alienates him from us, irretrievably. *(No Other God, pp. 28-30).*

I have said that if, for the New Testament, one must believe in Christ if one wants to believe in God, the problem we are faced with today is that without God we have no access to Jesus. I have also said that without witnesses and their works (i.e., man's given historical situation, his involvement in his world as an expression of his commitment to God) there is no God, at least none of whom the Christ-event is the empirical reality. Put differently this means that in order to speak about God one must speak about man. To do so, however, one must ultimately speak about Jesus Christ—that is to say, about God: exactly for this reason, however, nothing valid is said about Jesus (and, consequently, about God) if what is said overlooks the fact that Jesus was a man. The Johannine idea of the word become flesh stresses this fact as does Paul's Christological hymn of Philippians 2, not to mention the gospel passages where Jesus acts like a human being.

In biblical thought human existence is viewed both as nature and as history, as flesh and as spirit, as an empirical, physiological, or biological datum and as spiritual or eschatological reality, meaning thereby that man as spirit coincides with, and is identified *as* but not *with*, man as nature.

Man is created in the image of God. That this image is not a natural quality of man is evidenced by, or brings to light, the fact that even *qua* nature, let alone *qua* history, human existence is other than the sum total of its contradictions and achievements. And when one considers man *qua* history, it becomes all the more clear that this image is not so much a physical likeness as the verifying or authenticating act by which eschatological existence does not shun but assumes empirical existence in its totality. Indeed, man is created in the image of God only in the sense that God remains imageless.

Even in and through Christ, God remains imageless: Jesus is not a God, and Christ as God's empirical reality is so only from the standpoint of faith. And if Jesus said that "I and the Father are one" he did not, as Paul declares, "think to snatch at equality with God, but made himself nothing, assuming the nature of a slave. Bearing the human likeness, revealed in human shape, he humbled himself, and in obedience accepted even death—death on a cross." (Phil. 2/6-8)

From this we learn two things:

1) The human nature of Jesus is not the appearance of some divine nature; the divine nature manifests itself in no other way

than through the human nature. This is the same as saying that in Christ the word became flesh. This also means, however, that the human is the only access to the divine. To be human is to have access to the divine or, rather, to be accessible to the divine. Even death does not preclude that, much less the death of God if one does not hypostasize it into an article of "faith."

2) Jesus is not some kind of substitute for God. Not only the traditional doctrine of the two natures but also that of the Trinity stakes the otherness of God on man's being such that eschatological existence does not remove him from the arena of natural existence. Otherwise, faith in God would become belief that God is this or that, here or there, a thing, an object—a god that dies. This precisely is the meaning of the Trinity and, in particular, of the procession of the Spirit from both the Father and the Son. The Trinity thus ceases to be a concept or, at least, a glorified metaphor, and becomes the expression of the plain fact that no man can believe in God except in a given concrete situation and that faith in God is no faith at all if man's concrete situation is thereby obliterated. Indeed, faith is the price man must pay if he thus wants to assume his contingency.

It becomes quite clear at this point that from the point of view of the tradition, the doctrine of the Trinity itself was not some kind of esoteric description of the nature of God *per se* but the theonomous and iconoclastic expression of the conviction that eschatological existence must body forth into historical existence. The Trinity, so to speak, was no short-cut to God through the deification of the man Jesus—much less was it, therefore, a short-cut to Jesus. This amounts to saying that one cannot talk about Jesus without first talking about God. Nor can one do this without being asserted at the same time as a man of a given situation.

On this basis, any speech about God is also an iconoclastic speech about man, about his secularism as well as his religiosity. Indeed, human speech itself calls for just that iconoclastic understanding of the human experience.   *(No Other God, pp. 32-4).*

HARVEY COX

God comes to us today in events of social change, in what theologians have often called *history*, what we call *politics*. But events of social change need not mean upheavals and revolutions. The events of everyday life are also events of social change. The smallest unit of society is two, and the relationship between two people never remains just the same. God meets us there, too. He meets us not just in the freedom revolution in America but also in a client, a customer, a patient, a co-worker.

But how? God is free and hidden. He cannot be expected to appear when we designate the place and time. This means that God is neither close nor far *as such*, but is able to be present in a situation without identifying with it.   *(The Secular City, pp. 228-9).*

This biblical God's hiddenness stands at the very center of the doctrine of God. It is so commanding that Pascal was echoing its intention when he said, "Every religion which does not affirm that God is hidden is not true." It means that God discloses himself at those places and in those ways he chooses and not as man would want. And he always discloses himself as one who is at once different *from* man, unconditonally *for* man, and entirely unavailable for coercion and manipulation *by* man. *(The Secular City, pp. 225-6).*

But what part does Jesus of Nazareth play in this hiddenness of God? If Jesus were a theophany, an "appearance of God" in the customary religious sense, then in Jesus the hiddenness of God would be abrogated. But this is not the case. God does not "appear" in Jesus; He hides himself in the stable of human history. He hides himself in the sense that we have just mentioned,showing that He is not anything like what religions have wanted or expected from their gods. In Jesus God does not stop being hidden; rather He meets man as the unavailable "other." He does not "appear" but shows man that He acts, in His hiddenness, in human history.

No wonder the religious complusion of man, whether in its mythological or in its metaphysical form has never been too happy with Jesus. In Jesus, God refuses to fulfill either tribal expectations or philosophical quandaries. As Bonhoeffer says, in Jesus God is teaching man to get along without Him to become mature, freed from infantile dependencies, fully human. Hence the act of God in Jesus offers slim pickings for those in hope of clues for the erection of some final system. God will not be used in this way. He will not perpetuate human adolescence, but insists on turning the world over to man as his responsibility. *(The Secular City, p. 226).*

Jesus of Nazareth is God's Word to man. In him we find perhaps the only known person in whom word and deed always went together, for Jesus was as good as his word. He said, "I am the way, and the truth, and the life." In Jesus there was none of the schism between saying and doing which is in every one of us. As Rudolf Bultmann, the German theologian, pointed out, whatever Jesus says is a doing and whatever he does is a speaking, for his actions speak and his words act. So God has no wordy sermon for man, no choice aphorisms or religious maxims; he has but one Word, a life lived, Jesus of Nazareth. This is what we mean when we speak about the Word of God. *(God's Revolution And Man's Responsibility, p. 57)*.

We have misconstrued what the Word really is. When we look through the Bible, however, to discover what it says about the Word (*Dabar* in the Old Testament or *Logos* in the New Testament), then our whole understanding about words and talk is suddenly called into question. God's Word is *not* talk; God's Word is *action*, and this fact is very confusing to us.

When God talks, something happens. He *does* something. He speaks and the world is created. His Word brings light to the darkness. His Word judges, heals, cuts asunder. God's Word in the Bible is, in fact, not phrases and syllables, but ultimately it is hands and feet. In the final analysis God's Word for man is Jesus of Nazareth. He *is* God's Word. *(God's Revolution and Man's Responsibility, p. 54)*.

One could view the whole life of Jesus from first to last as a single continuing exploit in breaking down the walls that separate the people. The life of Jesus was a constant series of risky exploits, jumping over and short-circuiting the barriers which men erect between themselves. He broke down the walls between Jews and non-Jews, between the self-righteous Pharisees and the morally cynical publicans. His whole career presents a staggering series of calculated attempts to destroy the fictions that separate people from one another. Pursuing this indiscreet purpose, he shattered social conventions, trespassed on moral codes, and defied religious tradition. He simply refused to allow racial, class, or religious demarcations to hamper his movement, insisting that somehow in his own person all of these things were now abolished. *(God's Revolution and Man's Responsibility, p. 63)*.

Jesus Christ is the one who frees us, the Bible keeps saying. He is the one who makes us free. This idea is hard for us to understand today because we believe that, if anybody can make us free from anything, it is we ourselves. How, then, can we say that God in Jesus of Nazareth has made us free? What is this freedom all about?

Freedom, in the Bible, is first of all freedom for maturity. The opposite of bondage, as the Bible sees it, is not independence but responsibility. Freedom is the willingness to exercise responsible power and control over things which normally dominate us. The Bible talks about our liberation *from* and *for, from* bondage and *for* service. *(God's Revolution And Man's Responsibility, pp. 64-5).*

God's action, which goes on all the time but was made known in Jesus of Nazareth, is to call man to freedom *from* the powers and principalities, and to summon him at the same time to responsibility *over* and *for* them. *(The Secular City, p. 111).*

Here, perhaps, is the real scandal of the gospel, the thing that is really hard to understand and hard to believe: that in Jesus of Nazareth God has made us free from fate, from all the forces which distort and pervert human life. God's program in history is to "defatalize" human life, to put man's life into man's own hands and to give him the terrible responsibility of running it. *(God's Revolution and Man's Responsibility, p. 67).*

A biblical theology begins by viewing all of history since the coming of Jesus as the beginning of a new regime. But the new regime takes shape in the midst of the old. Consequently, a crisis of choice is presented which eventually confronts every man who hears about the new reality. In this respect it is essential to notice that Christian theology, unlike the Old Testament vision, claims that the seizure of power *has* already taken place. The revolutionary deliverer *has* come and *has* won the decisive battle. For this reason, all of human history takes place between the achievement of *de facto* power and the appearance of visible *de jure* authority. History does not take place between the black noon of Good Friday and the bright dawn of Easter. It takes place, rather, between Easter Day and the Last Day. History is a permanent crisis in which the defeated old regime still claims power while the victorious new regime has still not appeared publicly on the balcony. The New Testament looks forward not to the victory of Jesus, since that has already been won, but to the day when "every knee shall bow and every tongue confess" that Jesus is victor.

Exodus and Easter remain the two foci of biblical faith, the basis on which a theology of the church must be developed. The Exodus is the event which sets forth "what God is doing in history." He is seen to be liberating people from bondage, releasing them from political, cultural, and economic captivity, providing them with the occasion to forge in the wilderness a new symbol system, a new set of values, and a new national identity. Easter means that the same activity goes on today, and that where such liberating activity occurs, the same Yahweh of Hosts is at work. Both Exodus and Easter are caught up in the inclusive symbol of the Kingdom, the realization of the liberating rule of God. In our terms, God's action today, through secularization and urbanization, puts man in an unavoidable crisis. He must take responsibility in and for the city of man or become once again a slave to dehumanizaing powers.   *(The Secular City, pp. 113-4)*

The Kingdom of God, concentrated in the life of Jesus of Nazareth, remains the fullest possible disclosure of the partnership of God and man in history. Our struggle for the shaping of the secular city represents the way we respond faithfully to this reality in our own times.   *(The Secular City, p. 97).*

THOMAS J. J. ALTIZER

To confess that God has died in Christ is to believe that God Himself has truly, actually, finally and completely entered the world in Christ; that He has fully become embodied in time and space in Christ; that He has emptied Himself, as I said, of His own original plenitude. Therein He darkens and empties the transcendent realm, and releases the fulness of His own life and power into the world as a source of life and redemption so that finally, as Paul says, God may become all in all. So, to confess the death of God is simply a means of confessing the life, and indeed the redemptive life, of Jesus Christ.   *(The Altizer-Montgomery Dialogue, pp. 10-11).*

Why Jesus? Christianity has always been confronted from both within and from without by the primary question of why it makes such an absolute claim for the particular person of Jesus. At no time has this question become so compelling as it has today, as Christianity is attempting to move beyond its past historical expression to a universal form, and is inevitably being forced to face the full scandal of its own particularity. What is the intrinsic relationship between the Christian faith and Jesus of Nazareth? Can and should the Christian Word be divorced from the person of Jesus?   *(The Gospel Of Christian Atheism, p. 55).*

It's my conviction that we must realize that Christ is in no sense to be identified solely with Jesus of Nazareth, and despite scriptural statements to this effect, Christ is not to be thought of as being literally the same yesterday, today, and forever. Rather,

Christ is the embodiment of a forward-moving process, of a process which reverses all things making possible, in a certain sense, the renewal of all things and the coming together of all things into a new totality, a new life, a new energy, a new joy. *(The Altizer-Montgomery Dialogue, p. 14)*.

The problem that the theologian refuses to confront is the inevitable incompatability between the primordial Christian God and an incarnate or kenotic Christ, a refusal arising from a new epiphany of the primordial God-head in Christian history. Even as Christianity almost immediately came to worship Christ in the image of the Hellenistic mystery gods, the Christ of Christianity has almost invariably appeared in the form of a high god or heavenly deity which is found almost everywhere in the history of religions. Certainly the Christ who is fully God is not unique to Christianity, except insofar as he bears some sign of a concrete descent of God into human flesh. Such a descent cannot be truly meaningful unless it is understood as a real movement of God himself, a movement which is final and irrevocable, but which continues to occur wherever there is history and life. So long as the Christian God continues to be known as transcendent and impassive, or as a primordial deity who is unaffected by the processes of time and history, he cannot appear in his uniquely Christian form as the Incarnate Word and the kenotic Christ. Thus the radical Christian reverses the orthodox confession, affirming that "God is Jesus" (Blake's Laocoön engraving), rather than "Jesus is God." Before the Incarnation can be understood as a decisive and real event, it must be known as effecting a real change or movement in God himself: God becomes incarnate in the Word, and he becomes fully incarnate, thereby ceasing to exist or to be present in his primordial form. To say that "God is Jesus" is to say that God has become the Incarnate Word, he has abandoned or negated his transcendent form. *(The Gospel Of Christian Atheism, p. 43-4)*.

If we approach the meaning of the Incarnation by this means then we can see that a negation or emptying of God's transcendent manifestation makes possible a total realization and fulfilment of His immanent presence. It is precisely by negating Himself as transcendent Lord that God is becoming all in all, and only as that negation is embodied in history can the cosmos fulfil its movement towards an apocalyptic end. Yet in what sense can we speak of such a movement of God as a self-negation or movement through death? The Christian does so because he is bound in faith to the Christ who fulfils the movement of Incarnation in Crucifixion, in a passage through the actuality and finality of death. Unless the death of Christ is finally thought to be a façade or a Gnostic mirage, it cannot be thought of as a mere transition to a higher realm, or symbolically linked with an ascent into a transcendent realm or heaven. Should not the Christian more truly and more consistently come to understand the Crucifixion as a final negation of that transcendence which is pure transcendence?

Thereby God himself might be understood as freeing Himself from every dichotomy or opposition between His transcendence and His immanence, so as to make possible the apocalyptic triumph of a transcendence which would finally appear and be real as total immanence. Thus if the pure or radical transcendence of God is to be understood as passing into a pure or apocalyptic immanence, then the symbol and the reality of death must be evoked to speak of the finality of God's movement, and the symbol of the death of God will accordingly become a portal through which to pass to realize the meaning of God's evolutionary and apocalyptic movement. By this means we can also see that to limit the meaning of God to that meaning which is present in Christ is to accept God's self-negation in Christ, and to pass with Christ through the death of God's transcendence, so that the apostolic words may be fulfilled which promise that God will be all in all. ("Catholic Philosophy and the Death of God," p. 280).

Yet a danger lies here before us, one of understanding God's self-annihilation or self-negation as a simple or literal negation of His transcendence, and hence an understanding of God's transcendence as a purely negative or demonic pole or potency of the Godhead. This danger can be avoided if we can but realize that God's self-negation is consummated or fulfilled in the movement or transformation of transcendence itself into immanence. Once we come to understand God as moving or evolving through an organic and evolutionary process then we can come to a realization that God Himself dies to His previous epiphanies or manifestations, with the result that He progressively ceases to be truly present in His previous forms, even if those forms remain embedded in human memory and tradition. We must not, therefore, confine the death of God to a particular point or occasion, not even Calvary, for it issues out of the whole movement of revelation in the Old Testament, and it is successively and ever more comprehensively embodied in all of that history which is a consequence of Jesus Christ. As a result of that movement of history, transcendence has been manifest in

197

ever darker, emptier, and more alien forms, until, with the advent of the modern world, transcendence has been real in consciousness and experience only to the extent that it is totally empty or alien. When Christian theology speaks of the death of God it is taking with full seriousness the revolutionary movement of our history, is acknowledging that it is the movement of history and consciousness which has made the name of God unspeakable as a source of energy and life, and is attempting to understand the death of God as a consequence of God's own act of self-negation in Jesus Christ. ("Catholic Philosophy and the Death of God," p. 281).

In the Incarnation, God in Christ enters the world and *remains* in the world. There isn't a reversal process where Christ returns to heaven...We can most truly understand Christ insofar as we understand the uniqueness of the Incarnation, and the core of uniqueness does lie in the Incarnation, which embodies an actual divine movement from spirit to flesh, so that God actually becomes embodied in flesh. He becomes actualized in the world and in time. That's unique to Christianity. You don't find it elsewhere.

The significance is that we know that Christ is *not* present in heaven, that we don't meet Him by *isolating* ourself from the world or by seeking Him in a holy place or by turning away from the brute reality of life and existence. On the contrary, Christ is present and the very center—the brute, gut center—of existence in all its profane, concrete reality. We meet Christ in those moments which are most actual, most real, most immediate—not in those moments which are seemingly most holy, most isolated, or most heavenly. ("Can We manage Without God?" p. 62).

We cannot truly pronounce the name of Jesus if we isolate his name from the contingency and the actuality of our concrete existence in the world. It was the religious movement away from this immediate actuality that constituted an important dimension of Christianity's betrayal of Jesus, for when Jesus appears as an eternal and cosmic Word, he loses the immediacy of his original appearance. Yet it is no less true that to identify Jesus wholly with a particular and isolated person or event of the past is to foreclose the possibility of his present life or forward movement. Indeed, we can know Jesus as the ancient Jesus of Nazareth only insofar as we are closed to his contemporary presence. Not only is this ancient Jesus alien and lifeless, but precisely for this reason he can be manifest in a religious form only as an abstract and distant Word

198

or as an epiphany of a primordial Innocence. In either case we find a reversal of concrete experience, a flight from the actuality of consciousness and the body, a regression to a primordial moment of time. The uniquely Christian Jesus is the Jesus who is fully manifest in a present and actual moment of time. *(The Gospel Of Christian Atheism, pp. 57-58).*

By opening ourselves to the immediate actuality of the moment before us, we can know the Jesus who is present in the fullness of time itself, even if that time should prove to be a negation or reversal of the past event of Jesus of Nazareth. *(The Gospel Of Christian Atheism, p. 61).*

We might even say that Jesus is the Christian name of the totality of Experience, a new actuality created by the abolition of the primordial Being, whose death inaugurates a new humanity liberated from all transcendent norms and meaning. But with this new actuality there also comes a terrible darkness resulting from the obliteration of all inherited and established forms of judgment and understanding. So revolutionary was this acutality that it was not until after eighteen centuries that it penetrated the historical body of Christendom, first appearing in an anti-Christian form, and then finally eroding the foundations of the whole Western historical tradition. Yet the very darkness brought on by the historical actualization of the death of God makes possible the movement of the Incarnate Word into the universal body of humanity....

Jesus cannot appear as the "Universal Humanity" until the transcendent realm has been emptied and darkened; with the eclipse of that realm no primordial archetype or paradigm remains present in consciousness, since humanity evolves to a fully universal and historical form only with the disappearance of its ground in a Being that is confined to a primordial or particular moment of time . . . Despite the fact that modern Christian theologians have long lauded Christianity as a historical faith, they have for the most part conceived of salvation history in priestly terms as an isolated but absolute and once-for-all series of events of the past; or, insofar as they have identified the moment of salvation or "decision" with a contemporary historicity, they have conceived of historicity as a purely inward or subjective realm, existing totally apart from the actuality and the contingency of the concrete processes of history. If only in reaction against the "anti-Christian" Hegel, few if any theologians have been able to accept and affirm the actual process of history as salvation history.

Indeed, the theologian must inevitably remain closed to the redemptive possibilities of our history unless he is prepared to affirm the death of God as an epiphany of Christ.

True, our history has progressively but decisively dissolved every sign and image of the Christ who was once present in the Church. Yet the name of Jesus can continue to embody the innermost reality of faith if it can make concretely present the total union of God and man, even if that union should finally obliterate the God of a former faith. As the God who *is* Jesus becomes ever more deeply incarnate in the body of humanity, he loses every semblance of his former visage, until he appears wherever there is energy and life. Jesus is the name of the love of God, a love that eternally dies for man. Truly to pronounce his name—and for the radical Christian the names of Jesus and God are ultimately one—is to participate in God's death in Jesus and thereby to know the God who *is* Jesus as the expanding or forward-moving process who is becoming "One Man." *(The Gospel Of Christian Atheism, pp. 73-5).*

JOHN A. T. ROBINSON

One of the things that presents a major stop in the mind for our generation is the *uniqueness* of Christ. Of course, this is nothing new. It is an integral part of the 'offence' of the Gospel. Men have always stumbled at the 'scandal of particularity'—and never more than in a society which is conditioned by all its historical and scientific training to see the particular as but one instance of the general. But I get the impression that it is being made peculiarly and unnecessarily difficult by being presented as an objective fact to be swallowed at the beginning of the search. Men have Christ set before them as what appears to them a unique *kind* of being—half God and half man, quite different from the rest of us—whom they simply have to accept as such as part of 'Christian doctrine'. But, starting from the inductive end, I can only *begin* with the statement that Christ is a perfectly ordinary human being ('very man' in traditional terms) who is *unique for me,* in the sense that in him 'all things cohere': he is the one who co-ordinates and vindicates for me all that I believe most deeply true, in the way that Mahommed or Buddha does not. I can say with the early Church, 'Jesus is Lord', or with Thomas, 'My Lord and my God'. And I can go on to spell that out in terms of the Creeds, that this is one who is the unique expression of God in human life ('the only begotten Son of the Father'). But I am more concerned that

200

people should be able to set their foot on the path (and feel accepted for doing so) than with whether they have reached the end of it (and feel rejected for not having done so).

This inductive approach to Christian doctrine is, I am convinced, a discipline which the Church has got to re-learn. It is not conceived out an any desire to water down the faith. It does not prescribe the ends negatively. But it does insist that the ends are only to be reached from the beginning—and the beginning for men today, as for the first disciples, is from Jesus as a completely human man— *whatever more they may be compelled to see in him.* Indeed, I suspect that for our generation, 'a completely human man' is a better translation of the Greek *teleios* than ' a perfect man.' For the Church has succeeded in presenting the sinless perfection of Christ in a way that has failed to convince modern, Darwinian, Freudian, man that he could have been *completely* human. And for that reason contemporary man is inclined, understandably, to dismiss him as a possible definition, let alone as the unique definition, of a genuinely human existence. *(The New Reformation? pp. 41-2).*

The traditional supranaturalistic way of describing the Incarnation almost inevitably suggests that Jesus was really God almighty walking about on earth, dressed up as a man. Jesus was not a man born and bred—he was God for a limited period taking part in a charade. He looked like a man, he talked like a man, he felt like a man, but underneath he was God dressed up—like Father Christmas. However guardedly it may be stated, the traditional view leaves the impression that God took a space-trip and arrived on this planet in the form of a man. Jesus was not really one of us; but through the miracle of the Virgin Birth he contrived to be born so as to appear one of us. Really he came from outside.

I am aware that this is a parody, and probably an offensive one, but I think it is perilously near the truth of what most people—and I would include myself— have been brought up to believe at Christmas time. Indeed, the very word 'incarnation' (which, of course, is not a Biblical term) almost inevitably suggests it. *(Honest To God, p. 66).*

The Liberals were entirely justified in the courage with which they were prepared to abandon the supranaturalistic scaffolding by which hitherto the whole structure had been supported. That house had to collapse, and they had the faith to see that Christianity need not collapse with it. Moreover, however inadequate the Liberal theology may now appear to us, it undoubtedly helped many to hold on to their faith at a time when otherwise they might have thrown it up completely. As the supranaturalistic scheme of things became incredible, a naturalistic theology was all that stood between an entire generation and abandoning the spirit and power of Jesus altogether. And the spirit and power was able in many cases to prove itself greater than the theology. Yet equally the theology has not sufficed to commend the spirit and power. Modern humanistic naturalism has found less and less need to speak of Jesus as in any sense 'divine'. The belief that we are at this point and in this person in touch with God has increasingly been left to the religious minority that can still accept the old mythology as physically or metaphysically true. *(Honest To God, pp. 69-70).*

In many popular presentations of Christianity the line is taken that whereas in Hinduism and other religions there are numerous references to incarnations and virgin births, the difference in Christianity is that the incarnation and virgin birth of Jesus *really happened:* they were historical. There is indeed here a very real difference between Christianity and other faiths, and hitherto this was an adequate enough way of describing it. But we are being forced today to disentangle myth and history much more carefully than to say simply that 'our' myth is historical. Of course, what is recorded in the New Testament is claiming to be history in a way that is never claimed by the Hindu scriptures. But to say that 'the Incarnation' or 'the Virgin Birth' were historical events is to beg the question. That the man Jesus was born is a statement of history. That 'God sent his only-begotten Son' (which is what is meant by calling the birth at Bethlehem 'the Incarnation') is a mythological statement —*not* in the sense that it is not true, but in the sense that it represents (in the picture-language of the supranaturalist world-view) the theological *significance* of the history. ("The Debate Continues," pp. 265-6).

There is a paradox running through all the Gospels that Jesus makes no claims for himself in his own right and at the same time makes the most tremendous claims about what God is doing through him and uniquely through him. Men's response to him *is* men's response to God: men's rejection of him *is* men's rejection of God. And the fourth Gospel merely highlights this paradox (it does not, as is usually said, present quite a different picture of the claims of Jesus) when it combines the saying that 'the Son can do nothing of his own accord, but only what he sees the Father doing' with the uncompromising assertion, 'No one comes to the

Father, but by me'. Jesus never claims to be God, personally: yet he always claims to bring God, completely.

This paradox is the point from which our reinterpretation of Christology must start. *(Honest To God, p. 73).*

It is in Jesus, and Jesus alone, that there is nothing of self to be seen, but solely the ultimate, unconditional love of God. It is as he emptied himself utterly of himself that he became the carrier of 'the name which is above every name', the revealer of the Father's glory — for that name and that glory is simply Love. The 'kenotic' theory of Christology, based on this conception of self-emptying, is, I am persuaded, the only one that offers much hope of relating at all satisfactorily the divine and the human in Christ. Yet the fatal weakness of this theory as it is stated in supranaturalist terms is that it represents Christ as stripping himself precisely of those attributes of transcendence which make him the revelation of God. The underlying assumption is that it is his omnipotence, his omniscience, and all that makes him 'superhuman', that must be shed in order for him to become truly man. On the contrary, it is as he empties himself not of his Godhead but of himself, of any desire to focus attention on himself, of any craving to be 'on an equality with God', that he reveals God. For it is in making himself nothing, in his utter self-surrender to others in love, that he discloses and lays bare the Ground of man's being as Love. *(Honest To God, pp. 74-5).*

Jesus is 'the man for others', the one in whom Love has completely taken over, the one who is utterly open to, and united with, the Ground of his being. And this 'life for others, through participation in the Being of God', *is* transcendence. For at this point, of love 'to the uttermost', we encounter *God,* the ultimate 'depth' of our being, the unconditional in the conditioned. This is what the New Testament means by saying that 'God was in Christ' and that 'what God was the Word was'. Because Christ was utterly and completely 'the man for others', because he *was* love, he was 'one with the Father', because 'God is love'. But for this very reason he was most entirely man, the son of man, the servant of the Lord. He was indeed 'one of us'; and the symbol of the Virgin Birth can only legitimately mean what the fourth Gospel takes it to mean (if, indeed, its description of Christians reflects that of Christ), namely, that the whole of his life is a life 'born not of the will of the flesh, nor of the will of man, but of God'. He is indeed not 'of this world' but 'of love'. The source and spring of his whole being is God: his is a life conceived and sustained utterly by the Holy Ghost. But he is for that reason only the more truly the proper Man'. In the man Christ Jesus stands revealed, exposed at the surface level of 'flesh', the depth and ground of all our being as Love. The life of God, the ultimate Word of Love in which all things cohere, is bodied forth completely, unconditionally and without reserve in the life of a man—the man for others and the man for God. He is perfect man and perfect God—not as a mixture of oil and water, of natural and supernatural—but as the embodiment through obedience of 'the beyond in our midst', of the transcendence of love. *(Honest To God, pp. 76-7).*

Even in Christ, the Christian theologian is careful to say that God is not defined or contained, in the sense that Jesus *is* God or *vice versa.*. Nevertheless, the entire fullness of the Godhead was there bodily; he was the Word, the incarnation, of God. God is not for the Christian simply an *"x"* or an asterisk: the unconditional *is* met here, and from here we can recognize him in all else with which he cannot be equated. *(Exploration Into God, p. 53)*

III. WHAT IS RELIGION'S ROLE?

Our third area of inquiry into radical theology concerns the role of religious institutions in sustaining and implementing faith. Although often equated, religion and faith are no more synonomous than faith and belief. All three of these terms are used interchangeably in everyday conversation and dictionary definitions. But, in the technical nomenclature and careful precision of theological analysis, at least subtle distinctions must be made between faith, belief and religion. "Religion" has to do with the apparatus through which faith expresses itself and functions in the world. Theological traditions differ considerably in their views of the importance and forms of such apparatus. In fact, divisions over religious institutions are more clearcut and heated than over the theological underpinnings of faith. Without a doubt, religious institutions produce deeper divisions within Christianity than belief systems do because they are more obvious and less modifiable badges of faith. Religious institutions represent more concrete and immediate embodiments of faith than do belief systems. Therefore, the most obvious and controversial questions in any discussion of faith center in religion's role. What are the social and moral structures that sustain and implement faith's relationships to God and to others?

Religious groups usually live between the two extremes of dead formalism and formless spontaneity. The perennial danger of conventionalizing faith's activities and relationships is the loss of their vitality and reality. The spirit of faith is always threatened by

204

the letter of religion. Against the occurrence and even the threat of such dead formalism, sometimes a formless spontaneity in faith's activities and relationships is advocated. But faith cannot be sustained personally, shared socially or relevant culturally for long apart from *some* institutional embodiments. Institutional rigidity may stifle authentic faith but spontaneous enthusiasm eventually uproots living faith. As in politics and love, so faith needs institutional forms which will stabilize relationships and sustain commitment while still retaining spontaneity and permitting change. Maintaining such a delicate balance between stability and growth is notoriously and continually difficult. Furthermore, during times of great upheaval in the life and thought of faith, polarizations between uncompromised traditionalism and unchecked iconoclasm are certain to occur. But, apart from succumbing to lifeless rituals or engaging in polemic debates, faith always strikes a middle way between form and formlessness, changelessness and innovation.

But, although religious institutions are more visible and permanent embodiments of faith than belief systems, they are based upon the foundational principles and cardinal doctrines of a given theological system. The role of religious institutions depends upon how God, existence and Christ are conceived. Thus, each distinguishable theological tradition has its own answers to questions about the purpose of the Church and the duties of discipleship. Once again, Orthodoxy, Liberalism and Neo-orthodoxy will provide a theological and historical context for our investigation of religion's role in radical Christianity.

1. The Purpose of the Chruch

The term church is one of the most flexible words in Christian parlance. It may in a given context mean a particular building, a single congregation, a collective body, a national entity, all living Christians, Christians of all times, or all who live as Christians whether they are consciously Christians or not. This variety is often clarified by qualifying the word church in different ways to denote these different meanings. Thus, reference may be made to a church building, a local church, a denominational church, a national church, the militant church, the triumphant church or the latent church. But, despite this variety of meanings, fairly definite connotations prevail in discussions of the Church as a religious structure for sustaining and implementing Christian faith.

These connotations revolve around the nature and mission of the whole community of Christians near and far, united and divided, living and dead. Not surprisingly, theological traditions conceive of the essence and function of the Church in widely different ways. These differences are largely reflections of diverse accounts of faith's foundational principles and cardinal beliefs. But comparisons of differing concepts of the Church can be made by paying attention to how certain polar features of the Chruch's nature and mission are treated. The Church as a social and religious body involves relational and organizational, natural and supernatural aspects. Thus, views of the *nature* of the Church can be compared by weighing the place given to fellowship over against institution and to human association over against divine reality. Similarly, the Church as a worshipping and witnessing community involves prophetic and sacramental, verbal and actional aspects. Thus, concepts of the *mission* of the church may also be compared by noting whether worship is primarily spiritual edification or mystical union and whether witness basically means verbal declaration or concrete service. This very broad schemata provides a frame of reference for the comparisons that follow.

Orthodoxy embraces three distinct approaches to the Church's nature and mission. This diversity may come as a surprise since the purpose of the Church supposedly rests on a given theology's foundational principles and cardinal doctrines and Orthodoxy heretofore has been portrayed largely as a unified theological tradition. But, in actuality, these groupings concerning the Church rest on subtle distinctions concerning the mode of divine presence, the distortions of sin and the meaning of salvation which have been disregarded or merely indicated in the preceding discussions of Orthodoxy's basic tenets. Furthermore, these three families are bound together by certain concerns central to the Orthodox tradition as a whole. The first family, called the *Catholic* idea of the Church, sees the Church as a society supernaturally established and sustained by God to bring men into right relations with himself and with one another under him. This society is custodian of the sacramental means of God's mystical presence and is partner in the divine governance of man's secular life. In this view, the essential nature and mission of the Church can never change since they are given and protected by God. The *classic Protestant* idea views the Church as a human community ordained by God to make disciples through preaching and teaching and to nuture Christians through worship and good works. This community is identifiable by certain proper forms and functions of polity, ministry and ritual. But, although these forms and functions rest on biblical bases, they always remain imperfect means for serving God's Word and Will and thus are always subject to God's judgment and renewal. Finally, the *free Protestant* idea treats the Church as a fellowship of converted believers living under the sole authority of God's Word in the Scripture interpreted by God's Spirit to the believer. This gathered and covenanting community is not constituted or bound by authoritative ministries, fixed confessions or sacramental rites. Rather, it exists to evangelize individual sinners through preaching and exemplary life and to nurture personal piety through Bible study and devotional worship. Despite the differences between these three approaches, there are marked similarities. The classic Protestant retains much of the form of the Catholic view of the Church but significantly modifies its function. The free Protestant preserves the classic Protestant function of the Church but changes its structural forms and theological rationale. Furthermore, through all these views of the Church runs Orthodoxy's unmistakable stress on individual and otherworldly faith. The Church exists to solicit and sustain citizens for another world.

Liberalism finds an important role for the Church while rejecting some forms and almost all functions of the Church as seen by Orthodoxy. Similar to the free church concept, Liberalism rejects all supernatural, sacramental and authoritarian claims for the Church. The Church is a human community which is organized and maintained by human beings. But, quite unlike the free church concept in Orthodoxy, this human community serves the spiritual end of helping to create the Kingdom of God on earth. While the Church in liberal thought is never coextensive with the Kingdom of God, either as its sole content or creator, the Church is the pioneer community in the enlargement of the colony of God's people in the world. The Church plays this strategic role by enlisting and nurturing citizens in this Kingdom and by creating and permeating social institutions for this Kingdom. Countering Orthodoxy's individualism and otherworldliness, Liberalism sees salvation as a personal *and* social process. Man is both a center of individual responsibility and a product of environmental conditions. Therefore, the redemption of individual personalities is impossible apart from refashioning social institutions which will permit and enhance personal spiritual growth. Although often charged with advocating personal salvation through social engineering, Liberalism as a whole consistently recognizes the need for individual *and* social regeneration. The Church serves both dimensions of the redemptive process by educating and inspiring individuals in spiritual growth and by fashioning and ameliorating institutions with spiritual qualities. Thus, the venerable practices of preaching the Word and administering the sacraments are viewed as vehicles of this pedagogical and uplifting task. The Church's longstanding structures of polity and ministry are modified to sustain and implement authentic relations among men. All facets of the Church as a committed and organized community are directed toward the upbuilding of individual persons and social institutions into the Kingdom of God here and eventually hereafter.

Neo-orthodoxy draws from the catholic, classic and free concepts of the Church but these are understood and justified in a fresh way. The distinguishing feature of neo-orthodox treatments of the nature and mission of the Church is their Christological focus. As God's presence and activity were 'hidden' in the depth dimension of the life of an ordinary human being, so God dwells and works in and through an ordinary human community. Like all things human, the Church is a natural and imperfect association and organization. But this earthen and flawed vessel contains and conveys the saving truth and power of God's Word. Neo-orthodox theologians disagree over the importance of fixed structures of ministry, sacrament and liturgy. By and large, structures which are traditional in given denominations are retained although a few theologians have serious reservations about the propriety of some or all such institutional forms. But all agree that the Church is the vehicle God uses in calling and confirming men to faith. But faith is not an individualistic and otherworldly relation to God. Having learned from Liberalism's critique of Orthodoxy at this point, Neo-orthodoxy stresses the importance of the Church for the relational character of faith and the social dimension of salvation. The Church is a microcosm of the divine-human and interhuman relationships intended by God for life in the world among all men. As such, the Church's function goes far beyond mere teaching, preaching and worship. The Church uniquely embodies in itself and bodies forth in the world the revealing and redeeming activity of God for all men. Thus, Neo-orthodoxy combines prophetic and sacramental, verbal and actional emphases in a distinctive view of the Church as the continuing incarnation of God's revelatory and redemptive Word and Deed in Jesus Christ.

PAUL M. VAN BUREN

The Christian does not hold his historical perspective alone, but in company with others. He comes to this perspective, moreover, because other men have had it before him. In biblical language, in becoming a Christian, he becomes a member of the church. The difficulty is that we do not speak biblical language. In ordinary use, including the use of Christians when they are not rather self-consciously doing theology, the word "church" refers to a building: we go to church; the church is at such and such an address; it cost so many dollars to build. The linguistic difficulty arising from the difference between the biblical and ordinary uses of the word is nothing, however, compared to the theological problem of holding together biblical assertions concerning the *ekklesia* and descriptions of the sociological unit to which the biblical statements are supposed to apply. What appears sociologically to be an odd sort of club is often spoken of theologically as the "body of Christ." This is obviously not a description. It is a reference to the historical perspective which the members presumably have in common, and it suggests the harmony that would exist between people who shared this perspective.

A man becomes a Christian in the context of this community of believers, directly or indirectly. Conversion has not always come from hearing the Gospel spoken. It has also arisen from simply being with men set free "in Christ," so that the freedom of Jesus has been contagious through Christians.   *(The Secular Meaning Of The Gospel, pp. 183-4).*

One of the traditional "marks" of the "true church" is preaching. One member of the congregation stands before the others and speaks. In the Protestant tradition (and to some extent in Catholicism as well), this speaking has a peculiar relationship to the Bible. Passages of the Bible are read aloud. A particular passage is singled out as a "text," on the basis of which a "sermon" is preached. The sermon is primarily a proclamation, for it points to the free man of Nazareth as the story of Easter does; the sermon presents him as the source and the norm of the Christian's perspective and freedom. A sermon may therefore be an occasion for the renewal and deepening of the hearer's historical perspective. And if he has not previously been a Christian, it may become the occasion of a discernment that leads him to hold this perspective. This is the meaning of the traditional assertion that preaching which is faithful to the biblical witness to the "Word of God" may become itself the "Word of God."

Preaching has the further function of illustrating the perspective of Christian faith. The preacher points to the present situation of the world and suggests how some aspect of this world looks to "eyes of faith." The hearer is invited to stretch his imagination, to extend the range of his historical perspective, in order that he may see the world in which he lives in the light of Jesus of Nazareth as the liberator of the whole world, not just of believers. He is told that he may and that he can, rather than that he should, see the world in this way. The "blik" which is illustrated and commended in preaching will always be related explicity or implicitly to its historical basis, however. The sermon is said to be based on a text from the Bible, and this appeal to the documents which recount the history of Jesus, the people from which he came and of which he was a part, and the disciples who came to share in his freedom, reflects the historical aspect of the Christian perspective.

Preaching may also take the secondary form of exhortation...The hearer is invited to see a particular problem in a manner consistent with this perspective. The sermon suggests that if he does in fact have this perspective, he "ought" *logically* to see the problem in a certain way, and this would lead *logically* to certain acts. The "because it is God's will" is not an explanation of why a Christian ought to act in a certain way; it points to the historical perspective which provides a context for such an action. In this context, the statement is neither silly nor dishonest, but intelligible and meaningful. It may be granted, however, that "because it is God's will" appears to be an explanation and that other words might have been chosen to indicate more clearly that reference is being made to a historical perspective. *(The Secular Meaning Of The Gospel, pp. 185-7).*

Christians have continued and have led others to join them through telling and retelling an "old, old story," which they tell as being in some peculiar way the story also of their own lives. They tell this story and their faith lives off this story. He who performs the work of Christian education serves faith by teaching this story, making it familiar, tracing different ways in which it can be and has been told. He does not *tell* the story itself. That is for pulpit and holy table. He teaches the story as a story.

He teaches the story. It is nothing short of amazing that preachers still use, in whatever way, biblical texts, still make references to biblical passages. What sense can this make to those who do not even know the stories of the Bible? In order that the particular story or the particular form of the whole Christian story which is being told at any one time may be heard with even a fraction of the fullness which the preacher intends, it is necessary that the listeners know the whole range of biblical stories. If they do not learn these stories in Sunday school or Bible class, where shall they learn them? What is Easter without the story of Mary and the Gardener and also the story of the Exodus? What is Christmas without the nativity stories of both Matthew and Luke? What is Christian love without the stories of the Good Samaritan and of Lazarus and the rich man? Stories can be taught and learned. That is the task of Christian education.

Christian education involves the teaching of the stories of Christian faith as stories. ("Christian Education *Post Mortem Dei*," p. 7).

Christian education involves teaching 'about' Christian faith in a way which is comparable to teaching 'about' love. I should think that most people would agree that you cannot 'teach love,' that this combination of words does not go well together. You can love another person, and he may then respond with love, but it would also be rather awkward and inappropriate to say he had then learned 'how to love.' Love can, however, be 'taught about.'

How would you go about teaching about love? You might begin with the literature of love—love stories of ancient and more modern vintage. You might go on to the histories or stories of great lovers, including the reading of their letters. Then you could turn to the poetry of love. Finally, you could add other ways of talking about love—the analyses of anthropologists and psychiatrists—ways which would hardly be those of lovers. The differences between these various kinds of language are worth exploring.

In making this analogy, I do not wish to say that faith is in all respects of the same order as love. Like love, it is a human posture, a commitment, a way of seeing some people and things (but probably not a vision which governs all of man's thinking and activity in every realm of his existence), and it entails certain actions. Unlike love, however, its object is not at hand. Believers have stories to tell, not a photograph to look at. Since the death of God and the rise of the critical historical imagination, Christians have had to find analogies for the object of faith in myth, story and parable. They have always had to do this, but before the death of God they could always pretend that their faith somehow gave them an insight into 'ultimate truth.' Now that God is gone and with him the justification of faith, unjustifiable faith must live by faith alone, and in this sense it is not unlike love. Human love, therefore, provides a helpful analogy to human faith, and in this sense, those engaged in Christian education have the task of teaching 'about' faith. ("Christian Education *Post Mortem Dei*," pp. 9-10).

Those engaged in Christian education can serve Christian faith by clarifying the relation between believing and living. Christians have long insisted that how a man believes effects how he lives. One of them once said that if any man says that he loves God and at the same time hates his brother, he is a liar, and another early believer called Christianity "the way." On the other hand, believers frequently disagree about the precise consequences of believing when it comes to specific decisions. This disagreement appears to have led many Christians to conclude that the relationship between believing and living is so vague or general that nothing specific can be said, or even that faith has no concrete ethical consequences at all. We face today some of the painful consequences of this conclusion in the present sorry state of churches in which many believers see no conflict between Christian faith and the practice of racial discrimination. ("Christian Education *Post Mortem Dei*," p. 9).

He who serves in the work of Christian education serves faith, therefore, by teaching the role which story telling plays in human life, in the hopes of winning a frame of mind that will appreciate stories, not as 'facts,' not as 'critical history,' but as stories, as one of men's important ways of winning understanding and of being understood. ("Christian Education *Post Mortem Dei*," p. 7).

The mission of the Christian is the way of love upon which he finds himself, the way toward the neighbor, not the way of trying to make others into Christians. His mission is simply to be a man, as this is defined by Jesus of Nazareth. It is not particularly appropriate in our time, when the church has talked far too much to the world, for him to tell his neighbor why he is "for" him. It is quite enough that he practice the liberty for which he has been set free. *(The Secular Meaning Of The Gospel, pp. 191-2).*

WILLIAM HAMILTON

What is the relation of radical theology to the Church? It certainly must be clear that this theology has neither the power nor the ability to serve the Protestant Chruch in most of its present institutional forms. I do not see how preaching, worship,

212

prayer, ordination, the sacraments can be taken seriously by the radical theologian. If there is a need for new intitutional forms and styles, however, this theology doubtless has a great deal to say. If theology is tested by its ability to shape new kinds of personal and corporate existence in the times in which it lives, then it would seem that radical theology may be able to pass such a test. ("American Theology, Radicalism and the Death of God," p. 7).

If prayer is defined as a religious form of address to a personalized being called God, then we can make nothing at all of it. But this is a very poor definition of prayer, and radical theology will need to state more exactly than it is now able, just what it is that lies behind acts of adoration, intercession, and praise, for example, and to what extent these can be recovered without a doctrine of God. I would further assume that in certain techniques of meditation, particularly Buddhist ones where no God is involved, some ways of dealing with personal prayer in the radical context might be found. What public worship might mean, what the celebration of the "death of God" might mean as a liturgical act, this kind of thing we are just beginning to ask ourselves. ("Questions and Answers on the Radical Theology," p. 224).

Question: You wrote in an article some months ago that you couldn't see any value that the radical theology might have to the church as presently constituted. Do you still feel this way?

I received a good deal of very interesting criticism when I wrote that, and largely from pastors who had become interested in the radical theology and who felt that it was possible to be committed to that theology and still live in the pastoral ministry. Early in 1966, I held a continuing education seminar at Colgate Rochester Divinity School on the radical theology, and the majority of participants were pastors. Most of them began the seminar expecting that the measure of their commitment to radical theology would be the measure of their disaffiliation from the pastorate, and they found, to their surprise and mine, that they ended our period of study with a firmer confidence that radical theology could be put to responsible work in the parish. There are, of course, plenty of problems, but I am being wisely instructed by my friends at this point, and would by no means hold to my negative words. A very high proportion of my public speaking the last three months has been to pastors and they have taught me that the situation is more fluid than I'd thought. ("Questions and Answers on the Radical Theology," p. 237).

To be a Christian does not mean to be a member of a community whose social and intellectual structures are antiquated. There is no city of God unless it assumes the city of man, and there is no Christian community unless it asserts the community of man. A Church which is one institution among others ceases to be *in* the world and becomes part *of* the world.   *(No Other God, xii).*

The gospel need not stake its validity and actuality on the outdated structures of the Church. Because the Church is an eschatological reality and an article of faith *(Credo ecclesiam)* it must ·be careful not to perpetuate ecclesial forms that are due ·more' to historical contingencies than to its spiritual vocation in the world. The Church should be on its guard lest it transform itself into an empirical datum whose sociological aspects and intellectual values serve only to confirm its attachment either to a past social order, or to a now naive religious view of the world. A Church that came out of its ghetto but still kept its old ways and mentality would succeed merely in turning its faith into an anachronism. *(No Other God, pp. 15-6).*

The emergence of a post-Christian era makes it all the more imperative not only to rethink theology on the basis of a new model but also to recast the structures of the Chruch in terms of man's personal and social self-understanding today. A mobile and dynamic society has replaced the traditional stable structures in the light of which the nature of the Church was construed. In a post-Christian age the Church cannot remain at the center of the village if it wants to be present in the midst of life. Nor can it resort to becoming an enclave, a modernistic ghetto. Much less can Christianity forfeit itself by becoming merely a private matter. And inasmuch as all of the five types somehow imply that, so to speak, the Church is one side of the coin of which the other is the World, it would seem that unless Christianity wants to be wiped off the face of the earth, the Church must begin to think of itself not as a place of retreat from the world, not as a society within society, but as a community that has no reality other than *through* the society of men, as the avant-garde of society, as the axis of culture.

That, *mutatis mutandis,* the Church played such a role in the past is testified by the various ecclesiastical functions now taken over by the state (e.g., schools and hospitals). Instead of wondering what would be left for the Church to do should the state continue to infringe on the attributes of the Church and should sociology replace ecclesiology, Christians need to come to grips with the fact that there are always new things to do though they may not much resemble, at least superficially, those tasks the Church undertook in the past. Among other things, theology will have to enter the fields of, e.g., literature, politics, and economics, if it wants to tackle the chief problem of our age, namely, the problem of God. Otherwise, it will merely engage in the business of updating the Church. And that is not the position to take, especially if being the Church means also being the avant-garde of society, the axis of culture. *(No Other God, pp. 99-100).*

More than ever we have therefore the salutary occasion to realize that it is not the world which is made for the Church but the Church for the world. And we begin to grasp this occasion if, consciously or not, we do not transform the Christian faith into an ethico-social particularism. Such a particularism, even if one can consider it as having been the guarantee of the cultural and social vocation that the Church exercised for centuries, would today result in the conversion of the Church into a ghetto, and Church membership into a matter of private custom. This would no doubt be the easiest solution. But it would corroborate the demise of the Church.

To yield to the temptation exerted upon us by the cultural obsolescence of Christianity, as well as by the technological mentality for which moral problems tend to become equations to solve, would amount to acquiescing to the neutralization of the Christian tradition as a cultural ferment. But to sterilize the Christian faith would deviate the biblical message from its field of action—the world. Even if the precedent of apostolic times was claimed, by doing so the Church would not only constitute itself as an enclave off the mainstream of contemporary society but would also deceive itself into believing that the situation of the early Christians could be repeated. The circumstances are no longer the same, nor must one be isolated from the world in order not to conform to it. *(No Other God, pp. 91-2).*

HARVEY COX

In Christ, God discloses himself as present for men in the grime and blood, and in the parties and festivals of earth. Nor is the Incarnation to be understood merely as an isolated episode in God's life. It signifies that God is the One who is fully and irretrievably present in the life of men, that God takes our *saeculum* with life-and-death seriousness. A church which does not

215

identify with the world, with the same thorough solidarity that God does, betrays its mission.. ("Why Christianity Must Be Secularized," p. 15).

The church is a part of the world, and thus also a sphere of God's activity. It is part of the theater of God's reconciling work; it is the locus of the Christian life and of all the things we have said about the world....But we can say all this about the church because it is that part of the world which is privileged to recognize and to celebrate what God is doing in and for the *whole* world.

This, then, is the church: a people who live their lives in a pattern of scattering and then coming together, only to scatter again and come together again, very much as the heart sends out oxygenated blood to nourish every little capillary, then receives it again to be recharged with oxygen from the lungs for recirculation. This is the true pattern of the church's life, gathering and scattering, and our mistake has been to identify it only with the gathered phase. *(God's Revolution and Man's Responsibility, pp. 71-2).*

The church is a people who gather together and then scatter. It will always be this kind of people, but the character of what happens in the gathering and in the going forth may vary from age to age. Christians come together to sing, to be sustained by their mutual presence, to acknowledge the sovereign to whom they are obedient. But Christians must remain very open about the character of what happens when they do gather.

The church of the future will be smaller, more mobile, more flexible, much more disciplined, much more various in the ways in which it celebrates. It will be much more joyful, less solemn than we are when we come together. It will be much less preacher-oriented, much less cultic, much more open to discussion and give-and-take. This is the church we are moving toward... *(God's Revolution and Man's Responsibility, p. 98).*

I never intended to be anti-institutional, anarchistic or individualistic in *The Secular City,* but at times I allowed myself to use phrases which gave people that impression. I realize that the church is not pure spirit and cannot live in the modern world, or in any world for that matter, without some institutional expression. Nor is "institution" just a necessary evil. Institutions, as Arnold Gehlen has shown in his studies of the subject, really serve to liberate man rather than to imprison him. Institution is for man what instinct is for animal. Institutions make it possible for the organism to deal with certain levels of decisions by answering a whole range of questions before they are asked. The animal flees or freezes in the presence of danger without cogitating about it. It is a reflex action. Man goes through most of his life thinking only of day-to-day questions. He does not decide each morning whether family, property and the nation state (all arrangements unknown to animals) deserve his support and cooperation. Mostly, he goes to work, supports his family, drives his car, without much thought about the institutional assumptions that underlie these activities. In fact, if he had to think them through every time he acted, he would be like the centipede who became paralyzed when someone asked him how he moved all those legs at once. He would never get to anything else.

But we are not just centipedes. Sometimes we do question our assumptions about property or nation states. And sometimes we ask about the church as an institution. We do this because we now realize that property is not, as many once thought, an "order of creation" and that nations have no validity grounded in some natural law. Likewise, I believe that all the forms of institutional life we find in the church are open to change. There is no structure or practice so sacred that it is above critical reflection. Denominations? Residential parishes? Professional clergy? All these are institutional forms which arose in particular historical circumstances, to serve certain purposes. They can be altered or discarded if need be. But again, mere discarding will hardly suffice. What we need now is a willingness to *reinstitutionalize* the forms of church life based on a conscious theological recognition of what the church's purpose is. ("Afterword," pp. 186-7).

The forms of church life are dependent on the function, or mission, of the church. They must be designed to facilitate locating and participating in the "mission of God." They must effectuate rather than hinder the congregation's capacity to discover and cooperate in the work of God in the world. This means that the content of the church's ministry is simply the continuation of Jesus's ministry.

Jesus thought of his task as threefold. He was to announce the arrival of the new regime. He was to personify its meaning. And he was to begin distributing its benefits. Similarly the church has a threefold responsibility. Theologians call it *kerygma* (proclamation), *diakonia* (reconciliation, healing, and other forms of service), and *koinonia* (demonstration of the character of the new society). The church is the avant-garde of the new regime, but because the new regime breaks in at different points and in different ways, it is not possible to forecast in advance just what appearance the church will have. *(The Secular City, pp. 109-10).*

The ministry of the church is no more and no less than participation in the mission of God. This concept means that the first thing the church must always do is to find out where God is on the move in his world today, and then make all possible haste to be there with him. It does not mean, however, that the church must look back and forth between the world and somewhere else. The meaning of the life of Jesus of Nazareth is that God and the world can no longer be separated. We do not have to look back and forth now in harried anxiety between the world and God, trying to apply the one to the other. As Bonhoeffer once said:

Whoever set eyes on the Body of Jesus Christ in faith can never again speak of the world as though it were lost, as though it were separated from Christ . . . . It is only in Christ that the world is what is is . . . It is only in the midst of the world that Christ is Christ.

We have been emphasizing all along that in a secular age the mission of the church must assume a secular style. This idea should come as no surprise. God's becoming man in Jesus represents a kind of radical secularization. God laid aside his religiousness, his divine attributes, and took upon himself the form of a servant. This was a secular form. The church must learn to do the same today. *(God's Revolution and Man's Responsibility, pp. 104-5).*

1) A divided church will not speak to the man come of age. Mired in its own provincialisms, obsessed with defenses of its partial truths, it elicits hardly more than a yawn from the people Bonhoeffer wished to address. If reconciliation and authentic community constitute God's gift to the world, then a dismembered church contravenes its own message. Unity is not something for Christians to enjoy among themselves. It is a prerequisite of mission.

2) A church which eschews politics, or worse still, uses politics to shore up its own position in the world, will never speak to secular man. Ministers and nuns on picket lines for racial justice today are not just signs of the church's "social concern." They are evangelists, telling modern man what the Gospel says. The church which remains securely within the "spiritual realm" will annoy no one and convince no one, for secular man is a political animal *par excellence,* and that indispensable dimension of the Gospel which goes "beyond politics" begins after, not before, the political obedience of Christians.

218

3) A church whose ethical pronouncements remain generic and abstract will never speak to the secular man. He does not live "in general." He lives his life in a particular place, doing a certain job, faced with specific issues. Vague moral advice does not interest him. Specific ethical demands may infuriate him, stimulate him, or encourage him. But at least he will hear them, which is all the church can ever succeed in accomplishing. Whether he believes or obeys is not, in the final analysis, determined by the church but by the Spirit of God at work within him. ("Beyond Bonhoeffer? The Future of Religionless Christianity," pp. 213-4).

It is time that we Christians move our focus from the renewal of church to the renewal of world. M. M. Thomas, one of the leaders of the ecumenical movement and a great Indian Christian, said recently that the World Council of Churches, since its inception in 1948, has been far too obsessed with discussions about the church. His criticism applies to all of us. We have talked about the unity of the church, the mission of the church, the renewal of the church. We have talked far too much about the church, but not enough about God's world. This does not mean that we must devise some kind of nonchurch Christianity, but it does mean that we can correct our ecclesiastical overemphasis. *(God's Revolution and Man's Responsibility, p. 15).*

THOMAS J. J. ALTIZER

From the point of view of radical Christianity, the original heresy was the identification of the Church as the body of Christ. When the Church is known as the body of Christ, and the Church is further conceived as a distinct and particular institution or organism existing within but nevertheless apart from the world, then the body of Christ must inevitably be distinguished from and even opposed to the body of humanity....The radical Christian maintains that it is the Church's regressive religious belief in God which impels it to betray the present and the kenotic reality of Christ. So long as the Church is grounded in the worship of a sovereign and transcendent Lord, and submits in its life and witness to that infinite distance separating the creature and the Creator, it must continue to reverse the movement of the Spirit who progressively becomes actualized as flesh, thereby silencing the life and speech of the Incarnate Word. *(The Gospel Of Christian Atheism, pp. 132-3).*

Theologians must also take far more seriously than is their habit the identity of the Church as the full Body of Christ or the universal body of humanity. When this is done there can be no pretension that faith is confined to the institutional bodies of the Church or to that sphere or realm which is sanctioned by ecclesiastical authority. Indeed, if Christ is present wherever there is full human energy or life then it would seem to be apparent that He is more fully present outside rather than within ecclesiastical bodies. Why this idea should bring offense to a theologian today is beyond my imagination, but apparently it does so, and it should warn us ever to be on our guard against all forms of theology which are merely church or ecclesiastical theology. ("Catholic Philosophy and the Death of God," p. 276).

Christ is the embodiment of a forward-moving process, of a process which reverses all things making possible, in a certain sense, the renewal of all things and the coming together of all things into a new totality, a new life, a new energy, a new joy. Therefore, in a very real sense the body of Christ is an ever enlarging, ever more comprehensive, ever more universal body. It is not to be confined to particular space and time. It is in no sense to be confined to a particular image or shape, or a particular substance. Christ is most truly understood as the source of *all* life and energy whatsoever. *(The Altizer-Montgomery Dialogue, p. 14).*

A radical faith claims our contemporary condition as an unfolding of the body of Christ, an extension into the fullness of history of the self-emptying of God. No evasion of an autonomous human condition is possible for the Christian who confesses his participation in a Word that has negated its primordial and transcendent ground: the Christian who lives in a fully incarnate Christ is forbidden either to cling to an original innocence or to yearn nostalgically for a preincarnate Spirit. Indeed, it is precisely the Christian's life in the kenotic Word which impels him to accept and affirm a world in which God is dead as the realization in history of God's self-annihilation in Christ. *(The Gospel Of Christian Atheism, p. 111).*

We are living in a time in which the death of God is becoming corporately, communally present to all men. Every man who now lives in the history following the advent of Christ lives decisively in a time of the death of God. And inescapably he must live within a reality in which he no longer can know the presence of the transcendent Lord. He must inevitably live in a time of the eclipse of God, or the silence of God, or the absence of God. Now the common atheist or the unbeliever can know that ours is a time in which God is absent. There seems to be little controversy about that. But I believe that only in faith can we know that God is dead. Only in faith can we know that God is finally absent, that we are indeed heirs of a movement of God wherein this original death of God in Christ has finally penetrated the whole body of consciousness and experience in the world. So now every man who lives in the history following the advent of Christ lives the death of God insofar as he lives in history at all. And therein every man participates in the body of Christ insofar as the body of Christ incorporates and embodies the death of God.   *(The Altizer Montgomery Dialogue, pp. 16-7)*.

JOHN A. T. ROBINSON

A Reformation presupposes that the Church can be re-formed and a positive answer given to the question, 'Can these bones live?' There is, however, much from within the organized Church, and still more for those observing it from without, to raise the question rather insistently: 'Can it possibly be the carrier of the new life for the new age?' Is the Church not an archaic and well-protected institution for the preservation of something that is irrelevant and incredible? Because it is so dug in, it will not, of course, disappear overnight, at any rate in Europe and North America—though who can say even that for Afro-Asia? But will it necessarily be the channel of the Spirit? May not the really significant movements of renewal take place outside it and despite it? There are more in our generation than in any previous Christian century who would be inclined to return a reluctant, or not so reluctant, 'Yes' to that question.   *(The New Reformation? pp. 13-4)*.

Today, I believe, the main work of the manifest Church, certainly in terms of sheer numbers, is probably to make it possible for men and women to be met by Christ *where they are*—that is, within the context and thought-forms of the latent church. It has to ask itself whether what it really cares for most is that 'the poor *have* the Gospel preached to them'—if need be in the entirely non-religious terms announced by Jesus, of release for prisoners and recovery of sight for the blind—even if they never say, 'Lord, Lord'. If so, then it must, for the greater part of its work, be prepared to *respect* rather than remove (which is its instinctive urge) the incognitos under which the parable of the Sheep and the Goats alone shows it possible for the Christ to meet and to judge the mass of men. And the incognitos of that parable

221

are those of *humanity* and *secularity:* the Son of Man wills to be met in an utterly disinterested concern for persons for their own sake, and in relationships that have nothing distinctively religious about them. *(The New Reformation? pp. 49-50).*

To live for others means to accept life on their terms, to serve within the structures in which they live. The basic trouble is not that the Chruch has been too affluent — it is chronically short of money — but that it has used it on building its own structures (literally or metaphorically) rather than on serving in those of others. It has been an institution alongside, not the leaven within, the world it exists to change. Perhaps it can only hope to minister to that world by cutting down drastically on its own professionalism (by which I do not mean its own efficiency). I suspect that we should ordain fewer, rather than more, full-time professional clergy on the pay-roll of the Church. And I am sure that we could do with a great deal less ecclesiastical plant. We have got to relearn that 'the house of God' is primarily the world in which God lives, not the contractor's hut set up in the grounds. *(The New Reformation? p. 27).*

The house of God is not the Church but the world. The Church is the servant, and the first characteristic of a servant is that he lives in someone else's house, not his own. Paradoxically, the Church is also the son, the one who has the freedom of the house. But Christians only too often have celebrated this freedom, as soon as they have had the chance, by setting up on their own. *(The New Reformation? p. 92).*

'What is the place of worship and prayer in an entire absence of religion?' Bonhoeffer's question, which he never survived to answer, may sound too paradoxical to be intelligible. For worship and prayer would seem to be *the* expression of religion, the activities *par excellence* that distinguish a religious person from an irreligious. But we dare not simply dismiss the question. Rather, let it drive us to a more careful definition of terms. *(Honest To God, p. 84).*

The purpose of worship is not to retire from the secular into the department of the religious, let alone to escape from 'this world' into 'the other world', but to open oneself to the meeting of the Christ in the common, to that which has the power to penetrate its superficiality and redeem it from its alienation. The function of worship is to make us more sensitive to these depths; to focus, sharpen and deepen our response to the world and to other people beyond the point of proximate concern (of liking, self-interest, limited commitment, etc.) to that of ultimate concern; to purify and correct our loves in the light of Christ's love; and in him to find the grace and power to be the reconciled and reconciling community. Anything that achieves this or assists towards it is Christian worship. Anything that fails to do this is not Christian worship, be it ever so 'religious'. *(Honest To God, pp. 87-8).*

I wonder whether Christian prayer, prayer in the light of the Incarnation, is not to be *defined* in terms of penetration through the world to God rather than of withdrawal from the world to God. For the moment of revelation is precisely so often, in my experience, the moment of meeting and unconditional *engagement.* How easily one finds oneself giving pious advice to a person faced with a decision to 'go away and pray about it'. But, if I am honest, what enlightenment I have had on decisions has almost always come not when I have gone away and stood back from them, but precisely as I have *wrestled through* all the most practical pros and cons, usually with other people. And this activity, undertaken by a Christian trusting and expecting that God is there, would seem to be prayer. *(Honest To God, p. 97).*

My own experience is that I am really praying for people, agonizing with God for them, precisely *as* I meet them and really give my soul to them. It is then if ever, in this incarnational relationship, that deep speaks to deep and the Spirit of God is able to take up our inarticulate groans and turn them into prayer. It is *afterwards* that I find one needs to withdraw—as it were, to clarify on tablets and bring to obedience the revelation given on the mount. *(Honest To God, pp.99).*

Perhaps this is the starting point for a 'non-religious' understanding of prayer. We may begin from the fact that people do give themselves to people. There is nothing 'religious' about this. But to open oneself to another *unconditionally* in love *is* to be with him in the presence of God, and that is the heart of intercession. To pray for another is to expose both oneself and him to the commom ground of our being; it is to see one's concern for him in terms of *ultimate* concern, to let *God* into the relationship. Intercession is to *be with* another at that depth, whether in silence or compassion or action. It may consist simply in listening, when we take the otherness of the other person most seriously. It may not be talking *to* God, as though to a third person, about him at all. The *Thou* addressed may be his own *Thou,* but it may be addressed and responded to at such a level that we can only speak of knowing him in God and God in him. It may not be specifically religious, it may not be consciously Christian: but it may be a meeting of Christ in that man, because his humanity is accepted 'without any reservation'. The way through to the vision of the Son of man and the knowledge of God, which is the heart of contemplative prayer, is by unconditonal love of the nighbour, of 'the nearest *Thou* to hand'.

Prayer is the responsibility to meet others with *all* I have, to be ready to encounter the unconditional in the conditional, to expect to meet God in the way, not to turn aside from the way. All else is exercise towards that or reflection in depth upon it. *(Honest To God, pp. 99-100).*

If the Church is to travel sufficiently light, and to be flexible for a mobile society organized on functional lines, then it must be free to deploy much if not most of its manpower not for servicing units of ecclesiastical plant but for serving within the structures of the world. *(The New Reformation? p. 59).*

2.The Duties of Discipleship

Every theological tradition recognizes some relation between living faith and everyday life. Beliefs about God, Man and Christ are dead intellectual abstractions unless they are anchored in the daily activities of their adherents. As we have already seen from our discussion of the Church, faith's practice cannot be limited to the cultic activities of public and private worship or missionary and catechetical evangelism. The duties of discipleship extend to the moral conduct of the faithful as well. But the basis and scope of these moral duties are conceived of quite differently by theological traditions and individual Christians. Once again, these differences are reflections by and large of rival accounts of faith's foundational principles and cardinal beliefs. But these different views of Christian morality also reflect divergent estimates of the relation between ultimate principles and concrete situations, and between social structures and individual behavior.

Christian thinking about the basis of moral decisions range from an extreme legalism to an exaggerated situationism. *Legalistic ethics* bases morality on a code of rules ready made for every possible moral act. All phases of moral obligation are governed by an extensive body of "do's" and"don'ts" which stipulate behavior without regard for extenuating circumstances of time or place. More recently, *situation ethics* has argued that codes of laws distort the personal, spontaneous and novel character of Christian morality. Christians discover their moral duty only in a concrete situation of divine-human interaction. Since no two situations are ever identical, moral duties can never be codified or universalized. Between these polar positions, most Christians base moral duties on a combination of ultimate principles and concrete circumstances. Moral decisions are made by applying summary moral principles to a concrete situation. Thus, for example, the Golden Rule may encompass every moral duty though specifying none. Since this process of applying ultimate principles to specific situations is called casuistry, this mediating approach is often called *casuist ethics.*

Various conceptions of the scope of the Christian's moral responsibilities center in the relation between individual and social ethics. Since the early controversies over antinomianism, all Christian thinkers have insisted that authentic faith profoundly affects the moral quality of individual character and personal relations. Even theological traditions which base salvation wholly on God's initiative and supernatural resources point to the transformation of personal attitudes and actions as the sure fruit and evidence of saving faith. But most theological traditions extend the duties of discipleship beyond individual ethics. The Christian has public as well as personal moral obligations. But within this concern for social morality, at least three distinct conceptions of the Christian's relation to the offices and structures of society are represented. One theory of the Christian's role in political, economic and cultural activities draws a sharp distinction between social and individual morality although both are under divine jurisdiction. God has ordered the civil realm according to laws and structures which restrain evil and sustain life. Society is predicated upon the harsh but helpful necessities of restraint and requital. But in the realm of individual relationships, the Christian is governed by the spirit of love and sacrifice. This *dualistic social ethics* requires the Christian to support civil law and power in public life but to practice Christian love and sacrifice in personal relationships. In contrast, a *utopian social ethics* claims that the civil realm can and must be brought under the governance of Christian love and sacrifice. Dualistic social ethics lead to complacency and indifference over the injustice of laws and the inequities of power. The ideals of justice and equity can be achieved in political, economic and cultural life by men of good will who embrace Christian love and sacrifice as the social as well as the personal expression of discipleship. Still a third view rejects ethical dualism and utopianism as misleading half-truths. Dualism is too pessimistic while utopianism is too optimistic about man's moral capacities. On the one hand, the destructive behavior of

225

sinful men must always be restrained and requited by laws and structures of society. On the other hand, the constructive effort of redeemed men can transform civil laws and social structures. But Christians must adopt and maintain both of these strategies simultaneously. Christians must always seek to revise the laws and institutions of society toward justice and equity. But such revisions must devise ways of restraining and requiting evil since every moral gain is accompanied by new opportunities for the strong and ruthless to destroy the weak and acquiescing. This third position may be called *dialectical social ethics* since it holds seemingly opposite truths about social morality together dialectically.

Thus, theological traditions offer a number of different conceptions of the basis and scope of Christian morality. Similar to prevailing views of the Church, variety within encompassing theological traditions often occurs. These various combinations and alignments will become obvious in the following comparisons.

Orthodoxy exhibits a variety of ethical perspectives which can be roughly correlated to its differing views of the Church. Thus, the Catholic idea of the Church is typically joined to a casuist and dualistic ethics. As partner in the divine governance of men, the Church applies the supernaturally revealed principles of personal morality and the rationally discoverable principles of social morality to concrete situations. As custodian of the sacramental means of grace, the Church mediates the divine assistance necessary for Christians to practice love and sacrifice in personal relationships. The classic Protestant idea of the Church generally bases moral decisions on a casuistry of biblical principles, but both dualistic and dialectical emphases are common in social ethics. The Lutheran heritage traditionally draws a sharp distinction between the realm of society under law and the realm of the Church under grace. The Calvinist-Puritan strain dialectially relates the values of Christianity to the institutions of society. Finally, the free Protestant concept of the Church is characteristically legalistic and individualistic in its view of morality. Its emphasis on spiritual biblicism, fellowship and piety limits the duties of discipleship to the cultivation of individual spirituality under the guidance of biblical rules. But, despite their general accuracy, these correlations between views of the Church and of morality are not unabridgable. Furthermore, Orthodoxy as a whole, especially in its Protestant expressions, has become increasingly legalistic and either individualistic or dualistic in theory and practice. This trend

226

is due partly to the tendency for any theological tradition to be codified and simplified over a period of time and practice. But Orthodoxy has been profoundly influenced in the last two centuries by the rise of modern democracies and philosophical individualism. Therefore, a wide gap often separates earlier social theories from the actual moral practices of Orthodoxy today.

Liberalism closely joins both faith and morality and personal and social ethics. Faith means living in the brotherhood of man under the fatherhood of God. But this ideal Kingdom of God among men can never be attained by changes in individual character and personal relationships alone. Social institutions must also be changed so as to permit and encourage the growth of free and loving individuals. Liberalism thus scores Orthodoxy for ignoring or obscuring the social dimensions of redemption and discipleship. Whether dualistic or individualistic, Orthodoxy exhibits little or no concern for prevailing political, economic and cultural institutions which thwart and destroy the growth of whole persons. Such social evils must be endured as the consequences of human sin and divine judgment. Even where the attempt is made to apply love dialectically to social institutions, Orthodoxy's rigid biblicism and legalism hinder the development of moral strategies for dealing with evils peculiar to modern industrialized and urbanized societies. Against Orthodoxy's moral stance, Liberalism advocates a casuist and utopian approach to ethics. Concrete moral actions are based upon universal moral principles which are either innately known by all men or discovered by certain great men like Jesus. These encompassing moral absolutes apply not only to personal character and relationships but to problems of international and domestic politics, management and labor relations, racial and class prejudices. The emergence of democratic patterns and socialistic programs in the modern era are tangible expressions and evidences of such application. Although Liberalism is often censured for its unrealistic utopianism, most liberals have recognized that the drive toward the good world will progress gradually, encounter opposition, suffer setbacks and demand effort. But evil features of society can be eliminated and ideal possibilities for society can be eventually realized through the cooperation of human effort with divine immanence. Therefore, Liberalism offers a drastic reinterpretation and far-reaching extension of the duties of discipleship to the whole of individual and corporate life.

Neo-orthodoxy arose primarily as a protest against Liberalism's utopian ethics. Since ethics grows organically out of a total theological perspective, Neo-orthodoxy called for a thorough rethinking of the foundations and framework of liberal beliefs. Liberalism's moralistic faith, immanental God, developing man and humanistic Christ were charged with failing to preserve the distinction between God's and man's purposes, actions and achievements. But, though repristinating most of Orthodoxy's foundational principles and cardinal beliefs, Neo-orthodoxy in the main has not accepted Orthodoxy's moral outlook. Indeed, Neo-orthodoxy's ethical concerns make plain its deep debt to Liberalism's emphasis on the personal character of faith, the present activity of God and the social dimension of redemption. In working out these moral concerns, neo-orthodox theologians are divided over the basis of ethical decisions. Some argue for a casuist application of moral principles to concrete situations. Neo-orthodox casuists, however, rigorously guard against Orthodoxy's espousal or drift to legalism by subsuming broad moral principles such as the Ten Commandments or the Sermon on the Mount under an ultimate principle such as love. Other neo-orthodox theologians claim that the personal and contemporaneous character of divine-human interaction can not be reduced to specific rules or even to ultimate principles. The spontaneity of personal interaction and the novelty of concrete situations are obscured in a morality based on abstract and universal principles. Christian responsibility must be discovered anew in every situation where persons love, serve, reject and contend with one another. At most, moral principles like the Ten Commandments or the Sermon on the Mount throw light on a concrete situation of moral responsibility. But moral principles are always subservient to the demands of actual moments of divine-human interaction. Situational ethics, then, has arisen within Neo-orthodoxy as a fresh statement of the basis of moral decisions. Furthermore, differences of opinion over the scope of ethics also prevail with this movement. Both dualistic and dialectical forms of social ethics are typical. But, unlike Orthodoxy's development of these positions, God's will and work are related more intimately in the two realms of life under law and grace. Consequently, Christians are more explicitly responsible for serving and honoring God in both these realms. This stress on concrete divine governance and Christian responsibility in all areas of human existence leads to a virtual assimilation of the dualist to the dialectical position in Neo-orthodoxy. Christians must judge and permeate all laws and structures of society with God's ultimate purposes for human relationships. But, because of the persistence of human sin, this limiting and transfiguring work is a never-ending duty of Christian discipleship.

PAUL M. VAN BUREN

The man who says, "Jesus is Lord," is saying that the history of Jesus and of what happened on Easter has exercised a liberating effect upon him, and that he has been so grasped by it that it has become the historical norm of his perspective upon life. His confession is a notification of this perspective and a recommendation to his listener to see Jesus, the world, and himself in this same way and to act accordingly. It is an important perspective and it can be distinguished from other points of view. We may illustrate the difference by comparing the perspective of Christian faith and the point of view of the man whose perspective upon life is founded on the life of his nation. The nationalist understands himself first of all as a patriot and he defines his freedom in the context of loyalty to his country. He can understand the Gospel only as making a relative claim at most. He may allow that there is some freedom to be found in Jesus and in loyalty to him, but it is secondary to his freedom as a citizen. For the Christian, however, the situation will be reversed. His assertion, "Jesus is Lord," expresses the fact that Jesus has become his point of orientation, with the consequence that he is freed from acknowledging final loyalty to his nation, family, church, or any other person and is liberated for service to these other centers of relative loyalty. Because he sees not only his own history but the history of all men in the light of the one history of Jesus of Nazareth and Easter, he will not rest content when his nation, family, or church seek to live only for themselves; he will try to set them in the service of others.   *(The Secular Meaning Of The Gospel, pp. 141-2).*

He who asserts that the history of Jesus was a normative history of reconcilation means that he is committed to the *sort* of reconciliation revealed in that history. Reconciliation, for the Christian, will always have something to do with the freedom for which Christ has set men free, with being free for one's neighbor. To accept and live such a conception of reconciliation will tend to have serious social, personal, and political consequences...The Christian understanding of reconciliation has no limit to its application. It will bear upon all areas of human life, personal and public, local and foreign. It will bear upon the way in which the Christian thinks and acts concerning the relations between nations, peoples, and political groups, as well as upon relationships in his own family. Wherever he sees at work in the world any reconciliation at all like that which characterized the history of Jesus of Nazareth, he will support it, and he will rejoice over signs of such reconcilation accomplished, however partially, as much as he rejoices over the reconciliation with his neighbor which has been made possible by his having been set free for that neighbor. *(The Secular Meaning Of The Gospel, p. 149).*

The traditional doctrine of the Incarnation says that God entered the realm of history in the person of Jesus Christ. This is a statement of faith; it will no longer function as an empirical proposition, if indeed it could ever have been said to have done so. The doctrine is frequently cited as the "reason" for taking a positive attitude toward material things, or history, or people. Because, as he says, the Christian believes in the Incarnation, he is therefore impelled to take this world, men, and history seriously. Precisely. His attitude verifies, and therefore gives the meaning of, his faith. The doctrine of the incarnation of the Logos in the realm of human activity points toward history. It expresses the believer's deep concern with history, the world of men, and the world which man investigates; it indicates that this attitude toward men and their activities is related to his attitude toward a particular piece of history.   *(The Secular Meaning Of The Gospel, p. 160).*

He who says, "Jesus is Lord," says that Jesus' freedom has been contagious and has become the criterion for his life, public and private. As Jesus was led, because of his freedom, into the midst of social and political conflict, so it is with one who shares his freedom. The Gospel asserts that Jesus is Lord of the whole world. This means that the freedom for which the Christian has been set free allows him to see the whole world in its light. *(The Secular Meaning Of The Gospel, p. 142).*

WILLIAM HAMILTON

The death of God Protestant, it can be seen, has somewhat inverted the usual relation between faith and love, theology and ethics, God and the neighbor. We are not proceeding from God and faith to neighbor and love, loving in such and such a way because we are loved in such and such a way. We move to our

230

neighbor, to the city and to the world out of a sense of the loss of God. ("The Death of God Theologies Today," p. 48)

My Protestant has no God, has no faith in God, and affirms both the death of God and the death of all the forms of theism. Even so, he is not primarily a man of negation, for if there is a movement away from God and religion, there is the more important movement into, for, toward the world, worldly life, and the neighbor as the bearer of the worldly Jesus. ("The Death of God Theologies Today," p. 37)

Our being in the world, in the city, is not only an obedience to the Reformation formula, from church to world, it is an obedience to Jesus himself. How is this so? How is Jesus being disclosed in the world, being found in the world in our conrete work?

First, Jesus may be concealed in the world, in the neighbor, in this struggle for justice, in that struggle for beauty, clarity, order. Jesus is in the world as masked, and the work of the Christian is to strip off the masks of the world to find him, and, finding him, to stay with him and to do his work. In this sense, the Christian life is not a longing and is not a waiting, it is a going out into the world. The self is discovered, but only incidentally, as one moves out into the world to tear off the masks. Life is a masked ball, a Halloween party, and the Christian life, ethics, love, is that disruptive task of tearing off the masks of the guests to discover the true princess.

In the parable of the last judgment (Matthew 25:34 ff.) the righteous did not know it was Jesus they were serving. The righteous today don't need to know it either, unless they are Christian, in which case they will say that what they are doing is not only service, work, justified for this and that structural reason; it is also an act of unmasking, a looking for, a finding and a staying with Jesus.

In this first sense, the Christian life, ethics, love, is public, outward, visible. It is finding Jesus in your neighbor: "as you did it to one of the least of these my brethren, you did it to me" (Matthew 25:40).

There is another form of the presence of Jesus Christ in the world. Here, we no longer talk about unmasking Jesus who is out there in the world somewhere, we talk about becoming Jesus in and to the world. Here, the Christian life, ethics, love, is first a decision about the self, and then a movement beyond the self into the world.

The form, if not the content, of the parable of the Good Samaritan should be recalled. Jesus is asked a question: which one, among all the many claimants out there, is my neighbor? Jesus answers the question with one of his characteristic nonanswers: "Don't look for the neighbor, be one." Or, to put the form of his answer to work on our problem: "Don't look for Jesus out there, in scripture, tradition, sacraments, Ingmar Bergman movies, in the world behind a mask—become Jesus." Become a Christ to your neighbor, as Luther put it.

In this form the Christian life is not a looking outwards to the world and its claims, it is first a look within in order to become Jesus. "For me to live," cried Paul in one of his most daring utterances, "is Christ." Ethics and love are first a dangerous descent into the self. And in this form, the Christian life, ethics, love, are not so active or worldly. At this point the Christian is the passive man, and doubtless tempted into all of the easily noted dangers of confusing the self with Jesus.

The Christian life as the discernment of Jesus beneath the worldly masks can be called work or interpretation or criticism; while the Christian life as becoming Jesus looks a little different. At this point the Christian is the sucker, the fall guy, the jester, the fool for Christ, the one who stands before Pilate and is silent, the one who stands before power and power-structures and laughs.

Whichever of the paths one takes to find or define Jesus in the world, and perhaps some of us are called to choose both ways, and some only one, the worldliness of the Protestant can never, because of this, have an utterly humanistic form. ("The Death of God Theologies Today," pp. 49-50)

It is humanism, if humanism means a belief that there are no viable objects of loyalty beyond man, his values, his communities, his life. But it is a Christian humanism. ("Questions and Answers on the Radical Theology," pp. 214-5).

The question was posed whether the death of God might be a non-event, fashioned by nothing more substantial than the eager and empty publicity mills of our day. We radical theologians have found, I think, that it is something more. It is a real event; it is a joyous event; it is a liberating event, removing everything that might stand between man and the relief of suffering, man and the love of his neighbor. It is a real event making possible a Christian form of faith for many today. It is even making possible church and ministry in our world. ("The Death of God," p. 139).

GABRIEL VAHANIAN

Let us first of all rid ourselves of a few misunderstandings:

1. By claiming that the social ethics of the Bible no longer is valid in a universe where technology has upset our conceptions of man's relationship to the world, what is asserted is simply that the cultural framework in which (and thanks to which) this ethics took shape is today superannuated. Indeed, if Bible and Word of God must not be confused it is equally appropriate to distinguish carefully that which in the ethical teaching of the Bible is but the reflection of a certain natural cultural will—the social consciousness of which, though it was perhaps determined in terms of divine revelation, was nevertheless legitimatized by a conception of the world—and an image of man commensurate with this will. The conflict, or simply the lag we deplore between Christianity and the contemproary world, comes from the fact that the political and social involvement of the Church is not legitimatized by the master ideas of our period, nor is it supported by the goals implicit in our way of understanding the world today and of projecting the human adventure.

2. One can say of the Bible that it provides us with social teachings or with principles and values "for all times" only to the extent that these teachings, principles and values are frankly tributary of the cultural and social framework in whose terms they are enunciated. Unless this tributary character is recognized, "for all times" could only mean a surcease disloyally granted on Sunday at eleven o'clock to the universe of Ptolemy, to the Roman Empire, to the dialect of Canaan; the result of which is not, as one would be tempted to think, to underline the tributary aspect that I have just mentioned but to congeal divine revelation and make it depend upon certain conditions without which it would not be possible and could have no effect. And that would indeed be the surest way of turning the Church into its own caricature, a survival of the past. And yet there, more than anywhere else, faith should demonstrate its worldliness, its secularity. Not from the world is the Christian faith to be preserved but from its own loss of flavor, from its transformation into a kind of computer providing ready-made answers to questions we have survived.

3. If then the Bible itself, its social teachings, its ethical principles and its moral values are partly the expression of a cultural phenomenon it is not surprising that in this respect, too, Christianity has just completed a page of its history, that of the Constantinian period or "Christian" era. This page we have no

other choice but to turn, and we wish to turn it only because we believe that the Bible can still provide us with a social ethics attuned to our situation.

4. Finally, we must dissipate a misunderstanding which deals with the so-called Christian civilization. Against the despisers of Christianity one must have the candor to assert both the amplitude and originality of the successes won by Christianity as a cultural ferment in the field of political action as well as in shaping the type of humanism which is characteristic of Western culture. On the other hand, we must also snatch from the nostalgic adepts their illusions of Christian civilization as the golden age of the West, and bring them to recognize that the cultural triumph of Christianity does not make its cultural vocation or obligation dependent on the institutions we have inherited. *(No Other God, pp. 87-9).*

Part of our ethical dilemma today stems not from the impossibility of a sound theological ethics but from the fact that such ethics is deprived of the context in which to operate meaningfully. Equally a part of this dilemma is our traditional conception of ethics as a system of predicting human conduct, as if losing one's self in order to gain it could at all be codified. Accordingly, to advocate or to be shocked by the "new morality" scarcely faces the problem, certain aspects of which deal with the fact that if modern man has become emancipated from the Christian ethic this is because Christian thought has not been able to emancipate itself from its bondage to sclerotic concepts, to liquidate its own past in order to assume the obligations of the present time. *(No Other God, p. 90).*

Ethics makes sense only to the extent of the social relevance of the Church. The question is not simply whether or not ethics must be subsumed under theology, whether or not Christian ethics is "contextual," or "situational," or whether it should be pegged on some theory of natural law. As a matter of fact, what these alternatives themselves reveal is that without ecclesiology, i.e., a doctrine whereby the Church is understood as a dimension of the modern world, Christian ethics can only cease to be a live option. By and large, the present moral teaching of the Church only points to the fact that it was relevant as an institution in the past, let us say, in the Middle Ages. *(No Other God, p. 87).*

It is in and through the world that God's holiness manifests itself. It dwells in the world and, no matter whether the world be conceived as profane or religious, it is the world that constitutes the context where faith must assert its secularity and the Church its eschatological reality: "Religion that is pure and undefiled before God and the Father is this: to visit orphans and widows in their affliction, and to keep oneself unstained from the world," like Abraham who, through faith, "sojourned in the land of promise, as in a foreign land *(tanquam in aliena)*" (James 1/27; Heb. 11/9: R.S.V.).

Faith understood as eschatological existence can no more withdraw from the world than devaluate the world; it gives the world its worldliness, its secularity (John 17/15). By secularity I mean the attitude by which the Christian affirms faith as presence to the world at the same time that he affirms the original goodness of the world. It is in being in the world that it is possible for the Christian to be not of the world. *(No Other God, p. 18).*

One should not lament the fact that others, such as the state or private foundations have today assumed the great cultural, political, and social tasks that the Chruch in the past initiated and accomplished, and from which our civilization benefited before turning its back on Christianity. The essential thing today is that Christianity should not miss its vocation by not assuming even the humblest tasks to which its adherents may be brought in spite of their faithfulness to the Church. As in the parable of the last judgment, could it not be that these were the most urgent and decisive tasks? And could it not be that their style is the one that behooves the Church's involvement in the world? *(No Other God, p. 95).*

Today more than ever the structures of the Church should exist only to enable it to function within or, rather, *through* the structures of the world and not vice versa.

On the other hand, the Christian's freedom justifies the responsibility he must assume toward the world. The Christian's commitment to God should be matched by a reciprocal involvement in the world. Otherwise faith runs the risk of becoming sacral or spiritual religiosity (Col. 2/16-23), while the world is surrendered to the profane, to the *saeculum,* to secularism which is today underwriting the failure of both sacralism and spiritualism as the solution of the problem. This solution is proposed as consisting in a secularized and religionless Christianity. *(No Other God, p.20).*

This vulnerability of the Christian faith hinges today on the fact that there can be no faith in God which does not assume a concomitant cultural obligation. There can be no faith without secularity. But without God there can only be secularism, whether or not it masquerades as religion. Should, then, the Christian faith be unable to overcome its present cultural estrangement brought about by the death of God, its only alternative is to become an esoteric mystery cult, that is, the very antithesis of what it has claimed to be for twenty centuries. It will increasingly become a private religion, whether on an individual and domestic basis or whether on the basis of a spiritually segregated collective experience such as the Church affords today in the suburbs of life. And the trouble with this sort of eventuality is that most Christians do not have the stamina of the Amish. As Vinet says: "To believe in God and find oneself unable to draw from it any practical consequences is, if you will, to believe in God; it also is, however, to be without God."

Therefore, just as from the biblical point of view without witnesses there is no God, so also without a cultural vocation there can be, insofar as Christianity is concerned, no faith in God. And "faith apart from works is dead" (James 2/26). *(No Other God, p. 32).*

HARVEY COX

The world is the proper location of the Christian life. It is where the Christian is called to be a Christian. It is where his discipline and devotion, his defeats and victories occur. The world is the place of Adam's assignment, the place of Jesus' ministry, the place of the church's mission. The Gospel writers tell us that Jesus spent his time with people called the Am ha-Aretz, those beyond the pale of morality and law, including drunkards, winebibbers, and shady characters. He turned his back on the accepted moral and religious leaders of the day and spent his time in what we would call the seamy side of the world. Here were the people with whom and through whom he carried out his ministry. His career was climaxed in a clash with the urban power structures. He was executed on a public dump, and the sign over his gibbet was written in three languages. The crucifixion occured at a crossroads of the world. This is where it *continues* to occur, where languages and cultures clash, where the urban power structures in their injustices are challenged, where people are willing to turn their backs on the accepted religious and moral standards of the day in order to stand with God in what he is doing for the world. *(God's Revolution And Man's Responsibility, pp. 24-5).*

The world (by this I mean the political and secular world) is the

236

sphere of God's liberating and renewing activity. The world is the theater of God's being with man. The God of the Bible, in rather sharp distinction to the other so-called gods and deities of the ancient Near East was characterized precisely by the fact that he worked in and through political events. He would not share his deity with the stars, nor the sun, nor the moon. These bodies were merely things that God had created, not divine beings. The God of the Hebrews was the God who revealed himself in the exodus, in the conquest, in the exile, in the defeat of the kingdom. He revealed himself in political events, in the liberation of the people from economic serfdom and political slavery, in the military conquest of the land, in the defeat at the hands of a world power. Thus he used political and military events to get the things done in history that he wanted done. He was perfectly willing to use people who denied him, people who had never heard about him, and even people who defied him, to do his work. *(God's Revolution And Man's Responsibility, p. 21).*

In our particular time in history we need to devote more attention to those texts in the Bible which tell us about unclear boundaries between the church and the world, about the lack of assurance that we are "in" and someone else is "out." For example the text in Matthew 7:15 is one that should mean a lot to us today: "Beware of false prophets," Jesus says, "who come to you in sheep's clothing but inwardly are ravenous wolves." We might justifiably turn this around to read: "Beware of people who come to you in the costume of ravenous wolves but inwardly they may be prophets." *(God's Revolution And Man's Responsibility, p. 109).*

The church is an object of faith, not of sight. This is not to say that the church is "invisible." It is to say rather that whenever we say something is a church, biblically speaking, we are confessing our faith. We are *not* telling someone something he can find out by consulting a phone book. The church uses buildings, budgets, and bureaucracies, but it is not to be wholly identified with them. It is a people in motion, an "eventful movement" in which barriers are being struck down and a radically new community beyond the divisiveness of inherited labels and stereotypes is emerging.

It is clear, then, that this church-event, this reconciliation in action, cannot be either restricted to or excluded from the organizations called churches. God's reconciling work *may* be going on among them. It may not be. More likely it is and it isn't. More likely it is occuring within them and also at many places outside them. I believe that the real job of those in the churches today is to discern where God's reconciliation is breaking in and to identify themselves with this action. *(The Secular City. p. 198).*

Our social vision must be revolutionary. The difference between us and the Communists is not that they favor a world revolution and we do not. Rather, we must espouse a different *kind* of revolution, a revolution that makes the fruits of the earth available to all people without depriving them of the benefits of political and cultural freedom. We must be *more* revolutionary than the Communists and we must carry through the revolution first in the United States if it is to convince anyone anywhere else. *(The Secular City, p. 157).*

God through history summons man to affirm and celebrate what God wants him to be: Man, with all that implies. As Kierkegaard, Marx, and Nietzsche saw, to be a man involves personal, social, and cultural initiative and responsibility. It means accepting the terrifying duty of deciding *who I will be* rather than merely introjecting stereotypes that others assign to me. It means opening my eyes to the way power is distributed and wielded in a society and assuming a full measure of pain and temptation that goes with wielding it. It means defying any image of life which discourages criticism or undercuts human creativity. Metaphors which are allowed to become metaphysical become monsters. To be a man means to care for and name the fellow-man Eve, and with her to have dominion over the earth; to name and care for the creature whom God places in the human world of freedom. *(God's Revolution And Man's Responsibility, p. 47).*

Just turning our attention toward this world is not, in itself, a good thing. One can turn toward the world to exploit it, to debase it or to serve it. The Christian turns toward this world because God does in Jesus Christ, and he does so for the same reason, to "love it and give himself for it." ("An Exchange of Views," p. 120).

It was the mistake of our pietistic forebearers to believe that simply *coming out* of the world was enough—"don't be worldly." They forgot the second half which was to *go back into* the world, to identify with it, to love it, to serve it. It was the mistake of our liberal forefathers to believe that coming out of the world was unnecessary—that man could serve the world without first being freed from it. But God's way involves a two-way motion—to free his people from captivity and, in turn, to make them servants. He frees the church *from* the gods of the world, *from* the powers that decimate and deteriorate life, so that his people can live *in* the world as its servants. *(God's Revolution and Man's Responsibility, pp. 69-70).*

So God also makes us free for life, and not many of us are really ready to accept that kind of freedom. We are afraid of the freedom of defatalization. But to live with responsible freedom in today's world is what we mean by biblical faith. To answer God's call today is to respond in freedom and in responsibility to the tumultous events of our times through which he is calling us. Faith does not mean attaching one's signature to a series of religious propositions, whether Catholic or Unitarian or Baptist; it means living one's life in the freedom and responsibility that God makes possible. *(God's Revolution And Man's Responsibility, pp. 67-8).*

THOMAS J. J. ALTIZER

Christian theologians have told us that faith is a risk—despite the fact that few theologians have ventured to take upon themselves anything more than a token risk—and we must recognize that a faith which is not open to the loss of faith is not a true form of faith. A faith that is a haven from doubt and suffering is not only a false faith but is a reversal of the kenotic way of the Word. Moreover, the Christian can only participate in the suffering and broken body of the humanity of our time by freely sharing the depths of its anguish and despair, not with the self-conscious realization that his participation is vicarious, but rather with the certainty that there is no true suffering which is foreign to faith. If ours is a time that shatters the very possibility of faith, then the Christian faith is in vain, and the honest man can only renounce all faith. Therefore, for those Christians who have discovered that an established form of faith has become wholly unreal, there is really no choice, we must either open ourselves to a new form of faith or abandon faith itself.   *(The Gospel Of Christian Atheism, p. 28).*

With the death of the Christian God, every transcendent ground is removed from all consciousness and experience, and humanity is hurled into a new and absolute immanence. Our chaos becomes manifest as a uniquely modern chaos when it is ever more comprehensively present in response to the emptying of the transcendent realm, as its darkness fills every pocket of light, and night falls throughout the whole gamut of experience. Now an ultimate choice is thrust upon every man, as he can either turn back in horror at our chaos by engaging in a final No-saying, or he can turn forward and meet our darkness by means of an ultimate Yes-saying, a total affirmation of our actual and immediate existence. Such an acceptance and affirmation is possible only if man will give all of the energy which he once directed to a transcendent beyond to the immediate moment, thus releasing every source of energy so as to effect a total engagement with the actual present before him. *(The Gospel Of Christian Atheism, pp. 150-151).*

If we can find a way to understand and affirm absolute immanence as a contemporary and kenotic realization of the Kingdom of God, an expression in our experience of an original movement of Christ from transcendence to immanence, then we can give ourselves to the darkest and most chaotic moments of our world as contemporary ways to the Christ who even now is becoming all in all. Nothing less is demanded of the Christian who would truly and fully live in our world, and nothing less is promised by the radically kenotic way of Christ. *(The Gospel Of Christian Atheism, pp. 151-152)*

Once God has ceased to exist in human experience as the omnipotent and numinous Lord, there perishes with him every moral imperative addressed to man from a beyond, and humanity ceases to be imprisoned by an obedience to an external will or authority. *(The Gospel Of Christian Atheism. p. 127)*

Only by accepting and even willing the death of God in our experience can we be liberated from a transcendent beyond, an alien beyond which has been emptied and darkened by God's self-annihilation in Christ. To the extent that we attempt to cling to a transcendent realm, a realm that has become ever darker and emptier in the actuality of our experience, we must be closed to the actual presence of the living Christ, and alienated from the contemporary movement of the divine process. *(The Gospel Of Christian Atheism. p. 136).*

The Christian, however, cannot escape the fact that he must make a choice. He must either choose the God who is actually manifest and real in the established form of faith, or he must confess the death of God and give himself to a quest for a whole new form of faith. If he follows the latter course, he will sacrifice an established Christian meaning and morality, abandoning all those moral laws which the Christian Church has sanctioned, and perhaps even negating the possibility of an explicitly Christian moral judgment. Certainly he will be forced to renounce every moral imperative with a transcendent ground, and this means that he must forswear the possibility of an absolute moral law, and at best look upon all forms of moral judgment as penultimate ways which must inevitably act as barriers to the full realization of energy and life. Indeed, the Christian who bets that God is dead must recognize that he himself has not yet passed through the death of God at whatever point he clings to moral law and judgment. True, he can look forward to the promise of total forgiveness, but the forgiveness which he chooses can only be realized here and now; it must evaporate and lose all meaning to the extent that it is sought in a distant future or a transcendent beyond. Yet the Christian who wagers upon the death of God can be freed from the alien power of all moral law, just as he can be liberated from the threat of an external moral judgment, and released from the burden of a transcendent source of guilt. Knowing that his sin is forgiven, such a Christian can cast aside the crutches of guilt and resentment. Only then can he rise and walk. *(The Gospel Of Christian Atheism, p.147).*

We Christians are called upon to be loyal only to Christ, only to the Incarnate Word who has appeared in our flesh, and therefore we should already have been prepared for the appearance of Christ without God. We know that Christ is present in the concrete actuality of our history or he is not truly present at all. Rather than abandoning Christ by renouncing our history, we must confess that God has died if this is the path to the fully profane moment of our time. But we cannot meet our time if we remain bound to a God who no longer appears in time and space. It is precisely by freely willing the death of God that we can be open to our time and thereby open to the Christ who is always present, the Word that has actually become united with our flesh. ("Creative Negation in Theology," p. 866)

We must recognize that to cling to the Christian God in our time is to evade the human situation of our century and to renounce the inevitable suffering which is its lot. Already a Kierkegaard and a Dostoevsky knew that no suffering can be foreign to the Christian, not even the anguish that comes with the loss of God, for the way of the Christian is to bear with Jesus all the pain of the flesh. *(The Gospel Of Christian Atheism, p. 23).*

A love of the world is a total affirmation of an actual and immediate present: but in totally affirming the present, we must will that it recur, and that it recur eternally the same. A refusal to will the eternity of the present, the eternity of this actual present before us, can only proceed out of an attachment to transcendence, a bondage to a power lying outside the present, a power withholding us from a total affirmation of the world...Dare we bet that Christ is fully present in the actuality of the present moment? Then we must bet that God is dead, that a backward movement to eternity is a betrayal of Christ, and that a flight from the pain of existence is a refusal of the passion of Christ. The radical Christian calls us into the center of the world, into the heart of the profane, with the announcement that Christ is present here and he is present nowhere else. Once we confess that Christ is fully present in the moment before us, then we can truly love the world, and can embrace even its pain and darkness as an epiphany of the body of Christ. It is precisely by truly loving the world, by fully existing in the immediacy of the present moment, that we will know that Christ is love, and then we shall know that love is a Yes-saying to the totality of existence.

Christian love is an incarnate love, a self-giving to the fullness of the world, an immersion in the actuality of time and the flesh. Therefore our Yes-saying must give us totally to the moment before us, and if we accept its actuality as the "center" which is everywhere, then we can be delivered from every temptation of regressing to a backward movement which is a reversal and diminution of an actual and immediate present...Radical faith calls us to give ourselves totally to the world, to affirm the fullness and immediacy of the present moment as the life and the energy of Christ. Thus, ultimately the wager of the radical Christian is simply a wager upon the full and actual presence of the Christ who is a totally incarnate love. *(The Gospel Of Christian Atheism, pp. 155-157).*

The contemporary Christian who bets that God is dead must do so with a full realization that he may very well be embracing a life-destroying nihilism; or,worse yet, he may simply be submitting to the darker currents of our history, passively allowing himself to be the victim of an all too human horror. No honest contemporary seeker can ever lose sight of the very real possibility that the willing of the death of God is the way to madness, dehumanization, and even to the most totalitarian form of society yet realized in history. Who can doubt that a real passage through the death of God must issue in either an abolition of man or in the birth of a new and transfigured humanity? *(The Gospel Of Christian Atheism, p. 146).*

JOHN A. T. ROBINSON

Prayer and ethics are simply the inside and outside of the same thing. Indeed, they could both be defined, from the Christian point of view, as meeting the unconditional in the conditioned in unconditional personal relationship. And it is impossible to reassess one's doctrine of God, of how one understands the transcendent, without bringing one's view of morality into the same melting-pot. Indeed, the two are inseparable. For assertions about God are in the last analysis assertions about Love—about the ultimate ground and meaning of personal relationships. *(Honest To God, p. 105).*

No person, no society, can continue or cohere for any length of time without an accepted ethic, just as ordered life becomes impossible without a recognized legal system or a stable economy. And the Christian least of all can be disinterested in these fields. The more he loves his neighbour, the more he will be concerned that the whole *ethos* of his society—cultural, moral, legal, political and economic—is a good one, preserving personality rather than destroying it.

But he will also be the first to confess that Christ does not supply him with an ethical code, any more than he supplies him with a legal system, or a polity, or an economy. For it was not Jesus's purpose to provide any of these. Jesus's purpose was to call men to the Kingdom of God, to subject everything in their lives to the overriding, unconditional claim of God's utterly gracious yet utterly demanding rule of righteous love. And men could not acknowledge this claim without accepting the constraint of the same sacrificial, unselfregarding *agape* over all their relations with each other. It is this undeviating claim, this inescapable constraint, which provides the profoundly constant element in the distinctively Christian response in every age or clime. For it produces in Christians, however different or diversely placed, a direction, a cast, a style of life, which is recognizably and gloriously the same. Yet *what* precisely they must do to embody this claim will differ with every century, group and individual. *(Christian Morals Today, pp. 12-3).*

There is no such thing as *a* Christian ethic. The raw material of an ethic is provided by the ethos of a society or a century or a group. Times change and even Christians change with them. And, as we are increasingly aware in our complex technocratic society, our moral judgements have to take into account all kinds of purely technical assessments in which Christians have no peculiar or unchanging wisdom.

As long as we allow for this relativistic factor in all ethical judgements and are not afraid to face it as Christians, then we shall not be unduly disturbed by our divergent moralities. Of course, a sizable part of these differences must always be put down to slowness, stupidity and sin — and the blindness of Christians to such issues as slavery, war and race is, in retrospect, frightening. Nevertheless, the changes and differences are, I think, far more to be attributed not to moral enlightenment (if any) but to the fact that the non-moral factors are constantly shifting, so that what were not moral issues become so, and *vice versa*. A problem is redefined or its scale is altered until a difference in degree becomes a difference in kind. A change in biological or psychological knowledge may modify our understanding of the responsibility involved, or a shift in the structure of society may cause the same behaviour (such as gambling or drink) to have very different social consequences *(Christian Morals Today, p. 14).*

My plea is that Christians must not fear flux or be alarmed at the relativity of all ethics to the ethos of their day. We assume too readily that God is in the rocks but not in the rapids. We identify him instinctively with what is permanent and set ourselves commissioned to stand for the changeless in a welter of chaos not of his making. But that is a Greek assumption, not a Biblical. We are not here as Christians with changeless principles to *apply* to an alien process. God is *in* the history, addressing us and claiming us through it. And what he says will not always be the same as he said to our fathers. Yet if we are his sheep, we shall recognize his voice. For Jesus Christ is the same, yesterday and today and for ever. And yet the Jesus we serve is the Christ come and coming in the flesh. He wills to become incarnate in, the contemporary of, every generation; and this means that the Christ of today is not simply the Christ of yesterday. We must embrace the relativities and not fear them. For the assurance we are given is not of a fixity impervious to change, but of a faithfulness promising purchase over it. *(Christian Morals Today, pp. 18-9).*

The moral precepts of Jesus are not intended to be understood legalistically, as prescribing what all Christians must do, whatever the circumstances, and pronouncing certain courses of action universally right and others universally wrong. They are not legislation laying down what love always demands of every one: they are illustrations of what love may at any moment require of anyone. They are, as it were, parables of the Kingdom in its moral claims—flashlight pictures of the uncompromising demand which the Kingdom must make upon any who would respond to it. The word to the rich young man, 'Go and sell all that you have', is not a universal principle of the ethical life, but as it were a translation into the imperative of the parable of the rich merchant, who went and did just this for the pearl of great price. This transition to the imperative—'Go and do likewise'—is not legislation, but a way of saying, as Nathan said to David at the close of the classic parable of the Old Testament, 'You are the man'. It is a reminder that the parables are precisely not interesting stories of general application, but the call of the Kingdom to a specific group or individual at a particular moment. *(Honest To God, pp. 110-11)*.

In Christian ethics the only pure statement is the command to love; every other injunction depends on it and is an explication or application of it. There are some things of which one may say that it is so inconceivable that they could ever be an expression of love—like cruelty to children or rape—that one might say without much fear of contradiction that they are for Christians always wrong. But they are so persistently wrong *for that reason.* There is not a whole list of things which are 'sins' *per se.* That is not to say that there are not working rules which for practical purposes one can lay down as guides to Christian conduct—the catechetical passages in the New Testament epistles give plentiful examples. But in the last resort—St. Paul makes it as clear as Jesus—these various commandements are comprehended under the one command of love and based upon it. Apart from this there are no unbreakable rules. *(Christian Morals Today, p. 16)*.

Nothing can of itself always be labelled as 'wrong'. One cannot, for instance, start from the position 'sex relations before marriage' or 'divorce' are wrong or sinful in themselves. They may be in 99 cases or even 100 cases out of 100, but they are not intrinsically so, for the only intrinsic evil is lack of love. Continence and indissolubility may be the guiding norms of love's response; they may, and should, be hedged about by the laws and conventions of society, for these are the dykes of love in a wayward and loveless world. But, morally speaking, they must be defended, as Fletcher puts it, 'situationally, not prescriptively'—in other words, in terms of the fact that persons matter, and the deepest welfare of these particular persons in this particular situation matters, more than anything else in the world. Love's casuistry must cut deeper and must be more searching, more

245

demanding, than anything required by the law, precisely because it goes to the heart of the individual personal situation. *(Honest To God, p. 118).*

The plea for the priority of love fully recognizes the obligation upon Christians in each generation to help fashion and frame the moral net which will best preserve the body and soul of *their society*. We have seen the Christians of the first century seeking to relate the command of *agape* to their bewildering new environments, Jewish and Gentile, in the Graeco-Roman world. From their obedience we can indeed learn what the Spirit may be saying to the churches of the twentieth century. But we shall not do it by treating their formulations (any more than those of the Old Testament) as a permanent code—or by attempting to solve the perplexities of our generation with 'the Bible says.' *(Christian Morals Today, p. 31).*

Life in Christ Jesus, in the new being, in the Spirit, means having no absolutes but his love, being totally uncommitted in every other respect but totally committed in this. And this utter openness in love to the 'other' for his own sake is equally the only absolute for the non-Christian, as the parable of the Sheep and the Goats shows. He may not recognize Christ in the 'other' but in so far as he has responded to the claim of the unconditional in love he has responded to him—for he is in the 'depth' of love. The Christian ethic is not relevant merely for the Christian, still less merely for the religious. The claim of the Christ may come to others, as indeed it often comes to the Christian, incognito: but since it is the claim of home, of the personal ground of our very being, it does not come as anything foreign. It is neither heteronomous nor autonomous but theonomous.

Love alone, because, as it were, it has a built-in moral compass, enabling it to 'home' intuitively upon the deepest need of the other, can allow itself to be directed completely by the situation. It alone can afford to be utterly open to the situation, or rather ot the person in the situation, uniquely and for his own sake, without losing its direction or unconditionality. It is able to embrace an ethic of radical responsiveness, meeting every situation on its own merits, with no prescriptive laws. *(Honest To God, pp. 114-15).*

Our survey of the theological developments of the past two hundred years amply illustrates the interdependent character and the developmental impulse of Christian life and thought. Theological movements neither live nor die to themselves. Radical

Christianity is the latest but by no means the first significant transition in the way Christian faith has been interpreted and implemented. Liberalism arose partly as a rejection but partly as a continuation of Orthodoxy. Neo-orthodoxy similarly forged a new theological outlook by critically yet constructively responding to both Liberalism and Orthodoxy. Not surprisingly, we have found that radical Christianity's debt to the past seems more negative than positive, more reactionary than consolidatory. But our synoptic comparison between the new and the older theologies discloses numerous similarities, especially between radical and liberal thought.

Nevertheless radical Christianity represents a transition in religious thought which sets it apart from all previous theological realignments. The radicals relinquish the linchpins which, in one form or another, have held together all previous expressions of Christian life and thought. Faith can no longer rest on *absolute* standpoints for man or *special* places for God in nature, history or inwardness. Radical theologians like Hamilton and Altizer magnify this new assumption by stressing the discontinuity of their views with the Christian tradition in general and Neo-orthodoxy's reformulation in particular. In contrast, Robinson, Vahanian, Cox and even van Buren contend that their radical proposals are permitted if not required by the essential concerns of Christian faith from its New Testament beginnings. While such extreme claims about radical Christianity's relation to the Christian past are open to question, the qualitative differences between the new and older theologies can hardly be overemphasized and must not be underestimated. These men are the pioneering spokesmen for a radically new Christianity.

PART THREE

THE SIGNIFICANCE

OF

RADICAL CHRISTIANITY

As we have seen, the radical innovations of the new theologies reach from the center to the circumference of Christian faith as presently understood and practiced. Of course, at one time or another, every cardinal doctrine of Christian faith has been subject to debate. But seldom if ever has the place of God been so radically questioned as in the new theologies. The reality of God has always been the central datum of Christian faith and, thus, any radical rethinking of the doctrine of God will affect the whole circle of Christian beliefs. The radicals have focused on this crucial center of Christian faith, but they have also begun to unpack the implications of their new views on God for the whole of Christian faith. Understandably they have given most of their attention to the function of Christ, the meaning of existence and the duties of discipleship. Little more than sketches of how the other theological and practical expressions of radical Christianity will be developed have been offered. But, despite the fragmentary and piecemeal character of the writings of the radicals to date, a picture of the distinctive shapes and styles of radical Christianity has emerged.

Because this picture signals a break with most preceding ways of interpreting and implementing faith, some estimate of the significance of radical Christianity must be made. What will the lasting impact of this radical transition in Christian thought and life be? Is the radical thrust an aberrant *tour de force* or an irreversible new direction for future Christianity?

These questions cannot be answered by monitering public opinion polls and mass media communications alone. Churchmen who hoped (and perhaps prayed) that radical Christianity was the joint creation of publicity-seeking theologians and fad-mongering journalists take comfort in the public decline of "the death of God controversy." But surely their relieved pronouncements that "the death of God controversy" is dead and their official post mortems on the anatomy of this slogan are premature. No one can deny that what William Hamilton calls the "journalistic phase" of the movement has ended. Pronouncements concerning radical Christianity no longer merit front-page headlines or guarantee best sellers. Nor does anyone, least of all the radicals, deny that sensationalism and faddishness created a part of the impact of radical Christianity. Whether intended or not, the spectacular slogans and publicity surrounding the rise of radical Christianity has driven the Church further *into* the world. While theology may never again dominate the mass media, the 'publicizing' of theology is a lasting consequence of the radical debate. The Church can no longer protect herself or her children from doing theology in the public domain. The protective walls of dogmatic pronouncements, coercive authority and esoteric language have been leveled to the ground. But, this consequence aside, sensationalism and faddishness per se count neither for nor against the truth of ideas.

Describing or dismissing radical Christianity as nothing more than a theological and journalistic fad errs in two ways. The issues and alternatives being explored by the radicals will not disappear with the sensationalism surrounding the movement. For one thing, all six men treated in this book are in their 30's and 40's and are just entering the productive stages of their academic careers. They will all surely continue to build on what they have already taught and written. They readily admit that the careful and serious work lies ahead and they welcome the chance to pursue their concerns without the distracting and distorting influences of public controversy and fanfare. Their continuing work will be supported and perhaps surpassed by a number of theological unknowns in the Church and the universities who have begun to make their own contributions to the radical ferment. But the issues and concerns of radical Christianity are guaranteed an enduring significance for more substantive reason than the mere continuing presence of radical theologians. The radicals are dealing with issues that most contemporary theologians consider central. Radical views on the relations between church and world, faith and history, reality and language, theology and philosophy and Christianity and other religions cannot fail to contribute to differing theological approaches to these same problems. More important, the radicals are exploring forms of Christian faith which do not rest on absolute standpoints for man or special places for God in nature, history and consciousness. Their varied and fragmentary efforts are not always satisfactory to sympathetic critics, to fellow radicals or even to themselves. But they have accepted a theological challenge that cannot be reversed and must not be ignored. They have accepted the full weight of the threat and the promise that the modern world holds for Christian faith. Their responses to this crisis in Christian belief and behavior will not be rapidly completed or accepted. But the radicals have opened the door to a future for Christianity in a thoroughly relative and secular world.

More explicitly, what is the relation between the present and the future impact of radical Christianity? This question can be answered in two ways. The significance of radical Christianity may be measured generally in light of the value of any theological controversy. More specifically, each radical may be evaluated in terms of his fundamental insights and key contributions to present theological debate. A sketch of both kinds of answers will furnish our final perspective on the new theologies.

I. THE VALUE OF THEOLOGICAL CONTROVERSY

Traditionally the Church has found little value in theological controversy throughout her history. Concessions have been made to theological dissenters but these have been dictated by prudential concerns. Benefits have been realized from theological disputes but these have been rationalized in pragmatic terms. These typical responses are illustrated in the debate surrounding radical Christianity when creedal denominations have to *avoid* heresy trials and when orthodox Christians *laud* the radical debate for making religion newsworthy. But such concessions and benefits are only grudgingly allowed by religious leaders and theological orientations which claim to possess the infallible and indubitable truth and grace of God. Religious tolerance and theological diversity have no legitimate grounds in the basic assumptions and cardinal beliefs of Christian Orthodoxy.

But, as we have seen, profound changes concerning the task of theology have occurred in the last two centuries. The whole relativizing process has called into question traditional Christianity's claim to an authoritarian basis and unchanging content for theology. Accordingly, a variety of adjustments to this challenge have been made within the Church's life and thought. Prior to radical Christianity, Liberalism offered the most thoroughgoing accomodation to relativism by acknowledging the cultural influences operative in all expressions of Christian faith and the positive truth in all religions. Neo-orthodoxy took a different approach by claiming that God gives himself fully and freely through historically relative persons, institutions and beliefs. Even Orthodoxy reflects this climate of relativism and tolerance by combatting theological aberrations more humanely than with charred stakes and less obviously than with banned books. In short, the Church has decided to accept theological diversity and controversy as inevitable if not always desirable.

But good reasons exist for regarding theological controversy as a positive value rather than a tragic inevitability. These reasons are due as much to the nature of theology as to the inescapability of relativism. As we have seen from earlier discussion, theology and faith are broadly related as theory and practice. Faith is certainly more than mastering a body of information or espousing a system of beliefs. Faith involves the *whole* man as a feeling, valuing, relating and thinking creature. Faith denotes attitudes, actions and relationships as well as understanding. But the practice of a living faith is always related to some religious beliefs. Belief without practice is sterile intellectualism but practice without belief is humanly impossible. Some beliefs are operative in all but the most elemental human feelings, actions and relationships. Religious beliefs embody convictions about life's ultimate purposes and total environment. Religious beliefs express both a way of life and a vision of reality. These beliefs may not always be clearly formulated or cogently supported. But they are necessary conditions and inevitable conditioners of all religious behavior. Theology offers a clear formulation and cogent support of the religious beliefs involved in actual religious behavior. Like all theoretical activity, theology is one step removed from the concrete actions and assumptions of professing Christians. But the theoretical character of theology by no means separates it from the life and thought of faithful men and communities. Theory grows out of practice but practice grows up through theory. A way of life can be followed more consistently and shared more readily if it is given intelligible and coherent expression. A vision of reality can be employed more fruitfully and trusted more fully if it is related to all human experience and knowledge. Theology serves the Christian and the Church by reflecting and directing believing experience to all domains of human activity and knowledge.

Two implications of theology's service to faith are especially relevant to the issue of theological controversy. On the one hand, surprising as it might sound, genuine faith may be practiced *without* an adequate theology. A person may live faith better than he explains faith. Just as many people experience love deeply without profoundly understanding or poetically verbalizing their love, so most people experience faith without expressing it eloquently or grasping it theologically. Doing faith better than *theologizing* faith is always possible since practice always precedes theory in the order of their importance and often in the order of their occurrence. Even in those areas of human endeavor where theoretical grasp comes before practical mastery, theory arises out of practice originally and may be subsequently modified in practice. Furthermore, practice typically goes before theory in many domains of human activity. The most important activities of this kind are morality and religion. Both morality and religion basically involve attitudes and actions which are learned more by imitation and acculturation than by intellection and memorization. Children especially master a moral or a religious commitment without the burden or the benefit of its theoretical underpinnings. Even in most adult "conversions," changes in personal relations and conduct usually precede theological illuminations or inferences. Theology is a 'second order' activity and for this reason may remain absent or ambiguous in the believing experience of individual Christians.

Considering this distance between theology and faith, theological controversy appears to hold little immediate threat or promise to workaday Christians. This surmise held true in most of the Church's past theological altercations. Doctrinal disputes were waged behind the protective walls of political patronage, ecclesiastical structure, theological professionalism and technical literature. Translations of theological realignments into catechetic, liturgical and practical forms were so slow and slight that the pious and the public were seldom aware that any changes had been made. But the speed and the sound of theological controversy have increased dramatically in the last century. Modern revolutions in all areas of life, thought, education and communication have accelerated and popularized theological work. Consequently, the Church in the modern world must make up her mind more rapidly and publicly than in previous centuries. Theological upheavals now confront clergymen and laymen, engage believers and nonbelievers alike. People who might otherwise never raise questions or seek understanding of the theological underpinnings of their own life style and world view now face all the demands and dilemmas of theological inquiry. More and more modern Christians are becoming theologically curious and concerned about what and why they believe.

Thus, modern theological controversy serves a valuable purpose in making theology available and important to ordinary men. In a world increasingly unwilling to depend upon dogmatic authorities, men must learn to live without the guarantees of canonical scriptures and classical creeds. In a world increasingly required to tolerate conflicting viewpoints, men must learn to appreciate the concerns of competing faith commitments and religious communities. Neither of these demands, however, can be met unless men become aware of the theoretical foundations of their own and rival belief systems. The Church has taken steps in this direction previously, but the furor surrounding radical Christianity has greatly abetted the spread of theology to the common man. Denominational and parish education programs are being revamped to include serious studies in theology. Private and even public educational institutions are increasingly developing academic studies in religion. Both in and out of the Church, at least minimal theological understanding is becoming a personal possibility and necessity. Such understanding cannot help but clarify for all the meaning of Christian faith.

But this dissemination of theology to the common man could be nothing more than a by-product of theological controversy. The need for all men to have some awareness of the theoretical underpinnings of their own faith and the faiths of others may be a consequence of publicized theological disputes. But do doctrinal disputes do anything more than heighten and confirm doctrinal differences? Can theological controversy establish bridges of mutual understanding and even mutual enlightenment between rival faith commitments? More important, can theological revolutions alter the understanding and even practice of one's own believing experience?

These questions point to a second implication of the relation between faith and theology which bears on the significance of theological controversy. Genuine faith may be distorted by an inadequate theology. Confused and dubious beliefs can have a destructive effect on personal and social behavior. As we have seen, many Christians are simply ignorant of the theological underpinnings of their own life styles and world views. They have no clear understanding of what they believe or cogent explanation of why they believe. In all likelihood, their faith was acquired in the company of others largely through emulation and acculturation. Such persons are none the worse off for their theological illiteracy as long as their practical faith is realistic and responsible. Furthermore, their living faith could be and usually has been theologically formulated and justified by some persons within their community of faith. But religious beliefs which *cannot* be clearly formulated and cogently justified will distort in one way or another all religious behavior based upon them. Using again our earlier comparison between love and faith, people may experience love without having heard and learned of St. Paul or Hugh Hefner. But love consonant with St. Paul's thought will hardly be the same as love more nearly like Hugh Hefner's concept. Moreover, human relations modeled explicitly on *Playboy Magazine* rather than *I Corinthians 13* will offer minimal resemblance or opportunity to genuine love. Similarly, genuine Christians may be unaware of the many competing theological accounts of Christian faith. But the differences between these theological traditions are not matters of indifference. Theologies which fail to interpret and secure believing experience adequately mislead and undermine believing experience based upon them. Genuine faith may get along without a good theology but it cannot get along with a bad theology.

Because of the potentially adverse effects of inadequate theology, the Church has always been concerned with the problem of heresy. Ambiguous and indefensible beliefs create immediate problems only for those who consciously adopt and champion them. But confusion and insecurity may also be communicated indirectly and perpetuated indefinitely through religious communities and institutions. Theological traditions profoundly affect the ethos and ethics as well as the preaching and pedagogy of religious groups. When inadequate theologies are built into the spirit and structure of religious groups, they distort the attitudes and actions of future as well as present members of these communities. Recognizing these immediate and long range dangers of heresy, Christian thinkers have always sought to disavow and discredit religious beliefs and theological systems which undermine practical faith. As long as Orthodoxy had the political and ecclesiastical power to enforce its claim to absolute and unchanging truth, theological dissenters were routinely silenced, excommunicated and sometimes even executed for corrupting the "truth" and the "innocent." But this way of defining and dispelling heresy is no longer tenable. Orthodoxy's claim to have drawn a firm and final line between theological truth and error has been upset by both the cultural and the theological developments of the last two centuries.

The recognition that all theological reflection is fallible and mutable has overturned Orthodoxy's dogmatic way of defining and dispelling heresy. Culturally, this recognition rests on modern man's acceptance of the fragmentary and developmental character of all human knowledge. Relativism is the lot of every intellectual activity because men are always limited *to* and *by* a standpoint. No viewpoint offers more than a partial view since every viewpoint is conditioned by assumptions and expectations which never completely comprehend the subject matters at hand. Furthermore, such partial knowledge undergoes change when the assumptions and expectations of a given standpoint are modified. Theology, along with every other disciplined understanding of the real world, is never free from the limitations and vicissitudes of a concrete point of view. But this cultural argument against Orthodoxy's dogmatism and defensiveness has a counterpart in the theological developments of the last two hundred years. A broad spectrum of theological positions readily admit the ambiguous and developmental character of all theological reflection. Such relativism in theological work cannot be avoided because religious beliefs can never be perfectly or permanently formulated. Even deeply committed Christians cannot practice or understand faith perfectly because of the perennial tendencies toward self-deception and self-aggrandizement. Individual and collective egoism mar the most objective and ecumenical attempts to interpret believing experience. But, even if theological reflection were completely free from the distorting influences of man's sinfulness, a permanent theology could not be formulated. Theology arises out of a continuing dialogue between the lived experience of faith in the present and the trustworthy witnesses to faith from the past. Theology must be rewritten whenever significant changes occur in faith's wider intellectual and social milieu. Theology must be relative to a given situation for faith to be relevant in that situation. In brief, all religious beliefs and theological systems are subject to criticism and change because of their perspectival and dynamic character.

Exploring these limitations of theology further, the problem of heresy while still important is seen in a completely different light. A firm line between theological truth and error can never be drawn because all theological reflection is *situational*. At most, only tentative distinctions between adequate and inadequate belief systems can be made. Such judgments are by no means insignificant since beliefs always condition for good or for ill the behavior of individuals and communities. But even broad decisions about the adequacy or inadequacy of certain interpretations and justifications of the Christian faith can no longer be made by the whole Church. The Church embraces such a diversity of cultural and religious standpoints that unanimity on theological matters is simply impossible. Judgments of theological adequacy must be made by representative communities or even individual adherents of Christian faith. Thus, even a confessional preference of one theological formulation over others must always be tempered by the realization that such choices are made *from* a limited standpoint. Espousing a given theological formulation does not require or permit the denial of all truth and light to individuals and communities within the Church who hold different theological views. One man's 'heresy' may be another man's 'orthodoxy' since no *firm* line between adequate and inadequate formulations of Christian belief can be drawn. But the problem of heresy involves more than formulating an adequate theological position for and from a limited standpoint within the Church. An adequate account of believing experience requires criticism of these past and present formulations and justifications of Christian faith which are judged inadequate. Such criticism is required because of the dynamic relation between faith and life. A final line between theological adequacy and inadequacy can never be drawn because all theological reflection is *developmental.* Theology seeks to reflect and direct believing experience to all domains of human activity and knowledge. As such, theology always interprets and supports the life of faith within the limits of prevailing knowledge, political institutions, economic processes and cultural concerns. When this environing milieu changes, theology must reinterpret the meaning of faith in order for faith to remain intelligible and vital to the whole of a person's life and thought . The more dramatic and far-reaching the changes of life and thought 'in the world,' the more urgent and necessary the reinterpretation of life and thought 'in the Church.' Thus, theological positions which were once judged adequate by communities and persons in the past may no longer illumine and support believing experience adequately. Indeed, holding on to past formulations of belief may subvert the present practice of faith! Yesterday's 'orthodoxy' may become today's 'heresy' since no *final* line between adequate and inadequate formulations of Christian belief can be drawn.

These newer insights into the nature of theological controversy have instructive parallels in extra-religious life and thought. The genius of a free society is that it builds political conflict into its structures. Building perpetual revolution into the very fabric of society permits necessary changes and prevents power monopolies. A spectrum of opinions and a rivalry between parties help maintain a rough balance between order and justice in developing political institutions. This balance is often precarious because a free society progresses like a sailing ship tacking with and against the wind. But progress is made so long as a free society checks its own excesses of political rigidity and novelty. Similarly, the

259

essence of a free university is that it promotes exhaustive scrutiny of all ideas. Understandably, institutions of learning are expected to transmit the lessons and skills of the past to succeeding generations. But academic communities are responsible for challenging as well as perpetuating the past's fund of knowledge. The most dramatic strides in human understanding have come when men dared to view the familiar world in unfamiliar ways. The unhindered pursuit of the most controversial proposals as long and as far as evidence warrants is the hallmark of human intelligence and higher learning in an open society. When cherished opinions are supplanted by more adequate assumptions, persons and institutions are often uprooted in the process of transition. But truth is served as long as the academic community checks its own excesses of intellectual traditionalism and experimentalism.

In like manner, theological controversy serves a valuable purpose in keeping theology open to criticism and change. Happily, the Church has begun to learn from political and academic experiments in the open society. Diversity and even conflict are more and more seen as signs of vitality and creativity. The ecumenical movement has realized that unity need not mean uniformity. Even the creedal denominations have recognized that change need not mean chaos. Of course, tolerance and charity are often strained beyond the breaking point when theological quarrels divide denominations, families and persons within the Church. Nowhere in the twentieth century has this strain been more apparent than in the radical debate. But wise and patient churchmen seek to contain rather than dispel theological controversy, no matter how heated the clashes become. Such clashes of theological, ecclesiastical and liturgical traditions can expose the hidden errors and enrich the partial insights of all the traditions involved.

II. THE CONTRIBUTION OF RADICAL CHRISTIANITY

Granted that any theological controversy within the Church may correct and clarify believing experience, what contribution does radical Christianity make to the whole Church's understanding and practice of Christian faith? An overwhelming majority of churchmen presently question whether the radicals offer anything more positive than a boost to theological dialogue and perhaps even pose a serious threat to practical faith. Many of these same churchmen will admit the possibility of creative conflict over matters of belief and practice but will protest that the radical upheaval is qualitatively different from all previous theological debates. The Church has often disagreed over how best to describe God and relate faith to the world. These disagreements, though bitter and deep, were always variations on foundational assumptions and values which all disputants held in common. But the radicals are not merely quarreling over the most accurate interpretation of the Bible, or the most relevant expression of the ministry or the most compelling form for the liturgy. Rather, the radicals are cutting away from fideistic and exclusivistic assumptions which, in one form or another, have undergirded Christian life and thought from its beginning. Have not the radicals thereby excluded themselves from *Christian* disagreement and even *Christian* faith, despite their protests to the contrary? Should their proposals be any more welcome within the Church than are revolutionary political activities which undermine the very foundations of a free society? Are not the radical theologies, especially the more extreme versions, so patently inadequate interpretations of Christian faith that serious debate of these proposals is unnecessary and perhaps even harmful within the Church?

While these questions are understandable, the affirmative answers implied in them are shortsighted on two counts. On the one hand, radical thought should not be rejected simply because of its revolutionary character and disturbing effect. If truth were decided by majority vote or popularity poll, human life and thought would still be quite primitive. Every great breakthrough in scientific, artistic and religious understanding outraged prevailing opinion and upset standard procedures at the time. Unfamiliar ways of viewing the familiar world always disturb the intellectual, emotional and social status quo. New truth must always supplant cherished opinions which have been firmly believed and faithfully followed by the majority. But if such 'uncommon sense' proves more realistic and responsible than 'common sense,' then nothing of value is lost and much is gained by learning to think and live a new way. For this reason, the radicals should not be condemned simply because they reject past formulations of faith or disturb present practice of faith. They may in time prove to be the misunderstood and underestimated pioneers of the way Christian life and thought must travel in a relative and secular world. The Church dare not ignore the issues or dismiss the proposals raised by the radicals because today's 'heresy' has all too often become tomorrow's 'orthodoxy'.

On the other hand, the revolutionary claims and disturbing

implications of radical thought are the very reason for taking the radicals with utter seriousness. The Church must not ignore the strident urgings of men who claim to speak as Christian disciples and thinkers. If warranted, criticism from within always proves more penetrating and devastating than criticism from without. If adequate, revolution from within always proves more sympathetic and constructive than revolution from without. But, even if internal criticism and revolution prove too severe, such loyal opposition makes an indispensable contribution to Christian life and thought. The positive contribution of even inadequate theological effort is guaranteed by the very nature of theological controversy. "Better a live heresy than a dead orthodoxy!" once quipped the British theologian P. T. Forsyth, and for good reason. A 'heresy' is not sheer doctrinal error but an *over-emphasis* on one aspect of the truth. Sometimes this over-emphasis detracts from equally important aspects of the truth. But, if the 'heretic' sees one aspect of the truth that has been minimized or forgotten by the 'orthodox,' then he must be heard regardless of how lopsided or upsetting his convictions. The pendulum swing of 'heresy' is often necessary to counterbalance a lifeless permanence in 'orthodoxy.'

In any case, then, the radicals must be taken seriously by the whole Church. They are not inventing problems for more familiar and traditional ways of interpreting and implementing Christian faith. They are facing squarely the ways relativism and secularism have already captured life and thought both *in* as well as *out* of the Church. Unlike so many other moniters of these trends within the Church, the radicals are not engaging in breast-beating or browbeating over these encroachments. Rather, they are calling the Church to welcome relativism and secularism as irreversible and unavoidable. But they are also insisting that Christian faith *newly* interpreted and implemented has an indispensable place in the modern world. As we have seen, their efforts are still somewhat in flux and fragments. Even when fully developed, none of their constructive positions may prove wholly adequate. But the radicals alone have unmasked the momentous problems which must be solved in some way for Christian faith to survive as a vital force in human life and thought. They have also suggested a number of highly original ways for retaining a Christian faith while accepting the modern world. The radicals shed more light on the collision between traditional Christianity and modern world than any other spokesmen within the Church today. Therefore, a synopsis of their key insights and distinctive contributions will furnish the most reliable guidelines available for understanding and resolving the contemporary crisis of Christian belief and behavior.

1. John A. T. Robinson

Robinson's theological work is motivated by his concern over the growing gulf between traditional Christianity's supernaturalistic framework and the modern world's operating assumptions. Both the Bible and classical Orthodoxy assume a two-world framework in their expressions of Christian faith. The natural world is surrounded before, above and after by a supernatural world. Life in the natural world is created, controlled and consummated by the supernatural world. For the present, *religious* authorities, institutions and activities link these two worlds meaningfully and responsibly. But this familiar framework of otherworldliness and clericalism has been all but dissolved by modern life and thought, and therein lies the mandate for a *radical* reformulation of Christian faith. The vast majority of Christians and non-Christians equate Christian faith with this traditional framework. Unless a new framework is developed, Christian faith will not be an option for those who find otherworldliness and clericalism irrelevant and unacceptable. Convinced that more and more men are rejecting Christian faith *because* of these traditional theological underpinnings, Robinson has set out to develop a new theological framework which is adequate to the essence of historic Christian faith and to contemporary secular man.

Robinson believes that faith's essence can be adequately preserved without the supernaturalistic framework of biblical and orthodox Christianity. Although *Honest to God* marked a turn toward radical reconstruction, he claims that this book and all subsequent writings embody one conviction that he has held throughout his life. They all explore his commitment to 'the personal' as the ultimate reality in human life and thought. Traditional Christianity expresses this same central conviction in its view of God as the Personal Creator, Judge and Redeemer of the universe. But this traditional form of 'the personal' has become religiously misleading and rationally untenable for modern man. Not only does traditional theism portray God as overseeing and intervening the world process. It also focuses religion on a Super-Person beyond all things rather than on 'the personal' in the midst of all things. Speaking of the ultimate reality of 'the personal' as *a* Person makes God and faith increasingly remote from secular life and thought. Thus, honesty to the modern world and fidelity to historic Christianity requires a new way of expressing the ultimate reality of 'the personal.' The existential experience of God as an otherworldly Person has gone dead on modern man. But the rockbed reality of personal love at the heart of all things remains very much alive. Neither theism nor pantheism can adequately express this depth dimension. Thus, Robinson adopts a panentheistic model to represent and communicate the ultimate reality of 'the personal.' He portrays God as being neither apart from nor identical with the world by distinctively combining secularism's 'profane' approach with mysticism's 'sacred' approach to the whole of reality. God is the 'interpersonal field' at once in and beyond all things and persons, happenings and relationships. Robinson's future theological work will doubtlessly continue these explorations into God at the juncture of the secular and the mystical.

Nor surprisingly, Robinson's constructive efforts are criticized by his fellow radicals for remaining too traditional and by more traditional theologians for becoming too radical. But must not the Church emulate his concern for *the apologetic task of theology?* Here the word "apologetic" does not mean making an excuse for faith but rather making a case for faith. As such, apologetic theology has been variously defined and undertaken. For centuries Christian apologetics meant defending the Christian faith against all intellectual attacks from the world. More recently, especially in nineteenth century Liberalism, apologetic theology has come to mean commending Christian faith within the intellectual assumptions of the world. This newer sense of apologetic theology as dialogue rather than diatribe is the only viable intellectual stance for the Church in the modern world. But, unfortunately, biblicistic theology, preaching and piety systematically reject most if not all legitimate challenges to the thought-world of the Bible. How many theologians refuse to reinterpret religious beliefs which are clearly contradicted by scientific knowledge and human experience? How many ministers perpetuate the old tired clichés which have long ago lost all meaning in and out of the Church? How many believers blindly accept venerable doctrines which do not fit in or fill out the ways they really think and live? Even if Robinson's program for reconciling historic Christianity with the modern world is not entirely satisfying, he clearly represents the apologetic stance that must characterize Christian thought and life. The meaning of Christian faith must be harmonized with all trustworthy knowledge. The invitation to Christian faith must be intelligible to any modern man. The relevance of Christian faith must extend to all domains of life. We must learn such honesty, no matter how difficult or upsetting the process, before we or the world will truly know what and why we believe.

2. Thomas J. J. Altizer

Altizer characterizes his theological position as "Christian atheism." Behind this shocking and spectacular catchword lies a complex and controversial view of God's nature and activity. God is a living and growing Spirit rather than a static and changeless Being. As such God is continually in a process of self-expression and self-fulfillment. While a great deal of biblical and even traditional support can be found for a dynamic and developmental view of God, Altizer's explanation of where and how this process occurs has parallels or precursors in the history of Christian thought. God's self-expression is located in the concrete events of human history. Similar to the way an artist needs materials, so God needs the world to express himself. God is no more the world than artistry is its materials. But, similarly, God can no more be separated from some world than artistry can be separated from some media. God only lives, moves and has his being in and through a concrete world. Furthermore, Altizer sees God's self-fulfillment as a dialectical succession of self-expressions. God's worldly forms of self-expression are not timelessly and universally fixed. God is not expressed throughout the world everytime and everywhere the same. Nor do God's worldly forms of self-expression develop gradually and continuously. God is not fulfilled by cumulatively and quantitatively incarnating the world. Rather God moves toward self-fulfillment through a series of self-expressions which both *negate* and *transmute* earlier self-expressions.

This dialectical movement in which one form of God's self-expression passes over into a subsequent form through negation and transmutation underlies Altizer's entire thought. Like the nineteenth-century philosopher Hegel before him, he believes that the dialectical method of thinking furnishes the best human analogy for God's nature and activity. The dialectical mode of thinking is a process of entertaining an opinion, then a counteropinion, and finally reconciling these two apparent contradictions by combining their distinctive strengths while avoiding their respective weaknesses. In similar fashion, God moves toward a Final Completion through a continuing succession of self-expressions and self-emptyings which lead to even fuller self-expressions. Within this dialectical framework, Altizer's statements about the death of God become intelligible. The "death of God" is not a metaphorical phrase to denote a change in the way man previously perceived the universe or spoke of God. Rather, this phrase describes an event in history when God as an otherworldly Being and Power died in Jesus Christ. But this "death" was the *dialectical* emptying of an otherworldly into a this-worldly self-expression of God. Thenceforth a radically immanent participation in the world succeeded a radically transcendent relation to the world. Instead of being like an artist who expresses himself through materials while remaining personally apart and distinct from them, God now expresses himself through the world like a person expressing himself through his embodiment. As living and growing Spirit, God now totally indwells the concrete and actual world. Furthermore, within this view of the "death" of God's transcendent form Altizer's claim that a living faith must affirm God's "death" also becomes understandable. The transmutation of God's otherworldly self-expression into a radically immanent self-expression actually happened in the life and death of Jesus Christ. But this radically new presence of God in the world was obscured by the Church's adoption of thought patterns which still pictured God above and beyond the world. Even the doctrines of the Incarnation and the Crucifixion only ambiguously expressed this new nearness of God. Only the historical decline of Christendom and rise of secularism finally stripped Christian faith of its archaic and otherworldly gaze. The Church at last *can* because it *must* face the radical significance of Jesus Christ—God *is* everywhere in our world, especially in "every human face and hand." Thus, affirming the transcendent God's "death" really means sharing the living Spirit's presence and each concrete moment's eternity. For yet another dialectical transmutation lies ahead when God's this-worldly self-expression passes over into a Final Completion which will sum up all things in God's eternal self-fulfillment.

Obviously Altizer leaves himself wide-open for criticism because of his obscure language and controversial proposals. But can the Church afford to ignore his reminder of *the present reality of God?* Certainly the popular understanding of God's relation to the world localizes God in a this-worldly past or an otherworldly future. How many people imprison God in biblical history because they mistakenly believe God spoke only to biblical figures and came only in Jesus Christ? How many people exclude God from their worldly involvements because they completely separate spiritual and earthly things? How many people long to be with God in celestial places because they naively assume that God lies beyond time and space? Regardless of how bizarre Altizer's view of God's present reality, he does issue a timely warning to contemporary Christianity. We must cease mistaking indebtedness for bondage to the past. We must learn that God is not restricted or exhausted by an historical apprehension, even the Bible's or the Church's. More important, we must cease distinguishing God from the world by separating God from the world. Whatever meaning and reality the word "God" can have for us today must be found in and through our present world. Protecting or removing God from the changes and frailties of human experience neither honors God nor preserves faith.

3. Harvey Cox

Cox emphasizes modern secularity's enormous potentialities for man and its legitimate compatibility with faith. "Secularity" means that all human concerns and understanding are limited to the horizons of world and human history. These limitations have not been so much imposed as discovered as men gradually lost their interest in other worlds and outgrew their subservience to ecclesiastical domination. These changes involve great risks but the potential gains far outweigh the risks. The disappearance of otherworldliness and clericalism has bequeathed man the full freedom and responsibility for life in the world. Furthermore, this collapse of otherworldliness and clericalism is a legitimate extension if not a historical consequence of the trinitarian substance of traditional Christianity. The creedal portrayal of the Father claims that God expresses himself dependably and powerfully through the created world. If God is still alive, he must be involved in secular events today. The classical doctrine of the Son claims that God gives himself fully and irretrievably in human persons. If God is still available, he must be present in secular relationships today. Finally, the traditional doctrine of the Spirit claims that God discloses himself intelligibly and relevantly in concrete situations. If God is still knowable, he must be understandable in secular terms today.

But Cox believes that only a *secular theology* can develop these potentialities of modern secularization and conserve these insights from traditional Christianity. Secularizing Christian thought and life means centering them in the great moral issues of modern existence. Man's religious questions in the modern world are functional rather than ontological, political rather than cosmological. Men are basically concerned about how to achieve life's full meaning rather than how to define it, about how to persevere in this world rather than prepare for another world. If Christianity wishes to answer these questions, every doctrinal claim and religious institution must be reinterpreted so as to order and transfigure human life in the world. The most pressing problem for such a thoroughgoing reinterpretation is the doctrine of God. Traditional Christianity's emphasis on the transcendence of God has always furnished a way of judging human failings and inspiring human strivings. How can the Church dispense with otherworldliness and clericalism and still render moral judgments and offer moral inspiritation? Can there be transcendence "in and through the secular"? Cox answers these questions by suggesting a concept of transcendence which is temporal but not spatial. He believes that Christian faith can be kept open to criticism and change by anchoring world and human history 'ahead' rather than 'behind' or 'above.' Secular Christianity must relinquish authoritative revelations from the past and divine interventions from another world because clericalism and otherworldliness are dead. But God can still be conceived of transcendentally as the One who lures and leads man into the future. Faith as hope for the coming Kingdom of God can keep the historical process open to criticism and change but free from caprice and chaos. Christian faith can have a future by being anchored in the future. But, unlike early Christianity's similar emphasis on a coming Kingdom of God, secular Christianity hopes only for an interworldly rather than an otherworldly future.

Certainly Cox's secularized Christianity leaves many questions unanswered. But can the Church afford to ignore his emphasis on *the ethical focus of discipleship?* Surely the vast majority of Christians still judge discipleship by the norms of ecclesiasticism, ritualism and pietism. How many people gauge religious earnestness by frequency of church attendance and quality of institutional loyalty? How many people regard private devotion and public worship as the primary expressions of faith? How many people limit Christian morality to the inner attitudes and private relationships of individuals? Even though Cox is preoccupied with a limited range of problems and prospects for Christian faith in the midst of secularization and urbanization, he does properly center the duties of discipleship for contemporary Christians. We must engage religious loyalties for the redemptive renewal of the world.

268

We must orient liturgical activities to the redemptive renewal of the world. We must transform societal structures in the redemptive renewal of the world. Discipleship that smacks of 'churchianity,' otherworldliness or individualism offers no defensible rationale or vital contribution to modern life and thought. Every expression of discipleship should be geared to the growth of love among all men in the world.

4. Gabriel Vahanian

Vahanian's understanding of Christian faith grows out of his distinctive view of the relation between language and existence. Human existence is centered in man's capacity to project himself toward a destiny and a cause. Language furnishes the poetic and metaphorical images which enable men to seek a destiny and serve a cause. But such verbal "icons" perform this indispensable function only as long as they remain "iconoclastic." Only symbolic language which continually rebels against freezing reality in its own pictures and purposes keeps man from becoming static and normless. Only symbols which negate their own objectification enable man to escape his own objectification. Only lodestars which are 'imageless images' and 'impossible possibilities' keep human existence open-ended and goal-directed. According to Vahanian, this understanding of the linguistic and iconoclastic character of human existence underlies the biblical view of God and man. All men live by some poetic and metaphorical images. But life ceases to be authentically human when these *images* become *idols.* Men are always tempted to deify themselves, or some cultural extension of themselves, as a short cut to security and fulfillment. But such idolatries furnish spurious security and false fulfillment because they always close men to the future and to one another. Biblical iconoclasm stands in bold contrast to all latent or overt self-deification by grounding human existence in a Supreme Metaphor of reality, at once Wholly Other and Wholly Available to everything finite. The biblical God is an iconoclastic concept which frees man from self-deification in any of its forms—racial, national, cultural or religious. But while God is *only* a concept God is never *merely* a concept! God is at no place and in no time but God is everytime and everywhere human life is authentic. God is the Word that prevents man from equating his life with any racial, national, cultural or religious expression of his life. As such, God is the Word by which man's world and existence is continually created and redeemed out of nothingness.

But Vahanian charges that the iconoclastic character and

function of biblical faith has often been compromised in the Christian past and has been completely vitiated in the modern era. In the last two centuries, a religion of radical immanentism has replaced the faith of radical monotheism. Nineteenth-century Christianity reduced God in theory as well as practice to a cultural ideal and accessory by equating Christian faith with bourgeois religiosity. In turn, twentieth-century Christianity has eliminated God as a cultural reality and necessity by translating bourgeois religiosity into human sufficiency. Hence, Vahanian sees the 'death of God' as a cultural event initiated by the accomodation of Christian faith to modern culture in nineteenth-century liberal theology and consummated by the elimination of Christian faith from modern culture in the mid-twentieth century 'death of God' theologies. But he also sees two very beneficial consequences of this cultural event of the 'death of God.' First, this crisis in Christian thought and life demonstrates that God dies as soon as he becomes nothing more than a natural process, cultural ideal or human accessory. Using God as an intellectual or emotional stop-gap for human ignorance and weakness has been exposed as superfluous and irresponsible by the relativizing and secularizing of modern life and thought. On the other hand, the cultural demise of the self-idols of bourgeois religiosity prepares the way for the recovery of the iconoclastic power of religious symbols and the iconoclastic function of religious faith. In a cultural epoch where God has completely disappeared as an explanation of natural processes, as an agent in historical events and as a datum of human consciousness, God may reappear as the Supreme Metaphor of human existence. In the meantime, however, Vahanian counsels the Christian to wait without idols until literature or theology forges new "iconoclastic icons" for the believer, the Church and the world.

Certainly Vahanian's theological program sounds strange and remains obscure at many crucial points. But can the Church afford to ignore his strictures against *the perennial dangers of idolatry?* Unfortunately, individuals and groups too easily and too frequently confuse Christian faith with narrow self-images. How many people equate the reality of God with parochial outlooks such as creedal theologies or cultural mores? How many people reduce the purposes of religion to selfish interests such as personal prosperity or national security? How many people limit the community of faith to tribal in-groups such as denominational traditions or political parties? Even if Vahanian over-emphasizes the judgmental side of Christian faith, he does recognize that Christian faith becomes idolatrous whenever a partial viewpoint, restricted cause or exclusive group is absolutized. We must learn that God is not the personification of any religious or cultural group, that religion is not an instrument of individual or corporate aggrandizement, that churchmanship is not a haven for conditional and exclusive love. We must recognize that religiously disguised egoism is more difficult to detect and more destructive to life than any other form of human self-centeredness. For these reasons we must constantly guard against the deification of all selfish images, concerns and communities.

5. William Hamilton

Hamilton's major concern has been logging the cultural manifestations and theological implications of the "death of God." He uses the phrase "death of God" as a metaphor to describe modern man's loss of God as a miraculous problem-solver and need-fulfiller. No room for a personal and benevolent deity remains in a world subject to human control and caprice. The Christian God who supposedly indwells human history has been rendered superfluous experientially by modern man's growing capacities to explain, control and change his total environment. Secularism has laid the world at the door of human initiative, resourcefulness and responsibility. Viewed from another slant, the Christian God who allegedly controls human history has been rendered morally unthinkable because of modern man's self-destructiveness. The magnitude of modern man's inhumanity to man belies all convictions about a benevolent Father guiding history toward redemptive purposes. Modern Christians can no longer look for miraculous interventions in physical or psychic 'space' to solve human problems or fulfill human needs. Rather, the faithful must seek human solutions to the whole range of physical, social, psychic and spiritual ills that prevent life from becoming fully human. Furthermore, Hamilton believes such human solutions are attainable if men learn to live in the world after the pattern of Jesus Christ. When we look behind the strange words and ways in which the New Testament describes the importance of Jesus, we see a *man*—wholly free from self-interest, utterly committed to the neighbor, recklessly animated by love. By following this man, men learn what it means to be human rather than divine, men learn how they should be at work in the world rather than how God was once at work in the world. Although Christian faith must let go of God it can still hold fast to

271

Jesus.

This loss of God as an otherworldly problem-solver and need-fulfiller entails neither despair nor cynicism because it marks man's emergence from an adolescent dependence and irresponsibility. This loss is no more regretable than children becoming progressively free and independent of their parents. Modern man has simply reached a new stage of self-understanding when he can no longer look for supernatural guidance, assistance or comfort. Thus left to natural and human resources, men can at last learn to live in and for a world that contains in itself all the purpose and fulfillment life affords and needs. Such life in and for the world is still rich with mystery and sacredness. In time men may even learn to experience and interpret such mystery and sacredness in a *religious* though *non-theistic* way. But Hamilton believes that men for the present must move beyond their otherworldly ideas of faith and their problem-solver ideas of God before they can hope to discover a new religiousness. For the time being, men must learn to do without the Christian God.

Certainly criticisms of Hamilton's explorations come easily. But can the Church afford to ignore his challenge to *a new maturity of faith?* Surely the popular understanding of the relation between God's grace and man's efforts is a veritable haven for superstitious, irrelevant and irresponsible faith. How many people search frantically and superstitiously for ways to align God with their interests because they mistakenly assume God causes everything that happens in our world? How many people find God progressively and irrelevantly remote from real life because they stubbornly believe God works through miraculous interventions although few if any 'miracles' happen anymore? How many people wait piously and irresponsibly for God to transform the world's social and spiritual ills because they have dissolved even the classical tensions between grace and works by attributing everything to God? Regardless of how one-sided Hamilton's analysis of faith, he does sound an urgent note for contemporary Christians. We must give up our adolescent ideas and ways of faith. We must learn that there is no God who specially favors the faithful, who causes everything that happens or, indeed, who works apart from natural process and human instrumentality at all. The sooner we grow up in thought and deed to this maturity of faith, the sooner the world's inhumanity and ignorance, war and want will be accepted as human problems clamoring for human solution. Presuming upon God to show the way or do the work of making life fully human postpones human maturity and abdicates Christian responsibility.

6. Paul M. van Buren

Van Buren's theological program claims to show how a man may be thoroughly secular and genuinely Christian at the same time. His "secular meaning of the Gospel" rests on two complementary convictions. On the one hand, he argues that references to a supernatural realm, being or power are literally meaningless and religiously misleading. People who suppose that the word "God" refers to some entity or activity apart from the natural world and ordinary processes have no way of proving or disproving their suppositions. Since no empirical data counts conclusively for or against God's reality and activity, van Buren claims that such beliefs cannot be about real states of affairs. Indeed, such beliefs are literally meaningless since all beliefs about objective reality must be verifiable, at least in principle, by empirical data. But, while denying them *literal* meaning, van Buren admits that statements about "God" could and once did have *religious* meaning. Statements about "God" are actually oblique ways of expressing a personal commitment to a moral perspective. But men forget that references to "God" are really poetic devices for acclaiming the absoluteness and universality of their own moral perspective. Beliefs about "God" become religiously misleading when such forgetfulness occurs because men fail to see that Christian faith is a distinctive form of ethical humanism. Therefore, van Buren wishes to translate all statements about "God" into statements about man in order to free the Christian Gospel from literal nonsense and religious confusion.

The other side of van Buren's secular reinterpretation of the Gospel is his claim that Christian faith is based upon Jesus. Christianity is a distinctive form of human life. It involves a commitment to certain patterns of human relationships and norms of human attitudes. Jesus originally embodied these patterns and norms in his own living and communicated them to his immediate followers. This same distinctive and contagious life style confronts and attracts men today through the stories about Jesus set down by his early followers in the New Testament. Living under the Lordship of Christ means living for others in modern parallels to the New Testament portraits of Jesus as "the man for others." Christian faith has never been anything more than this ethical perspective modeled and motivated by Jesus. But as long as men acclaimed the Lordship of Christ in theistic language, the human and ethical focus of Christian faith was easily blurred. Van Buren believes that such confusions will become less and less likely as secularism continues to undermine the literalistic and religious confusions concerning language about "God." For this reason, he insists that the *secular* meaning is the *essential* meaning of the Gospel.

Certainly van Vuren's views may be criticized at many points. But must not the Church accept his insistance on *the functional meaning of beliefs?* Surely popular definitions of faith as believing the invisible, the impossible and the incomprehensible separate religion from real life. How many people assume that religion is primarily concerned with an unseen world behind and beyond our experiential world? How many people firmly believe that faith begins where human explanations and resources end? How many people affirm unintelligible beliefs because they are told that God's mysterious ways are beyond finite comprehension? Even though van Buren may define rational and verifiable knowledge too narrowly, he does lay down a crucial guideline for contemporary theological work. We must discard religious beliefs which cannot be expressed in functional terms. We must recognize that religious beliefs, no less than scientific beliefs, must be based on the real world, must be concerned with everyday life and must be intelligible to any man. Religious beliefs which do not function as instruments for coping with our total environment are empty palliatives at best and misleading illusions are worst. Religious beliefs can be maintained and practiced consistently only if they illumine vital human experiences and relationships. Our hearts cannot find true what our heads find false. Believing the unbelievable is not a requirement or a sign of faith.

Comparing the radicals to one another, we find them saying very different things about the theological underpinnings of faith but nearly identical things about the practical expressions of faith. The radicals disagree in their accounts of God, man and Christ but these diverse accounts support their shared conviction that Christian faith frees man for creative and responsible life in and for the world. This ambivalence will not surprise or disturb us if we remember our earlier discussion of theological controversy. A living faith can be described quite differently without destroying personal confidence and interpersonal companionship in faith's reality. Furthermore, not only is such creative disagreement *possible* in the Church but is also *necessary*. The Church is a diverse society "for the mutual extraction of motes and beams." Even theological positions which may be judged inadequate in the long run have a vital role in this on-going process of self-understanding through self-criticism. Every earnest attempt to correct the Church's vision serves the whole Body of Christ regardless of how much or how little light is readmitted.

Finally, then, the radical theologians make significant contributions to any understanding and resolution of our unprecedented crisis in Christian belief and behavior. Their diagnoses and prognoses of the radical ills besetting traditional Christianity are not without fault. Their views are and must be subject to thorough critical analysis. But most discussions of radical Christianity thus far have sought to discredit the radicals from theological standpoints which do not take relativism and secularism seriously. Even sympathetic commentators have all but buried their positive affirmations beneath their negative criticisms of radical Christianity. For this reason, the critical perspective of this book has been limited to the positive contributions of radical Christianity. The full weight of traditional Chrisitanty's problems and of radical Christianity's alternatives must be felt by everyone concerned with the radical impasse between traditional Christianity and the modern world. The radicals get at the roots of this crisis from different perspectives and with different concerns. But taken together they levy trenchant criticisms against still-prevelant theological assumptions and religious actions which are no longer realistic and responsible expressions of Christian faith. They also furnish a spectrum of 'fixed points' for guiding the Church through the dangers and difficulties of reformulating Christian faith in relative and secular terms. All Christian thought and life must take seriously the apologetic task of theology, the present reality of God, the ethical focus of discipleship, the perennial dangers of idolatry, the new maturity of faith and the functional meaning of belief. However the circle of Christian faith is drawn in the future, these criteria must prevail from center to circumference.

SELECTED BIBLIOGRAPHY

Part One THE RISE OF RADICAL CHRISTIANITY

Altizer, Thomas J. J., ed., *Toward a New Christianity: Readings in the Death of God Theology,* New York: Harcourt, Brace & World, Inc., 1967 (paperback).

Cooper, John Charles, *The Roots of the Radical Theology,* Philadelphia: The Westminster Press, 1967.

Dewart, Leslie, *The Future of Belief: Theism in a World Come of Age,* New York: Herder and Herder, 1966.

Herberg, Will, *Protestant-Catholic-Jew: An Essay in American Religious Sociology,* Garden City, New York: Doubleday & Co., 1960 (paperback).

Jenkins, David E., *Guide to the Debate About God,* Philadelphia The Westminster Press, 1966 (paperback).

Loen, Arnold E., *Secularization: Science Without God?,* Philadelphia: The Westminster Press, 1967.

Macquarrie, John, *God and Secularity (New Directions in Theology Today, vol. III),* Philadelphia: The Westminster Press, 1967 (paperback).

Marty, Martin E., *The New Shape of American Religion,* New York: Harper & Brothers, 1959.

Marty, Martin E., *Varieties of Unbelief,* Garden City, New York, Doubleday & Co., 1966 (paperback).

Miller, W. R., ed., *The New Christianity: An Anthology of the Rise of Modern Religious Thought,* New York: Delacorte Press, 1967.

Rubenstein, Richard L., *After Auschwitz: Radical Theology and Contemporary Judaism,* Indianapolis: The Bobbs-Merrill Co., 1966 (paperback).

Williams, Colin, *Faith in a Secular Age,* New York: Harper Chapelbooks, 1966 (paperback).

1. General Surveys of Contemporary Theology

Averill, L. J., *American Theology in the Liberal Tradition,* Philadelphia: The Westminister Press, 1967.

Carnell, E. J., *The Case for Orthodox Theology,* Philadelphia: The Westminster Press, 1959.

Cobb, Jr., John B., *Living Options in Protestant Theology: A Survey of Methods,* Philadelphia: The Westminster Press, 1961.

DeWolf, L. H., *The Case for Theology in Liberal Perspective,* Philadelphia: The Westminster Press, 1959.

Hordern, William, *The Case for a New Reformation Theology,* Philadelphia: The Westminster Press, 1959.

Hordern, William, *Introduction (New Directions in Theology Today,* vol. I), Philadelphia: The Westminster Press, 1967 (paperback).

Marty, Martin E. and Peerman, Dean G., *New Theology,* nos. 1-4, New York: The Macmillan Co., 1964-67.

Vidler, A. R., *Twentieth-Century Defenders of the Faith,* New York: The Seabury Press, 1964.

Williams, D. D., *What Present-Day Theologians Are Thinking,* New York: Harper Chapelbooks, 1967 (paperback).

2. Important Writings of the Radical Theologians

Paul M. van Buren

The Secular Meaning of Gospel, New York: The Macmillan Co., 1963.

"Theology in the Context of Culture," *The Christian Century,* 82 (1965), pp. 428-30; reprinted in *Frontline Theology* ed. by Dean Peerman, Richmond: John Knox Press, 1967, pp. 46-51.

"The Dissolution of the Absolute," *Religion in Life,* 34 (1965), pp. 334-42.

"Christian Education *Post Mortem Dei,"* *Religious Education,* 60 (1965), pp. 4-10.

"Straw Men and the Monistic Hangover," *Religious Education,* 60 (1965), pp. 40-42.

"Bonhoeffer's Paradox: Living with God without God," *Union Seminary Quarterly Review,* 23 (1967), pp. 45-59.

278

William Hamilton

The New Essence of Christianity, New York: Association Press, 1961.

"American Theology, Radicalism and the Death of God," *Radical Theology and the Death of God,* ed. by Thomas J. J. Altizer and William Hamilton, Indianapolis: The Bobbs-Merrill Co., 1966, pp. 3-7.

"The Death of God Theologies Today," *Radical Theology and the Death of God,* pp. 23-50.

"Banished from the Land of Unity," *Radical Theology and the Death of God,* pp. 53-84.

"Thursday's Child," *Radical Theology and the Death of God,* pp. 87-93.

"Deitrich Bonhoeffer," *Radical Theology and the Death of God,* pp. 113-18.

"The New Optimism — from Prufrock to Ringo," *Radical Theology and the Death of God,* pp. 157-69.

"The Shape of a Radical Theology," *The Christian Century,* 82 (1965), pp. 1219-22; reprinted in *Frontline Theology* ed. by Dean Peerman, Richmond: John Knox Press, 1967, pp. 69-76.

"The Death of God," *Playboy,* 13 (August, 1966), pp. 79, 84, 137-39.

"Questions and Answers on the Radical Theology," *The Death of God Debate,* ed. by J. L. Ice and J. J. Carey, Philadelphia: The Westminster Press, 1967, pp. 213-41.

Gabriel Vahanian

The Death of God, New York: George Braziller, 1961.
Wait Without Idols, New York: George Braziller, 1964.
No Other God, New York: George Braziller, 1966.
"Beyond the Death of God," *The Meaning of the Death of God,* ed. by Bernard Murchland, New York: Vintage Books, 1967, pp. 3-12.

Harvey Cox

God's Revolution and Man's Responsibility, Valley Forge, Pennsylvania: Judson Press, 1965.

The Secular City, revised edition, New York: The Macmillan Co., 1966.

On Not Leaving It to the Snake, New York: The Macmillan Co., 1967.

(ed.), *The Church Amid Revolution,* New York: Association Press, 1967.

"The Place and Purpose of Theology," *The Christian Century,* 83 (1966), pp. 7-9; reprinted in *Frontline Theology* ed. by Dean Peerman, Richmond: John Knox Press, 1967, pp. 149-55.

"Secularization and the Secular Mentality," *Religious Education,* 61 (1966), pp. 83-87.

"Response to My Critics," *Religious Education,* 61 (1966), pp. 110-13.

"An Exchange of Views," *The Secular City Debate,* ed. by Daniel Callahan, New York: The Macmillan Co., 1966, pp. 113-20.

"Afterword," *The Secular City Debate,* pp. 179-203.

"Beyond Bonhoeffer? The Future of Religionless Christianity," *The Secular City Debate,* pp. 205-14.

"The Death of God and the Future of Theology," *The New Christianity,* ed. by W. R. Miller, New York: Delacorte Press, 1967, pp. 379-89.

"Why Christianity Must Be Secularized," *The Great Ideas Today 1967,* Chicago: Encyclopedia Britannica, Inc., 1967, pp. 8-21.

Thomas J. J. Altizer

Oriental Mysticism and Biblical Eschatology, Philadelphia: The Westminster Press, 1961.

Mircea Eliade and the Dialectic of the Sacred, Philadelphia: The Westminster Press, 1963.

The Gospel of Christian Atheism, Philadelphia: The Westminister Press, 1966.

The New Apocalypse: The Radical Christian Vision of William Blake, East Lansing, Michigan: Michigan State University Press, 1967.

The Altizer-Montgomery Dialogue, Chicago: Inter-Varsity Press, 1967.

(ed.) *Toward a New Christianity: Readings in the Death of God Theology,* New York: Harcourt, Brace & World, 1967.

"Creative Negation in Theology," *The Christian Century*, 82 (1965), pp. 864-67; reprinted in *Frontline Theology* ed. by Dean Peerman, Richmond: John Knox Press, 1967, pp. 77-85.

"America and the Future of Theology," *Radical Theology and the Death of God,* ed. by Thomas J. J. Altizer and William Hamilton, Indianapolis: The Bobbs-Merrill Co., 1966, pp. 9-21.

"Theology and the Death of God," *Radical Theology and the Death of God,* pp. 95-111.

"Word and History," *Radical Theology and the Death of God,* pp. 121-39.

"The Sacred and the Profane: A Dialectical Understanding of Christianity," *Radical Theology and the Death of God,* pp. 139-55.

"The Significance of the New Theology," *The Death of God Debate,* ed. by J. L. Ice and J. J. Carey, Philadelphia: The Westminster Press, 1967, pp. 242-55.

"Catholic Philosophy and the Death of God," *Cross Currents,* 17 (1967), pp. 271-82.

"Can We Manage Without God?" by Kenneth L. Wilson (a report of an interview with Altizer), *The Christian Herald,* 90 (January, 1967) pp. 16-18; 60-68.

John A. T. Robinson

On Being the Church in the World, Philadelphia: The Westminster Press (London: SCM Press), 1960.

Honest to God, Philadelphia: The Westminster Press (London: SCM Press), 1963.

Christian Morals Today, Philadelphia: The Westminster Press (London, SCM Press), 1963.

The New Reformation? Philadelphia: The Westminster Press (London, SCM Press), 1965.

Exploration into God, Stanford, California: Stanford University Press, 1967.

But That I Can't Believe, New York: The New American Library, 1967.

"Comment," *The Honest to God Debate,* ed. by D. L. Edwards, Philadelphia: The Westminster Press (London: SCM Press), 1963, pp. 228-31.

"The Debate Continues," *The Honest to God Debate,* pp. 232-75.

Bent, S. J., Charles N., *The Death-of-God Movement,* Glen Rock, New Jersey: Paulist Press, 1967.

Callahan, Daniel, ed., *The Secular City Debate,* New York: The Macmillan Co., 1966 (paperback).

Christian, C. W. and Wittig, G. R., eds., *Radical Theology: Phase Two; Essays on the Current Debate,* Philadelphia: J. B. Lippincott, 1967 (paperback).

Edwards, D. L., ed., *The Honest to God Debate,* Philadelphia: The Westminster Press, 1963 (paperback).

Hamilton, Kenneth, *God Is Dead: The Anatomy of a Slogan,* Grand Rapids, Michigan: Eerdmans, 1966 (paperback).

Harrison, Ernest, *A Church Without God,* Philadelphia: J. B. Lippincott, 1967 (paperback).

Ice, J. L. and Carey, J. J., eds. *The Death of God Debate,* Philadelphia: The Westminster Press, 1967 (paperback).

Murchland, Bernard, ed., *The Meaning of the Death of God,* New York: Vintage Books, 1967 (paperback).

Montgomery, John W., *The 'Is God Dean?' Controversy,* Grand Rapids, Michigan: Zondervan, 1966 (paperback).

Ogletree, Thomas W., *The Death of God Controversy,* Nashville: Abingdon Press, 1966 (paperback).

Smith, Ronald G., *Secular Christianity,* New York: Harper & Row, 1966.